THE
INTENTION
ECONOMY

THE
INTENTION
ECONOMY

When Customers Take Charge

DOC SEARLS

HARVARD BUSINESS REVIEW PRESS

Boston, Massachusetts

10 9 8 7 6 5 4 3 2 1

No part of this publication may be reproduced, stored in or introduced into
a retrieval system, or transmitted, in any form, or by any means (electronic,
mechanical, photocopying, recording, or otherwise), without the prior permission
of the publisher. Requests for permission should be directed to permissions@
hbsp.harvard.edu, or mailed to Permissions, Harvard Business School Publishing,
60 Harvard Way, Boston, Massachusetts 02163.

Library of Congress Cataloging-in-Publication Data

Searls, Doc.

  The intention economy : when customers take charge / Doc Searls.

    p. cm.

  Includes bibliographical references.

  ISBN 978-1-4221-5852-4 (alk. paper)

  1. Customer relations. 2. Customer service. 3. Consumers' preferences. 4. New
    products. I. Title.

  HF5415.5.S448 2012

  658.8'342--dc23

                                2011053277

The paper used in this publication meets the requirements of the American
National Standard for Permanence of Paper for Publications and Documents in
Libraries and Archives Z39.48-1992.

For Joyce

CONTENTS

Part III **The Liberated Customer**

16 Personal Freedom   153

17 VRM   163

18 Development   167

19 The Four-Party System   177

20 The Law in Our Own Hands   181

21 Small Data   189

22 APIs   197

23 EmanciPaytion   207

24 VRM + CRM   217

Part IV **The Liberated Vendor**

25 The Dance   223

26 Commons Cause   239

27 What to Do   245

Epilogue Almost There   253

Notes   257
Bibliography   275
Index   281
Acknowledgments   291
About the Author   301

As for the future, your task is not to foresee it, but to enable it.

—Antoine de Saint-Exupéry

Paying Attention
to Intention

In matters of style, swim with the current.
In matters of principle, stand like a rock.

—Thomas Jefferson

Words may show a man's wit but actions his meaning.

—Benjamin Franklin

The Insight

Work on this book started in March 2006, when I was covering O'Reilly's Emerging Technologies (eTech) conference in San Diego for *Linux Journal*. The conference theme was "The Attention Economy." Sitting in the audience taking notes, I thought, *Why build an economy around attention, when intention is where the money comes from?* So I wrote an article, on the spot, titled, "The Intention Economy." An excerpt:

> The Intention Economy grows around buyers, not sellers. It leverages the simple fact that buyers are the first source of money, and that they come ready-made. You don't need advertising to make them …
>
> The Intention Economy is built around truly open markets, not a collection of silos. In the Intention Economy, customers don't have to fly from silo to silo, like a bees from flower to flower, collecting deal info (and unavoidable hype) like so much pollen. In The

Intention Economy, the buyer notifies the market of the intent to buy, and sellers compete for the buyer's purchase. Simple as that ...

The Intention Economy is about buyers finding sellers, not sellers finding (or "capturing") buyers.

In The Intention Economy, a car rental customer should be able to say to the car rental market, "I'll be skiing in Park City from March 20–25. I want to rent a 4-wheel drive SUV. I belong to Avis Wizard, Budget FastBreak and Hertz One Club. I don't want to pay up front for gas or get any insurance. What can any of you companies do for me?"—and have the sellers compete for the buyer's business.[1]

Positive buzz followed, but development didn't, and that's what the Intention Economy needed. So, several months later, when I was given a fellowship at Harvard University's Berkman Center for Internet & Society, I decided to launch a development project toward making the Intention Economy happen. We called it ProjectVRM.[2]

VRM stood for vendor relationship management—the customer-side counterpart of CRM, or customer relationship management, a business that appears to most of us in the form of junk mail and call centers. Project-VRM's goal was to cause development of tools that would make individuals both independent of vendors and better able to engage with them. In other words, to fix a broken system from the customer side by developing a new system complementary to existing businesses and built on the natural independence and agency of human beings.

Behind ProjectVRM was a thesis:

Free customers are more valuable than captive ones.

And, as a corollary,

Free markets require free customers.

Since CRM was already a multibillion-dollar business category, ProjectVRM was a highly ambitious undertaking. But I was neither alone nor early. In the United Kingdom, Iain Henderson, Alan Mitchell, and others had already started the Buyer Centric Commerce Forum and were doing work on what they called personal data stores—an essential VRM tool. Adriana Lukas, also in the U.K., had similar goals for both her consultancy and her blogging company, and was encouraging development work as well. The digital identity development community had also been working on some of the same problems, encouraged by the twice-yearly Internet Identity Workshops (IIWs), which Kaliya Hamilin, Phil Windley, and I started in 2005.

At Berkman, ProjectVRM consisted of myself, a mailing list, a blog, a wiki, and gatherings in the form of meetings and workshops. It still does. Out in the world, however, it has grown to consist of dozens of development efforts and hundreds of individuals, all working in their own ways to create tools that liberate customers and build the Intention Economy. This book is a progress report on that work and the evolving ideas behind it.

The Book

I hadn't planned to write this book before we had lots of working code, but two events in early 2009 changed my mind. The first was a breakfast in Toronto with my friend Rick Segal, who was then a venture capitalist there. Rick told me, in a way that could hardly be more emphatic if he had slammed me into a wall, "You have to write a book! You already have a title! It's *The Intention Economy*! Stop screwing around! Go write it!" The other was a talk I gave by the same title a few weeks later at the Berkman Center.[3] Among those at the talk was Jeff Kehoe of Harvard Business Review Press. Jeff came up to me afterward and asked if I had considered making my talk into a book. With Rick's command still ringing in my ears, I said yes. The result is now in your hands.

Most VRM tools today are either early in development or just starting to be adopted. Many of the ideas and assumptions about VRM and the Intention Economy are also far from proven and easy to dismiss in proof's absence. We are at the early edge of the technology adoption cycle. Author Geoffrey Moore's famous chasm between innovators and early adopters is still ahead of us.[4]

So why would both Rick and Jeff want me to write a book about something that hasn't happened yet and probably will not start to happen for another several years? Two reasons: reality and promise. In reality, e-commerce—a huge forward leap on the economy's supply side—had already happened. But it was only the first shoe to drop. The promise was a forward leap on the demand side, by individual customers. That shoe is VRM. We don't know where it will drop first, but do we know the foot wearing it will be the customer's. The Intention Economy will then step forward with both shoes, on both feet: supply on one side and demand on the other. No more hopping along on the supply side alone.

Because we are dealing with the future here, much of what you read in this book is speculative. In fact, I am willfully practicing what Nassim Nicholas Taleb (in *The Black Swan*) calls "epistemic arrogance." He says this "bears a double effect: we overestimate what we know, and underestimate uncertainty, by compressing the range of uncertain states (i.e., by reducing the space of the unknown)."[5] But I am not just making guesses here. I am also looking for effects, and I have influence over the causes of those effects. So do many others in the VRM movement, some far better equipped than I. Those intentions add up. After that, they multiply.

I have also seen this kind of intention work before—in particular with free software, open source, and Linux, all three of which I've been covering since the mid-nineties for *Linux Journal*. So, while I base what I can on facts and solid sources, I am also working with a lot of other people to *make* the Intention Economy happen.

There are sure to be many different kinds of responses to this book and its purposes, but the only ones that matter are ones we can use. Thus, I invite you to use the tools we develop, to give helpful feedback, and to weigh in with your own ideas and development efforts. The frontier is wide open, and opportunities abound. You can see them best if you realize the full value of free customers and how much work we have left to do. If this book succeeds, some of that work will be yours.

Free Markets Require Free Customers

Perspective

This book stands with the customer. This is out of necessity, not sympathy. Over the coming years, customers will be emancipated from systems built to control them. They will become free and independent actors in the marketplace, equipped to tell vendors what they want, how they want it, where, and when—even how much they'd like to pay—outside of any vendor's system of customer control.[1] Customers will be able to form and break relationships with vendors, on customers' own terms, and not just on the take-it-or-leave-it terms that have been pro forma since industry won the industrial revolution.

Customer power will be personal, not just collective. Each customer will come to market equipped with his or her own means for collecting and storing personal data, expressing demand, making choices, setting preferences, proffering terms of engagement, offering payments, and participating in relationships—whether those relationships are shallow or deep, and whether they last for moments or years. Those means will be standardized. No vendor will control them.

Demand will no longer be expressed only in the forms of cash, collective appetites, or the inferences of crunched data over which the individual has little or no control. Demand will be personal. This means customers will be in charge of personal information they share with all parties, including vendors.

Customers will have their own means for storing and sharing their own data and their own tools for engaging with vendors and other parties. With these tools, customers will run their own loyalty programs—ones in which vendors will be the members. Customers will no longer need to carry around vendor-issued loyalty cards and key tags. This means vendors' loyalty programs will be based on genuine loyalty by customers and will benefit from a far greater range of information than tracking customer behavior alone can provide.

Thus, relationship management will go both ways. Just as vendors today are able to manage relationships with customers and third parties, customers tomorrow will be able to manage relationships with vendors and fourth parties, which are companies that serve as agents of customer demand, from the customer's side of the marketplace.

Relationships between customers and vendors will be voluntary and genuine, with loyalty anchored in mutual respect and concern, rather than coercion. So, rather than "targeting," "capturing," "acquiring," "managing," "locking in," and "owning" customers, as if they were slaves or cattle, vendors will earn the respect of customers who are now free to bring far more to the market's table than the old vendor-based systems ever contemplated, much less allowed.

Likewise, rather than guessing what might get the attention of *consumers*—or what might "drive" them like cattle—vendors will respond to *actual intentions of customers*. Once customers' expressions of *intent* become abundant and clear, the range of economic interplay between supply and demand will widen, and its sum will increase. The result we will call the *Intention Economy*.

This new economy will outperform the *Attention Economy* that has shaped marketing and sales since the dawn of advertising. Customer intentions, well expressed and understood, will improve marketing and sales, because both will work with better information, and both will be spared the cost and effort wasted on guesses about what customers might want, flooding media with messages that miss their marks. Advertising will also improve.

The volume, variety, and relevance of information coming from customers in the Intention Economy will strip the gears of systems built for controlling customer behavior or for limiting customer input. The quality of that information will also obsolete or repurpose the guesswork mills of marketing, fed by crumb trails of data shed by customers' mobile gear and Web browsers. "Mining" of customer data will still be useful to vendors, though less so than intention-based data provided directly by customers.

In economic terms, there will be high opportunity costs for vendors that ignore useful signaling coming from customers. There will also be high opportunity gains for companies that take advantage of growing customer independence and empowerment.

Customer independence and empowerment have always been implicit in the nature of the marketplace and in the nature of the Internet as well. But while the marketplace is as old as civilization, the Internet is still new. Born in 1994, the graphical browser is still a teen. And while the Net has already transformed business and society throughout the world, it has done so mostly on the supply side, with tremendous innovations in production, supply chain management, marketing, sales, and other functions. Synergies between online and offline business operations and practices have also improved to the point where it is impossible for most businesses, especially large ones, to imagine working without the Internet.

But much has not yet changed. The legal frameworks for doing business online are as absurd and broken as they were in the age of shrink-wrapped software. Marketing and sales have made great efforts to become more "conversational" and "social," but customers in too many cases are still "assets" to be "managed." Implicit in this mentality is a belief that the best customers are captive ones and that therefore a "free market" for customers means "your choice of captor."

This twisted norm will end because free markets require free customers. The Internet by its nature invites developments that will equip customers with tools for both independence and engagement. Over the last decade, many developers have accepted that invitation and have started work on tools that will make customers both independent of vendors and better able to engage with them. These tools will also become the means by which individuals control their relationships with multiple social networks and social media.

These tools comprise a new category of capabilities called VRM, for vendor relationship management. VRM tools work as the demand-side counterpart of vendors' CRM (customer relationship management) systems. In the highly competitive CRM marketplace, winners will be those that best engage customers' VRM systems.

Creating the Intention Economy won't be easy or smooth. The flywheels of business as usual are huge. The Attention Economy is deeply normative and entrenched. Google alone has advanced the science and practice of advertising to the point where advertising pays not only for all of Google's many free services, but also for much of the other stuff we take for granted on the Net. The upward trends of both revenue and investment in advertising remain steep. Today, many millions (perhaps billions) of dollars per annum are being invested in start-ups with advertising either as a purpose or as a revenue model.[2] Many companies are also working hard to improve advertising by personalizing it to the nth degree.

But perfectly personal advertising is a dream of advertisers, not of customers. In the last few years, the online advertising business has become obsessed with mining, harvesting, and crunching large sums of personal data, in ways that are invisible to ordinary users of computers and phones. A backlash against this is underway, with predictable appeals for government intervention and other countermeasures. This book, however, is not part of that backlash. Nor is the VRM movement. The case for customer liberation and the Intention Economy is not one against advertising or its excesses. It is the case for a new set of customer capabilities and the effects of those capabilities on vendors, markets, society, and the whole economy. It is the case for vendor liberation as well.

Freedom requires means. Freedom of speech began with the human voice and grew from stone tools through pens, typewriters, computers, networks, and software for writing, editing, publishing, and syndicating. Likewise, our freedom to build things, which also began with stone tools, now includes nail guns, drills, and power saws.

The VRM tools in development today are still at the hammer and screwdriver stage. But the nail guns and power saws are not far behind, because even primitive VRM tools will prove that free customers are more valuable than captive ones—to themselves, to vendors, and to everybody else. Once that starts to happen, investment and development will snowball.

This book makes a case for that snowball. It begins with:

Chapter 1. The Promised Market describes a near future in which the Intention Economy is a fact of life. Four parts follow.

Part I. Customer Captivity examines dysfunctions in the marketplace today: in law, advertising, networking, and customer relations.

Part II. The Networked Marketplace explains how the Internet creates an entirely new environment for business, and privileges scale in the quality of genuine relationships with customers—not just a maximized sum of users.

Part III. The Liberated Customer examines ways that VRM developments reduce or eliminate the market dysfunctions listed in part I, while opening and taking advantage of opportunities visited in part II.

Part IV. The Liberated Vendor discusses what vendors—and all parties on the supply side of the marketplace—can expect of liberated customers and the changes required for dealing productively with them.

The *Epilogue* sums things up and offers questions to get conversations started.

Design and Style

This book covers too much territory—literally, the future of business—to be a linear work. Still, it has arguments to make, so each chapter starts with one. Then, to summarize or make a transition to the following chapter, each closes with the heading, "So, then."

Because I am accustomed to working both as a researcher and as a writer of linky posts and essays on the Web, I include many more footnotes than you'll find in most other business books. The bibliography is also long, for the same reason. So are the acknowledgments.

I also use a lot of quotes. This is because I like to give full respect to my sources, especially when they make their points in better ways than I might rephrase or summarize them. I also use epigraphs—opening quotes for book parts and chapters. While most books don't endnote epigraphs, this one does (in most cases, anyway).

All these choices are also matters of style. Mine is not just to stand on the shoulders of giants, but to stand astride as many as I can.

Since I know many of my cited authorities personally, I sometimes use their first names after introducing them. Again, that's just my style. I hope you appreciate all of them as much as I do.

1

The Promised Market

The only way to deal with an unfree world is to become so absolutely free
that your very existence is an act of rebellion.[1]

—Albert Camus

Amara's Law says we overestimate in the short term and underestimate in the long.[2] So, when I ask you to look at a number of Intention Economy scenarios that should be common a few years from now, I probably overestimate the speed at which this new economy will develop. I do not, however, overestimate the ambitions of developers or the eventual effects of their work.

What follow are scenarios from the near future—say five or ten years out—involving an American mother traveling with her family, experiencing the Intention Economy at work. I address her in the present tense.

While the scenarios are idealized, I don't mean to present this woman or her lifestyle as ideals. I choose them simply as a way to string together pearls of work already going on today. Where the work is on specific topics that will come up later in the book, I've italicized them. The names of companies, organizations, and tools are also real ones. They are not the only companies and organizations working toward the Intention Economy, and the tools described are not the only ones being made. What matters is that this work, and much more like it, is already underway.

Waking Up from Adhesion

You've had trouble sleeping lately. Your husband says you're snoring less, but you wake up tired, even after a long night in bed. When you look for help on the Web, you find Zeo, a company that sells a sleep-monitoring gizmo you wear like a headband.[3] It watches your brain waves, respiration, and other activity (such as your husband's snoring and your dog barking) while you sleep at night. When you dock it in the morning, it produces detailed data that you can use any way you want.

On the menu bar of your browser are two buttons that look like magnets facing each other: ⊂ ⊃. These are called "*r-buttons.*" The "r" stands for "relationship." Yours is on the left and the site's is on the right. You notice that Zeo's r-button is a solid color, while yours is gray. The solid color on Zeo's side is a signal that says, "We are open to dealing with you on *your* terms and not just ours." This doesn't mean it accepts your terms, but rather that it is open to them.

This is a huge change from the old commercial Web, where most sites had lopsided terms of service that gave you no choice but to take them or leave them. In law, these are called "*contracts of adhesion,*" because they hold the submissive party (that's you) to terms the dominant party (that's them) is free to change at will. These contracts became pro forma on the Web at the dawn of e-commerce (1995) and didn't change until corresponding mechanisms showed up on the users' side. But now we have mechanisms. For example, your terms might say,

- You may only collect data I permit you to collect.

- Any data you collect—for me, from me, or about me—is mine as well as yours, and will be made available to me in ways I specify (and here they are).

- You can combine my data with other data and share it, provided it is not PII (personally identifiable information).

- If we cease our relationship, you can keep my data but not associate any PII with that data.

- If we enter a paid relationship for services, you will spare me advertising and promotion for products or services other than yours. You will also not follow my behavior for the purposes of promotion or advertising. Nor will your affiliates or partners.

- You will put nothing on my computer or browser other than what we need for our own relationship. That includes cookies. (And here are the specific kinds of cookies I allow.)

It's Your Law

These terms, which respect ancient *freedom of contract* values, are standard ones chosen by you from a list at Customer Commons (Customer Commons.org), which was organized in 2011 and grew out of Project-VRM at the Berkman Center for Internet & Society at Harvard University, with help from the Information Sharing Workgroup.[4] By now, Customer Commons has compiled many choices of standard terms for individuals and organizations—all described in ways that can easily be compared and matched up automatically. As with Creative Commons (on which Customer Commons was modeled), computers, lawyers, and ordinary people can easily read the terms.

It Takes Four

Later, after kicking a few more tires, you get your Zeo sleep-monitoring gizmo and improve your sleep with the help of coaching provided on its Web site and from other users of the same service. When you go to the Zeo site now, you see both r-buttons are solid. Clicking on either opens links to details for each side of the relationship you now have with Zeo. Details on your side are filled out from your *personal data store (PDS)*, either directly or by the *fourth party* you've hired to help manage your many relationships.

Fourth parties are distinguished from second and third parties by working as agents for first parties: customers like you. Their business is helping you manage relationships, and they carry out your intentions in the marketplace. Fourth parties belong to a larger class of what blogger and software developer Joe Andrieu in 2009 called *user-driven services*.[5] The first example of a VRM-based fourth party was Mydex, a community interest company in London.[6] Early fourth parties in the United States were Azigo, Personal.com, Connect.me, and Singly. In the years since these companies began their pioneering work, fourth parties have turned into a very large category. Many old-line business categories, such as banking and brokerage, are now considered fourth-party services, for the simple reason that they work primarily for individual customers.

New Rules

Your new Zeo joins an assortment of other devices and apps that produce data on your health and lifestyle. Those include your Withings bathroom scale, Fitbit, Digifit, and RunKeeper gear and mobile apps, the Nest thermostat in your home, the exercise machines at the gym, and GPS chips in your smartphone and other devices. The companies that make all this stuff have *open APIs*, or application programming interfaces. In simple terms, APIs provide ways for programs to communicate with each other. On the old *Static Web* (where the sites were in charge, and you always had to agree to those icky contracts of adhesion), APIs simply produced data, such as maps or stock charts, for use on Web sites and in apps of various kinds. On today's *Live Web*, APIs have become *interactive* or *evented* and are simply resources, but fully interactive ones. Nearly all companies, stores, apps, devices, and services—including government agencies and nonprofits—now have interactive APIs. You do too. Anything ready to engage with anything else through digital data streams now has an interactive API.

Think of APIs as exposed competencies, for which engagement is an open choice. In this way, they are a lot like any store, but with the entire inventory exposure-ready (at the store's selective discretion), along with location data and means for shipping and accepting payment. In fact, this kind of thing has been normal for e-commerce from the start.

In your case, you have *rules* written in *KRL* (Kinetic Rules Language) to connect multiple APIs and sources of data, such as all the gizmos and apps you use. You easily arrange cause-effect relationships between them, saying what data can be pulled from where, how data might be combined and put to use, and what rights might accompany data that's shared with other parties.

Your professional life is also thick with rules, but they're yours and not just ones others make for you. For example, you can make connections between your travel services, your preferred airlines, car rental agencies, and hotels, so that much of the selecting, booking, and back-end paperwork is handled automatically and accountably, your trip runs smoothly, and at the end a report in the right format is submitted automatically to your company's systems.

Demand Finds Supply

Among other things, fixing your sleep problems will be good for helping you manage your family of six. Right now, you're on a family trip, having just arrived in San Diego for a wedding and a couple of extra days off. For reasons unknown, the airline has lost your twin toddlers' stroller. While the airline might find the stroller eventually, you need one now. So, rather than searching through countless commercial offerings on the Web—which was your only choice back in the Static Web days, you get on your smartphone and issue a *personal RFP*—a notice of intent to purchase a stroller for twins in the next two hours.

In technical terms, your personal RFP is an *event* that triggers *rules* that are written in KRL and executed by a *rules engine* that's under your control, in this case, at your fourth party (though it could be anywhere). The rules are ones you or your fourth party write. They say what kinds of information can be released, to whom, and under what conditions. They also say what other information might be brought in to help move things along, such as banking and credit information, general or specific locations, time frames, and other data that can be released securely, at the right time, on a need-to-know basis, and auditable later.

All the retailers in your current area are also on the Live Web and ready to receive notice of intents to buy (what used to be called "leads") from potential customers. Your fourth party sends out your RFP to qualified sellers, and in a few minutes, you have serious responses from stores with strollers to offer. After a couple of conversations with stores that have the most attractive offers, you decide that a place about two miles from the airport has the stroller you want. You tell them you'll pick it up after you get your rental car. The store's systems and yours both record the same intention in their respective databases. The same shows up in your smartphone's calendar, along with directions to the store on your phone's map.

The car you're getting is a minivan that seats six. That's what you requested in the personal RFP you sent out to car rental agencies a month ago, when you planned the trip. In years past, you had little control over what kind of vehicle you might get. Shopping around required going from one agency's Web site to another or hoping that a travel site might help find what you wanted. In most cases, however, renting was a cross between a crapshoot and a bait-and-switch scheme. The agency would half-promise a certain car "or similar," and "similar" would turn out to be a less desirable alternative. In this case, you said you wanted to rent a Toyota Sienna with a bike rack, but would be willing to take a Honda Odyssey. Since you are a member of Budget's Fastbreak, Avis's Wizard, and Hertz #1 Club programs, your system matched up with their systems first, and the company with the best offer got your business. Your fourth party also got a piece of the action.

Strolling

After picking up the van and the new stroller, you decide to drop by the nearest Peet's Coffee & Tea for a couple of cappuccinos before heading to the hotel. Using an AR (augmented reality) application from Layar on your smartphone, you can see (literally) a Peet's along the way. So you reserve the cappuccinos through your smartphone.

Since your phone knows your location (though it isn't telling anybody other than your fourth party), it will notify Peet's two minutes before you arrive, so the barista can start making your drinks. After you arrive and pick up the cappuccinos at the counter, you pay through your *digital wallet*. Peet's was a pioneer on the Live Web when it started working with Google's Wallet app and service back in 2011. That early work resulted in open source code and infrastructural modeling now used by all wallet apps.

Real Loyalty

You've been loyal to Peet's for years. Both you and Peet's know that, because you've let it know. Peet's is among the vendors you care about and with which you have a relationship. In some cases, you initiated those relationships. In other cases, those relationships migrated from those vendors' own loyalty programs. In the old days, loyalty programs were run entirely by vendors. Each was different, and all knew only as much about you as their systems were built to comprehend. Then, as the Live Web came along, customers developed their own ways of expressing loyalty, which included solid, reliable, and secure information about themselves and their other relationships in the marketplace. Vendor loyalty programs then adapted and coevolved with customer systems, following customers' leads.

Before customers took the initiative, Peet's didn't have a loyalty program; nor did it see a need for one, since its customers were clearly loyal in any case. The same was true for Trader Joe's, your favorite grocery store. It was a matter of pride for Trader Joe's that it had no loyalty program, no discount cards, and no coupons. Like Peet's, it earned loyalty by avoiding gimmicks and being its own unique kind of store.

You were one of many customers who reached out to both companies, just to let them know how loyal you were, right down to the sums you had spent at their retail outlets over a recent period of time. You could do this because you had *VRM* tools ready to engage with retailers' *CRM* systems.

In the old world, where nearly every store had a different loyalty program, you carried an extra wallet in your purse, just to organize the cards of stores where you shopped frequently. You also carried a number of plastic tags on your key ring, each for a different store, each with its own bar code.

Once *VRM and CRM systems connected* on the Live Web, the need to carry many cards ended, and loyalty programs on the vendors' side were improved by new standards, protocols, and code (as well as data) originating on the customers' side.

Real Relationships

After the social network crash of 2013, when it became clear that neither friendship nor sociability were adequately defined or managed through proprietary and contained systems (no matter how large they might be), individuals began to assert their independence and to zero-base their social networking using their own tools and asserting their own policies regarding engagement.

Customers now *manage relationships in their own ways*, using standardized tools that embrace the complexities of relationship—including needs for privacy (and, in some cases, anonymity). Thus, *loyalty to vendors now has genuine meaning* and goes as deep as either party cares to go. In some (perhaps most) cases, this isn't very deep, while in others, it can get quite involved.

For example, you've let your new favorite airline, Virgin America, know that you had already racked up many miles with Delta, plus more on United and American. In response to your notification and those of other customers, Virgin America adjusted its loyalty program to include personal communications with interested frequent flyers of all airlines. This helped Virgin America improve its own service while offering attractive perks to all frequent flyers.

Personal Pricing Gun

Your hotel is La Jolla Shores, which you chose based on a variety of considerations. One, of course, was price. You named a fair price, and the hotel agreed to it. This isn't new, since prices for many things (including travel accommodations and big-ticket items like houses and cars) have always been somewhat flexible, and services such as Hotwire and Priceline modeled customer-set price offerings long ago.

What's different today is that you have a standard tool for communicating what you are willing to pay, along with your preferences, policies, and whatever else you might choose to share. This tool, called *EmanciPay*, is most useful for product or service categories where prices are already flexible or have prices that have been absent or set by the customer from the start.

EmanciPay also supports *ascribenation*, which expresses your interest in how your payment might be distributed to each party that contributes value to what you pay for.[7] So, for example, you have an EmanciPay button on the screen of your smartphone, which also works as a radio in your rental car. So, when you hear a jazz program you like on KSDS in San Diego and decide to throw $2 to the station for a job well done—your ascribenation— the station also learns that you'd like some of that money to go to the program source and not just the station. You can make this as simple or as complex as you like.

Empathic Supply and Demand

All up and down the world's *supply chains*, connections have become what Michael Stolarczyk, author of *Logical Logistics*, in the 2000s began calling "empathic" and not just mechanical. Today, the supply chain and the *demand chain* have become funicular, constantly pulling on each other at every level, but through teamwork, which requires a "feel" as well as a strong mechanical connection to what others are doing.

Beyond Guesswork

Advertising still pays for much of what you see, hear, and read, but the trade-offs have evolved. In the old world, advertising was mostly an annoyance you put up with in order to watch a TV show, listen to a radio program, or read a newspaper or a magazine. Even on the Web, where Google, Facebook, and others built elaborate systems to improve their guesswork about what you might want, truly interesting and relevant ads were rare.

A few years back, as *VRM and CRM systems pulled together*, with better signaling between them, the reduced need for old-style vendor-driven guesswork caused a crash in what came to be called the *advertising bubble*. Sites and services that depended totally on advertising had a hard time adjusting to a marketplace where free customers were more valuable to sellers than captive ones. But some of the same companies that made big money in the old advertising game adjusted by becoming fourth parties, taking advantage of opportunities in helping customers buy and not just helping vendors sell. These included some of the biggest players, including Google and Microsoft.

Finding

Ever since 1995, when the Web went commercial, search has been the primary means by which users looked for what they wanted among billions of Web sites. Providing this service was very resource-intensive for search engine companies, but they made so much money on advertising that they were able to provide many other services, all for free. By 2012, it became clear that the business model of search was overcoming its original mission, which was simply to help people find stuff. The ratio of commercial to noncommercial sites became so lopsided that for countless keyword combinations, the only noncommercial result to appear in the first page of countless search results was Wikipedia. All the other sites were selling something—or so it seemed. Search engine guesswork about what people wanted to find had been optimized entirely for advertisers, not for users, whether or not they were being customers at the moment.

This changed when the advertising bubble popped. It would have popped in any case, but the introduction of new user-driven search models helped hasten history. Starting with Andrieu's SwitchBook, *new search systems* (not just "engines") began to appear. These new systems gave users control of input, output, storage, and management of their own search history and results. A user could easily, for example, view and construct "search maps" for topics, separating the vacation stuff from the sports stuff and the work-related stuff. Thus, users began to manage search with the same level of control and intentionality as they managed their calendars and wallets.

So the searching you do now on your San Diego trip is remembered in your personal data store and shared with other parties on your own terms, with lots of control over how you organize and interpret queries and results.

Individuals also play the role of sources in searches. So, for example, you can ask a question requiring an expert answer and get it quickly—and even pay for it, if it is worthwhile, using EmanciPay. In your own case, you want to know if it's true that some wallabies have escaped from the San Diego Zoo and are running wild (because one of your kids says she heard something to that effect). After a quick Web search brings up nothing, you tweet the question and get a good answer from a local who works at the zoo. It's only a rumor, the guy says. You thank him, tweet what you just learned, and use EmanciPay to donate a couple dollars to the zoo.

Your tweeting also does not have to involve Twitter, as it did in the early days, when one company owned and defined tweeting. Thanks to work by

Dave Winer (creator of RSS—Really Simple Syndication) and others, tweeting is now as free, open, and as far outside any company's control as e-mail has been from the start.

Everyware

A decade or so back, Bob Frankston, who coinvented spreadsheet software, began forecasting what he called "*ambient connectivity*." That is, Internet connectivity you just assume is available. This hasn't happened yet, but there is progress. For example, few reputable hotels still charge for Internet access (a business roughly equivalent to pay toilets), and none force you to endure a welcome page on your Web browser. Instead your laptops, tablets, and other mobile devices move seamlessly between cellular, wi-fi, and wired connections. This is why you usually don't bother seeing how you are connected, most of the time. Nor do your husband and kids.

Still, there are costs involved, and you are in a position to monitor those. You are also in a position to name your preferred connection providers when there is a choice to be made.

For example, since you'll be shooting a lot of photographs and video footage at the wedding and on the beach and you store those over the Live Web "in the cloud," you have a preference for maximized upstream speeds when there is a choice of connection paths and you express a willingness to pay a bit more for that privilege.

At this point in history, Internet service providers are still mostly a combination of what used to be phone and cable TV companies. The difference now is that their offerings are much more à la carte and responsive to customer demand. Since one common demand is that providers not shackle customers to complicated plans and adhesive contracts, those have gone by the wayside. Those same companies now compete to provide the best possible connections and services, and earn customer loyalty in the process. The company that pioneered this shift was Ting, which began to offer "a mobile service that makes sense" back in 2012.

So, while the primary provider of connectivity at your house is Verizon FiOS and you continue to express a preference for Verizon over other connectivity providers when you are on the road (because you have a genuine relationship with Verizon and appreciate its high level of personal service), you are not locked into using Verizon connections alone when you travel. You are also not subject to the punitive roaming fees for traveling outside

Verizon's service areas. If additional costs come up, services inform you directly or through third or fourth parties.

As a result of ambient connectivity, the sum of business supported by the Internet has gone up rapidly over the past several years, and economic prosperity has also been the result. That's because, in the old system, business could grow only as much as phone and cable companies (and their captive regulators) allowed. In the new system, Internet-based business opportunities are as wide and unrestricted as the Net itself.

SO, THEN

All these scenarios are optimistic—or perhaps even utopian—extrapolations of current technology developments. These developments are all moving fast, and all are bound to change, even before this book is published. What I've done with this exercise is mark the elevation and slope of developers' aspirations, and what they imply in the Intention Economy as it unfolds.

PART I

Customer Captivity

The Matrix is a computer generated dream world built to keep us under
control in order to turn a human being into this (a battery).

—Morpheus, in *The Matrix*, by Lana and Andy Wachowski

2

The Advertising Bubble

Half the money I spend on advertising is wasted; the trouble is,
I don't know which half.

—John Wanamaker[1]

Advertisements are now so numerous that they are very negligently
perused, and it is therefore become necessary to gain attention by
magnificence of promises, and by eloquence sometimes sublime and
sometimes pathetic.

—Samuel Johnson[2]

THE ARGUMENT

Advertising is a form of one-way signaling defined from the
start as guesswork. As more ways are found for customers
and vendors to signal their intentions directly to each other,
advertising as we know it will shrink to what only one-way
guesswork can do.

Good journalists respect what they call the "Chinese wall." That's the
virtual partition between what they do and what their business sells. For
the most part, the latter is advertising. Journalists don't want their interests
conflicted, so they stay disinterested in the advertising side of the business.

There is a similar wall in the minds of advertising people, separating
their inner John Wanamaker from their inner Samuel Johnson. On one side,
they do their best to make good advertising. On the other side, they join the

rest of us, drowning in a flood of it. Like journalists, advertising folk are aware of what's happening on the other side of the wall. Unlike journalists, it's not in their interest to ignore it.

Nobody is in a better position to understand what's happening on both sides of both walls than Randall Rothenberg. For three decades, he's worked as an author and journalist, covering marketing and advertising for *Bloomberg*, *Wired*, *Esquire*, *Advertising Age*, the *New York Times*, and other publications. For most of the time since 2007, he has been president and CEO of the Interactive Advertising Bureau (IAB). Here's how he explains the role of advertising's Chinese wall:

> There are two discrete conversations taking place in our realm
> that simply don't ever intersect. One conversation posits that the
> future of marketing will be based entirely on the reduction of all
> human interactions and interests into sets of data points that can be
> analyzed and traded. The other conversation posits that marketing
> success derives entirely from content, context, environment and the
> qualitative engagement of human emotion.[3]

Both conversations are professional factions, and both have their own approaches to the separate problems of Wanamaker and Johnson. The quantitative faction works on ways to make advertising as personalized and efficient as possible, with or without voluntary input from the persons targeted. The emotional faction works to improve advertising by changing its mission from targeting to engagement.

I think the emotional faction has the edge, because engagement is the only evolutionary path out of the pure-guesswork game that advertising has been for the duration. It's what will survive of advertising when the Intention Economy emerges. In the short run, however, the quantitative faction is driving growth in the Attention Economy, and the flood of advertising output continues to rise. In June 2011, eMarketer estimated that the annual sum spent on advertising would exceed half a trillion dollars in 2012 and pass $.6 trillion in 2016.[4] Four months later, eMarketer moved the dates closer by one year apiece.[5]

These numbers measure tolerance more than effects.

Tolerance

No medium has tested human tolerance of advertising more aggressively than television, which has long been the fattest wedge in advertising's pie chart of spending[6] (40.4 percent of the projected total worldwide in 2012, according to Zenith Optimedia;[7] and around 72 percent in the United States, according to Nielsen and AdCross).[8] So let's dive into TV for a bit. How much advertising do we tolerate there? And how much less will we tolerate after we do all our TV watching on devices that are not designed and controlled by the TV industry?

In the United States, the typical hour-long American TV drama runs forty-two minutes. The remaining eighteen minutes are for advertising. Half-hour shows are twenty-one minutes long, with nine left for advertising. That's 30 percent in each case. The European Union sets a limit of twelve minutes per hour for advertising on TV, which comes to 20 percent. Ireland holds broadcasters to ten minutes per hour, or 16.7 percent. Russia by law sets aside nineteen minutes per hour for advertising: four for "federal" messages and the rest for "regional" ones. Russia is also considering lowering those numbers, due to a decline in viewing.[9] Thus, eighteen minutes seems to be the upper limit.

So far, nobody is pushing that limit online, except with simulcasts. On the Web, Hulu sells only two minutes of advertising per half hour.[10] Commercial podcasts and streaming videos tend to have only "bumper" ads at the front and back. As viewing and listening migrate from TV and radio to the Net, however, it's only natural for producers to look for ways to increase revenues by loading more advertising into content. To help with that, comScore in 2010 released a research report titled, "Great Expectations: How Advertising for Original Scripted TV Programming Works Online."[11] From the introduction:

> Eager to sustain growth online both in audience size and time spent
> viewing long format TV content, publishers have erred on the side of
> fewer ads against a typical TV program. However, although audiences
> continue to grow in both size and engagement, this approach has
> resulted in challengingly low ratios of ads to content—typically,
> 6–8% of viewing time is ads against most long format TV programs
> viewed online, compared to 25% on television. Consequently,
> the business model around online distribution of TV programs is
> becoming difficult to sustain for many content providers.[12]

Note the perspective here. Publishers "have erred" by running fewer ads. To comScore, the problem is *not enough advertising*. So it surveyed to see how large an advertising load the audience will bear when viewing scripted TV on devices other than TVs. Not surprisingly, it found "cross-platform viewers" (ones that watched TV online as well as the old-fashioned way) were much more positive toward advertising than were TV-only viewers, that "43% of all cross platform viewers stopped watching a TV program online in order to visit an advertiser's website," and that "over 25% of the audience who were reached by online video advertising felt that the commercials were enjoyable."[13]

Thanks to advertising's Chinese wall, the reciprocal numbers don't get mentioned. Here, they are: 57 percent didn't stop to visit a promoted Web site, and 75 percent did not find commercials enjoyable.

ComScore also did a "sensitivity meter analysis" to find "ad load tolerance levels." It surveyed 640 people and spread the results across a graph titled "Desired Length of Commercials Online: 18–49." ComScore came to the conclusion that around six minutes was most "desirable," because 50 percent or more of those surveyed considered six minutes to be either "long enough" or "too long."[14]

Now, if you're not in the advertising business, you might ask, *Is advertising something viewers desire at all?* In fact, comScore's findings show that nearly all people find some level of advertising intolerable. Asking how much of an ad load people will bear is like asking how much brown matter they can stand in their water, or how many extra pounds of fat they're willing to carry.

If advertisers would peek over on our side of the Chinese wall, they would see two icebergs toward which TV's Titanic is headed, and both promise less tolerance for advertising. One is demographics and the other is choice.

The Ageberg

We can see the demographic iceberg approaching in the comScore's breakdown, in the same study, for five demographics (see table 2-1).[15]

TABLE 2-1

Demographic breakdown of viewers by platform

Age range	TV-only	Cross-platform	Online-only
18–24	45%	42%	13%
25–34	53%	38%	9%
35–49	68%	28%	4%
50–64	81%	17%	2%
65+	87%	12%	1%

Already, the majority ages eighteen to twenty-four watch TV on devices other than TVs, and TV-only as a platform is going down while online-only is going up. At some point, it will become clear that TV is a video format and not a platform, and that the only platform still worthy of the noun is the Internet.

The Choiceberg

The tip of the choice iceberg is TiVo, which has been around for more than a decade. TiVo was the first digital video recorder (DVR, aka PVR). It gave users a way to store TV shows as files and to skip over ads when viewing shows later. The full implications of TiVo still haven't fully sunk in, although there are plenty of people in The Industry (as they call it in L.A.) who saw the end coming from the start. One is Jonathan Taplin, a veteran Hollywood producer, writer, entrepreneur, and currently a professor at the USC Annenberg School for Communication & Journalism.[16] At the Digital Hollywood conference in September 2002, Taplin was on a panel during which the moderator asked the audience to raise their hands if they had a TiVo.[17] Nearly every hand went up. Then he asked them to drop their hands if they didn't use their TiVo to skip over ads. The hands stayed up. "There goes your business model," Taplin said.[18]

Six years later, in 2008, engadget published a press release by the management consulting firm Oliver Wyman reporting that 85 percent of those surveyed by the company used their DVR to skip at least three-quarters of all commercials. Those surveyed also said they would not want to "watch advertising even when it underwrites free content." Nor would they pay extra to remove ads.[19]

These findings were published in the *Oliver Wyman Journal*, in a long report by John Senior and Rafael Asensio, titled "TV 2013: Is It All Over?"[20] In it, they look at two scenarios they call "Non-TV" and "Next TV." With Non-TV, video is just video. Watch it on anything: your flat screen, your laptop, your phone, your tablet, or any other device you like. Today's TV content sources go direct, and sell or give you whatever you like. With Next TV, the cable and satellite systems continue couch potato farming the old-fashioned way, but with better Internet integration.

Non-TV is what the cable industry calls "over the top." It's a good metaphor, since the bottom is its whole old system, and it's a dam that's breaking down. What's spilling over it isn't a brook or a river anymore. It's an ocean of video files and streams from millions of sources, most of which

TABLE 2-2

Viewers' platform choices

	Streams	Files
	(sent live over the Internet)	(either downloaded or on demand from "the cloud")
Paid	Original basic and premium cable channels	Movie and program rentals
	Paid subscription services, such as Hulu+	Free subscription services, such as basic Hulu
Free	Original over-the-air stations and networks	YouTube and others like it

are already available à la carte through YouTube and other online distributors. So far, most "original scripted programming" is still confined to old-fashioned TV, but in time, that stuff will move online as well. Consider the choice. With TV, your choices are sphinctered through a set-top box. With the Internet, you can watch on whatever device you like. It's no contest.

Meanwhile, we're willing to put up with what's left of TV, for two reasons: (1) because it's still normative, and (2) because the stuff we want most is still trapped inside TNT, ESPN, HBO, and other cable-only networks. But how long will those networks put up with being stuck inside an old system that's breaking down? They'll bolt for the Net as soon as they're sure they will still get paid for their goods. Once that's worked out, your choices as a viewer will be simple: you'll watch some mix of live streams and stored files, some of which you'll pay for and some of which you won't. Table 2-2 shows a possible sorting out.

How it all sorts out matters less than the fact that all of it will be "over the top" on the Internet.

More of Less

When TV's sources go direct through the Internet, what happens to advertising? The old TV system was built to make you watch advertising, while the Internet is built to let you do whatever you like. Yes, there are ways you can be forced to watch ads on cable-over-Internet services such as Hulu and Xfinity. But we still have the "load" tolerance problem that comScore probes. We'll put up with some advertising, but far less than we did in captivity. If the most we'll tolerate is six minutes per hour, as comScore says, that's a two-thirds drop from what you got over the old tube. You might put up with eighteen minutes per hour on a live sportscast, no matter what glowing rectangle you watch it on. But will you put up with it on everything else? Doubtful.

After reading the comScore study, Terry Heaton, one of the top consultants in the TV industry, posted an essay titled, "Media's Real Doomsday Scenario." An excerpt:

> The advertising hegemony used by Madison Avenue is about to collapse, and when it goes, it will take traditional media with it. As alarming and preposterous as that might seem, it is exactly the impossibility of such a situation that makes it so likely and so dangerous. When it happens, those involved will look around in astonishment and insist that it couldn't have happened and that, indeed, either advertisers or media moguls have lost their minds.[21]

Heaton isn't alone. Bob Garfield, author of *The Chaos Scenario*, cohost of NPR's *On the Media*, and veteran columnist for *Ad Age*, shook the walls of the advertising world in March 2009 with an *Ad Age* column titled, "Future May Be Brighter, but It's Apocalypse Now." He writes,

> Chicken Little, don your hardhat. Nudged by recession, doom has arrived. The toll will be so vast—and the institutions of media and marketing are so central to our economy, our culture, our democracy and our very selves—that it's easy to fantasize about some miraculous preserver of "reach" dangling just out of reach. We need "mass," so mass, therefore, must survive. Alas, economies are unsentimental and denial unproductive. The post-advertising age is under way.[22]

The Greater Unknown

So why is advertising's apocalypse running late? One reason is that the TV programs viewers like best (especially sports) are still trapped on cable, and cable isn't giving up easily. (Even the live streaming of HBO GO requires a cable or satellite subscription.) The other is that online advertising is growing rapidly, thanks partly to a growth in the number of places where ads can be placed and partly to innovations in tracking, targeting, and personalization. This is the quantitative conversation Randall Rothenberg talked about, and it has become a craze.

The *Wall Street Journal* began following this craze in the summer of 2010, when it launched an investigative series titled, "What They Know."[23] The first article, which ran on July 30, 2010, said,

> One of the fastest-growing businesses on the Internet ... is the business of spying on Internet users. The *Journal* conducted a comprehensive study that assesses and analyzes the broad array of cookies and other surveillance technology that companies are deploying on Internet users. It reveals that the tracking of consumers has grown both far more pervasive and far more intrusive than is realized by all but a handful of people in the vanguard of the industry.[24]

Over the following months, the *Journal's* series grew to dozens of reports, polls, and graphical illustrations. The findings were many. Here are a few, in summary form:

- Data gathering is a new and lightly regulated industry based on surveillance, harvesting, and selling data and data-educated guesses about what users might want, in real time.[25]

- All the largest commercial Web sites in the United States put intrusive tracking devices in computers visiting their sites. Some installed more than a hundred of these things in a single visit. Forty-nine of the fifty most popular Web sites installed a total of 3,180 tracking files on the *Journal's* test computer. Twelve (including IAC/InterActive Corp.'s Dictionary.com, Comcast Corp.'s Comcast.net, and Microsoft's MSN.com) had each installed more than a hundred files.

- It's worse for kids. The top fifty sites targeting teens and children installed 4,123 tracking files on the *Journal's* test computer: 30 percent more than for sites targeted at adults.[26]

- In response to the poll question, "How concerned are you about advertisers and companies tracking your behavior across the Web?" 85 percent of respondents were "very alarmed" or "somewhat concerned."[27]

- In the back-end market for buying and selling personal data in real time, the biggest player is BlueKai, which "trades data on more than 200 million Internet users, boasting the ability to reach more than 80% of the U.S. Internet population."[28]

- Most users had few if any clues that they were being tracked. Case in point: many phone apps share the customer's user name, password, location, contacts, age, gender, location, unique phone ID (equivalent of a serial number), and phone number with third parties, which in turn represent countless advertisers.[29]

- The biggest exposure comes not from location-oriented apps like Foursquare, but from apps that do not appear to be location-based, or even advertising-supported—and quietly make money by selling users' location data to advertisers, without users' knowledge or permission. One app tested by the *Journal* sent personal data to eight different ad networks.[30]

- There is a big business in building detailed information about people, gleaned from tracked browsing and digital crumb trails. Writes the *Journal*,

  > firms like [x+1] [sic] tap into vast databases of people's online behavior—mainly gathered surreptitiously by tracking technologies that have become ubiquitous on websites across the Internet. They don't have people's names, but cross-reference that data with records of home ownership, family income, marital status and favorite restaurants, among other things. Then, using statistical analysis, they start to make assumptions about the proclivities of individual Web surfers. "We never don't know anything about someone," says John Nardone, [x+1]'s chief executive.[31]

- Companies such as Kindsight and Phorm do "deep packet inspection"—the same technology used by spy agencies for surveillance of terrorism suspects—to "give advertisers the ability to show ads to people based on extremely detailed profiles of their Internet activity."[32]

- "Scraping"—copying every message an individual posts, even on private sites—is another popular way for advertisers to gather information about individuals. The *Journal* found a number of companies that live to "harvest online conversations and collect personal details from social-networking sites, résumé sites and online forums where people might discuss their lives."[33]

- Answering the poll question, "Would you use an Internet 'do-not-track' tool if it were included in your Web browser?" more than 92 percent said yes.[34]

Not surprisingly, on December 1, 2010, the Federal Trade Commission issued recommendations for a "do not track" mechanism on browsers.[35]

Picking up on the FTC's cue, *USA Today* and Gallup conducted a poll of a random-dialed sample of 1,019 adults over eighteen years old on December 11–12, 2010.[36] To the question, "Should advertisers be allowed to match ads to your specific interests based on Web sites you have visited?" 67 percent said no. And, while 30 percent agreed with the statement, "Yes, advertisers should be allowed to match ads to interests based on websites visited," and 35 percent also agreed with, "Yes, the invasion of privacy involved is worth it to allow people free access to websites," the reciprocal numbers—70 percent and 65 percent—show negative demand by its recipients for tracking and advertising personalization.

At some point, The Market—meaning people gagging on advertising—will pull their invisible hands out of their pockets and strangle the source.

Waste

One might think all this personalized advertising must be pretty good, or it wouldn't be such a hot new business category. But that's only if one ignores the bubbly nature of the craze or the negative demand on the receiving end for most of advertising's goods. In fact, the results of personalized advertising, so far, have been lousy for actual persons.

Chikita Research, a primary source for online advertising statistics, published a report in September 2010 with the headline, "Ad Layout Series: Above The Fold Ads Get 44% Higher CTR."[37] The *fold* is an old newspaper term and was meant literally. Full-size papers (non-tabloids, such as the *New York Times*) are folded, and in the caste system of newspaper advertising and editorial placement, "above the fold" is always better, no matter what the page. Online, "below the fold" refers to space outside the typical browser's viewing area. Chikita found that CTRs both above and below the fold run at less than 1 percent (0.939 percent and 0.651 percent, which combined are 0.818 percent).

From advertising's side of its Chinese wall, all this waste is okay, because advertising is guesswork, and online the waste is easier to ignore because it has been relocated: moved from airwaves, billboards, and newsprint to server farms, pixels, rods, and cones. But it's still there. So are the costs, which far exceed zero.

Branding

Of course, that's the view from *our* side of the Chinese wall. From the side where advertising comes from, most of that waste can be excused, because even its failures can be rationalized as "branding." Within the industry—and even outside it (see the sidebar, "Nothing Personal")—branding is a subject of countless books, articles, and postings on the Web. What was once an "image" is now a "promise," an "experience," and an "asset" that has "equity."

It's easy to forget that the term *branding* was borrowed from the cattle industry. The idea was to burn the name of a company or a product onto the brains of potential customers.

Procter & Gamble's first brand was Ivory soap, in 1878. The product and its strategy were so successful over the following decades that *brand management* eventually became a serious business discipline.[38] This happened in the 1930s, when America was getting hooked on radio, and women listening at home were entertained by soap operas, which were mostly sponsored by brands of cleaning products. It was in this era that grocery store chains also grew, and "shelf wars" were won by companies that maximized varieties of packaging and promises, while minimizing the actual differences between the products themselves. This is also when the first jingles came along. Hence the old industry adage, "If you've got nothing to say, sing it."

NOTHING PERSONAL

Personal branding in the social networking age has become a calling card for countless marketing-advice givers (bringing up many millions of results in a Google search). But the term is oxymoronic. Branding is a corporate practice, not a personal one. Branding works for companies and products because those things are not people. That is, buildings and offices and ballparks and shoes may have human qualities, but are not themselves human. Likewise, humans may be industrious or durable or attractive, but that doesn't make them companies or products. You and I are not brands. Our parents did not raise us to be brands. Nor would we want our children to be brands, any more than we would want them to be logos.

At its best, branding is unforgettable. For example, I remember fondly the words to beer-brand jingles I heard endlessly as a kid listening to Dodgers, Giants, Yankees, and Mets games on the radio. Here's one:

Schaefer
Is the
One beer to have
When you're having more than one.

Schaefer
Pleasure
Doesn't fade
Even when your thirst is done

The most rewarding flavor
In this man's world
For people who are having fun.

(repeat first verse)

Four facts are worth noting here. First, Schaefer's brand was burned into my cortex long before I was old enough to drink. Second, Schaefer has never been anywhere on my list of adult beer preferences, even back when I was in my twenties and Schaefer was still popular. Third, Schaefer at its peak was the world's best-selling beer. Fourth, branding couldn't save it. In 1981, Schaefer sold out to Stroh's, and in 1999, Stroh's sold out to Pabst. Schaefer survives today as one of Pabst's many labels: small-bore ammo in liquor store shelf wars.[39]

At its worst, branding is brutal. My vote for the most memorable characterization of branding brutality is a scene in *The Hucksters*, a movie in which Sydney Greenstreet plays Evan Evans, a soap industry magnate whose crude style was modeled on George Washington Hill of the American Tobacco Company. After spitting on the glossy surface of a conference table, Evans says, "Gentlemen, you have just seen me do a disgusting thing. But you will always remember it!"

My favorite response from our side of the Chinese wall is a Hugh MacLeod cartoon (see figure 2-1).[40]

Today, the fastest-growing category of advertising is online, where effects are easier to measure than in the old offline world and far more accountable. Google launched advertising's accountable age with AdWords—text ads placed in the margins of search results—in October 2000.[41] AdWords was

FIGURE 2-1

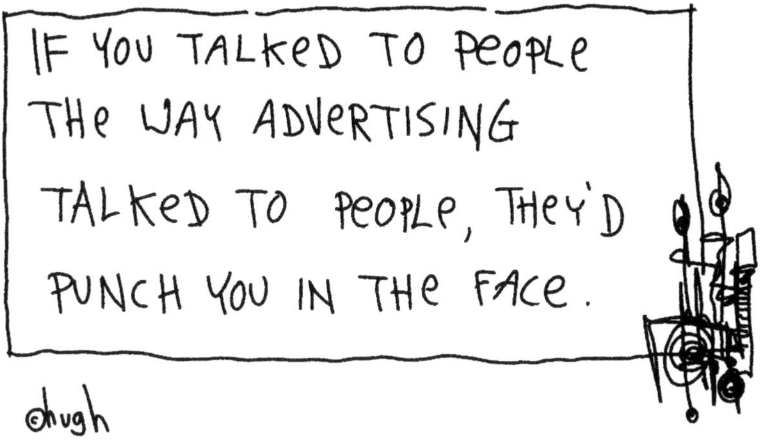

IF YOU TALKED TO PEOPLE
THE WAY ADVERTISING
TALKED TO PEOPLE, THEY'D
PUNCH YOU IN THE FACE.

@hugh

Source: Hugh MacLeod, reprinted with permission.

revolutionary in several ways. First, advertisers paid only for click-throughs. Second, the ads were text-only and as nonbrutal as possible. Third, ads were ordered in respect to how well they worked. Those earning more click-throughs were placed higher among ads accompanying a given search result.

Online advertising has grown at double-digit rates every year of its existence. In 2010, Google's annual revenues, derived almost entirely from advertising, passed $30 billion.[42] According to the IAB, Internet advertising in the United States sold at a $25.4 billion annualized rate in the third quarter of 2010, up 17 percent from the same period one year earlier.[43]

Within the online sector, the fastest growing subsector is mobile. In April 2010, AdMob bragged about serving 16.7 billion ads to mobile phones in the prior month.[44] The next month, Google acquired AdMob for $750 million.[45] In September 2010, MobileSquared, a research company, said it expected mobile advertising revenues in the United Kingdom alone to grow 850 percent by 2015.[46] Reports from other sources are no less optimistic and ambitious.

Raise your hand if you like seeing ads on your phone. (And drop that hand if you make money from advertising.) In fact, most of us ignore or avoid the torrent of unwanted messages we slog through every day. That same "most of us" includes everybody in the advertising business. They're not impressed either, even if they don't admit it.

Clogged Filters

In *The Filter Bubble: What the Internet is Hiding from You*, Eli Pariser writes,

> "You have one identity," Facebook founder Mark Zuckerberg told journalist David Kirkpatrick for his book *The Facebook Effect*. "The days of having a different image for your work friends or coworkers and for the other people you may know are probably coming to an end pretty quickly ... Having two identities for yourself is an example of a lack of integrity."[47]

Later, Zuckerberg discounted the remark as "just a sentence I said," but to Facebook, the only *you* that matters is the one *it* knows. Not the one you *are*.

In the closing sentences of *The Shallows: What the Internet is Doing to our Brains*, Nicholas Carr writes,

> In the world of 2001, people have become so machinelike that the most human character turns out to be a machine. That's the essence of Kubrick's dark prophecy: as we come to rely on computers to mediate our understanding of the world, it is our own intelligence that flattens into artificial intelligence.[48]

Even if our own intelligence is not yet artificialized, what's feeding it surely is.

Pariser sums up the absurdity of it all in a subchapter titled, "A Bad Theory of You." After explaining Google's and Facebook's very different approaches to personalized "experience" filtration and the assumptions behind both, he concludes, "Both are pretty poor representations of who we are, in part because there is no one set of data that describes who we are." He says both companies have dumped us into what animators and robotics engineers call the *uncanny valley*: "the place where something is lifelike but not convincingly alive, and it gives people the creeps."[49]

Lost Signals

The ideal of perfectly personalized advertising is also at odds with the nature of advertising at its most ideal. This ideal is perhaps best expressed by the most canonical of all ads for advertising: McGraw-Hill's "The Man in the Chair." Of it, David Ogilvy (the most respected—and certainly the most widely quoted—figure in the history of advertising) wrote, "This ad summarizes the case for corporate advertising." It features a bald guy in a suit and bow tie, sitting in an office chair with his fingers folded, looking out at the reader. Beside him, in the white space of the ad, runs this copy:

> "*I don't know who you are.*
> *I don't know your company.*
> *I don't know your company's products.*
> *I don't know what your company stands for.*
> *I don't know your company's record.*
> *I don't know your company's reputation.*
> *Now—what was it you wanted to sell me?"*

> MORAL: Sales start *before* your salesman calls—with business publication advertising.

In economic terms, what the man wants are signals, and those signals are not just about what's for sale. In "Advertising as a Signal," Richard E. Kihlstrom and Michael H. Riordan explain how advertising signals the substance of the company placing it:

> When a firm signals by advertising, it demonstrates to consumers that its production costs and the demand for its product are such that advertising costs can be recovered. In order for advertising to be an effective signal, high-quality firms must be able to recover advertising costs while low-quality firms cannot.[50]

In "The Waste in Advertising is the Part that Works," Tim Ambler and E. Ann Hollier compare advertising to the male peacock's tail: a signal of worthiness that a strong company with a quality product can afford to display, but a weak company cannot.[51]

Therefore, placing an ad in a McGraw-Hill publication wasn't just a branding effort or a briefing in advance of a sales call. It was a signal of financial sufficiency. But that ad ran back when Mad Men ruled the advertising world, and print publications conveyed the most substance. Today, the grandchildren of the man in the chair get their news from the Net. Thus, Don Marti, former Editor-in-Chief of *Linux Journal*, suggests one more item for the Man In The Chair's list: "I don't know if your company is really spending a lot on advertising, or if you're just targeting me." He explains,

> Here's the problem. As targeting for online advertising gets better and better, the man in the chair has less and less knowledge of how

much the companies whose ads he sees are spending to reach him. He's losing the signal ... On the web, how do you tell a massive campaign from a well-targeted campaign? And if you can't spot the "waste," how do you pick out the signal?[52]

Perhaps the financial sufficiency signal doesn't matter much in a time when advertising from a zillion unknown sources is the norm and companies come and go at the speed of fads. But if that's the case, advertising itself might not matter much, either. In other words, advertising may now be giving away some of the soul it has left.

The true lodestar of advertising has always been the customer. This is why "the man in the chair" ad was so important. It was a signal sent by McGraw-Hill to advertisers on behalf of its readers. It spoke of the company's relationship with those readers and said to advertisers that it stood on the readers' side. It demanded substance, relevance, and earned reputation from its advertisers. It said relationships were possible, but only when customers sat with companies at the same table, at the same level.

Anonymity

Tracking and "personalizing"—the current frontier of online advertising—probe the limits of tolerance. While harvesting mountains of data about individuals and signaling nothing obvious about their methods, tracking and personalizing together ditch one of the few noble virtues to which advertising at its best aspires: respect for the prospect's privacy and integrity, which has long included a default assumption of anonymity.

Ask any celebrity about the price of fame and he or she will tell you: it's anonymity. This wouldn't be a Faustian bargain (or a bargain at all) if anonymity did not have real worth. Tracking, filtering, and personalizing advertising all compromise our anonymity, even if no PII (personally identifiable information) is collected. Even if these systems don't know us by name, their hands are still in our pants.

SelectOut.org is a "privacy manager" Web site that cleverly surfaces all the advertising companies with tracking hands inside your browser's trousers. Table 2-3 shows a list of the company hands SelectOut just found inside one of my browsers.

TABLE 2-3

Results of SelectOut's browser search

24/7 Real Media	BrightRoll	Lucid Media
33Across	Brilig	Magnetic
aCerno	BTBuckets	Maxpoint Interactive
Acxiom	BuySight	Media6degrees
Adara Media	BuzzLogic	MediaMath
AdBrite	BV! Media	MediaMind
AdBuyer	Casale Media	Mediaplex
AdChemy	Choice Stream	Microsoft Advertising
adConductor	CPX Interactive	Mindset Media
Adconion	Crimson Tangerine	Navegg
AdGear	Criteo	Netmining
Adify Media	Dapper	NexTag
AdInterax	DataLogix	OpenX
AdJuggler	DataXu	Outbrain
AdMeld	Datran Media	PeerSet
AdMotion	Demdex	PointRoll
adnetik	Dotomi	PrecisionClick
Adnologies	Double Verify	PrecisionClick Ads
Adperium	echoSearch	PredictAd
Adroit Interactive	Efficient Frontier	Proximic
AdShuffle	eXelate Media	Pubmatic
AdSpeed	Facilitate Digital	Quantcast
AdTech	FetchBack	QuinStreet
Advertising.com (AOL)	Freewheel.tv	Quisma
AggregateKnowledge	Full Circle Studies	RapLeaf
AlmondNet	Google (DoubleClick)	Red Aril
AppNexus	Groupon	Reedge
Atlas Technology	i-Behavior	richrelevance
BeenCounter	Infectious Media	Rocket Fuel
Bizo	interCLICK	Safecount
BlueKai	Invite Media	Smart AdServer
BlueStreak	Lijit	Specific Media LLC
brand.net	Lotame	SpongeCell Ads

(Continued)

TABLE 2-3

Results of SelectOut's browser search (Continued)

Tatto Media	Tumri	Wall Street on Demand
TellApart	Turn	[x + 1]
Traffic Marketplace	Undertone Networks	XGraph
Travel Ad Network	ValueClick Media	Xtend Media
Tribal Fusion	Vibrant Media	YuMe
Triggit	Vindico	

If you're not familiar with the companies listed in the table (and this is just a subset of the whole business), it helps to look at what they say about themselves. I'll choose one at random: Reedge. This is from Reedge's "Our Company" Web page:

> Reedge offers online software that helps site operators to identify and track user behavior, optimize the site performance and serve customized pages to improve conversion and drive more transaction revenue. Reedge customers pay a monthly subscription fee and receive unlimited access to Reedge tools, software and professional support.
>
> Reedge works by segmenting the audience based on their browser type, location and online behavior to identify their *intent*, then dynamically customizes the text, images, pop-up offers and other content to improve conversion and boost sales.[53]

And here's what Rocket Fuel says on its "About" page:

> Rocket Fuel goes beyond other audience targeting technologies by combining demographic, lifestyle, purchase *intent* and social data with its own suite of targeting algorithms, blended analytics and expert analysis to find active customers. Rocket Fuel uses its technology to deliver better ROI for premium brand marketers— whether their objectives are brand-oriented or designed to drive a conversion event.[54]

The italics are mine.

Note how both these companies assume that user *intent* is something *the company* needs to figure out. They are not alone in this. All the companies on the list in the table have the same ambition.

The distance between what tracking does and what users want, expect, and *intend* is so extreme that backlash is inevitable. The only question is how much it will damage a business that is vulnerable in the first place.

Terminal Delusions

Eric K. Clemons, professor of operations and information management at the Wharton School of the University of Pennsylvania, visited those vulnerabilities in a March 2009 guest post on TechCrunch titled, "Why Advertising Is Failing On The Internet."[55] His post is long and detailed, but compressed to its essence, it says this:

1. There must be something else. (There will be other business models.)

2. We don't trust advertising. (It's among the least trusted forms of communication.)

3. We don't want to view advertising. (Given the option, we avoid it.)

4. We don't need advertising. (There are plenty of other ways to get information.)

TechCrunch readers didn't like what Clemons wrote. Of the six hundred comments below the post, nearly all were negative. "WOW!" wrote one reader, "This is one of the most ignorant and misinformed articles I have ever read! First, Internet advertising is one of the most profitable, fastest growing industries in existence."

Clemons replied,

> I've been attacked and ridiculed before. I warned the floor traders in New York about the coming of online trading back in 1989 and was fired for it. I warned traditional people-based travel agents about dropping commissions and their eventual bypass through online booking systems and was ridiculed ...
>
> And even if you continue to ridicule my piece, there are too many other professionals noticing the same thing. Consider the recent article in the *Economist*[56] on essentially the same thing: advertising cannot fully support the net. You cannot ridicule everything you do not like off the net.[57]

Yet we can't ignore the huge numbers of people who live within or on the shores of the vast money river that flows through advertising, especially online. That's where the ridicule comes from, and it won't stop until the bubble pops.

Advertimania

The etymologist Douglas Harper calls mania "mental derangement characterized by excitement and delusion," adding that it has been used in the "sense of 'fad, craze'" since the 1680s, and since the 1500s "as the second element in compounds expressing particular types of madness (cf. nymphomania, 1775; kleptomania, 1830; megalomania, 1890)."[58] I believe we have *advertimania* today.[59] Here's why:

- **An overly generous infusion of liquidity**, in the form of venture capital. This capital is invested both in companies that expect to make money through advertising, and in advertising for those companies and others. This was rampant in the dot-com boom and is again today.

- **Faith in endless growth** for advertising and in its boundless capacity to fund free services to users.

- **Herd mentality**—around advertising itself and in faith that ad-supported social media will persist and grow indefinitely.

- **Huge increase in trading**. This is happening with user data bought and sold in back-end markets, employing the same kind of "quants" who worked on Wall Street during the housing bubble.[60]

- **Low quality of personal information**, despite the claims of companies specializing in personalization.

And that's just on advertising's side of the Chinese wall. Over here on our side, we can add to that list (especially the last item) six delusions, inclusive of the ones listed by professor Clemons:

1. **We are always ready to buy something**. We're not. In fact, most of the time we're not about to buy anything. Even if we don't mind being exposed to advertising when we're not buying, nearly all of us do mind being watched constantly—especially by parties whose main interest is in selling us stuff.

2. **People will welcome totally personalized advertising**. Even if people allowed themselves to be tracked constantly through the world and

to be understood in great detail (a privilege that advertisers have done little if anything to earn), the result would still be guesswork, which is the very nature of advertising. For customers, rough impersonal guesswork is tolerable, because they're used to it. Totally personalized guesswork is not. At least not by advertising. To become totally personal, advertising needs to cross an existential bridge, to become a different corporate function. It must become sales—without the human sound or the human touch.

3. **The market for tracking-based advertising is large enough to justify the huge investments being made in it.** Christopher Meyer, founder of Monitor Talent and frequent author on the impact of technology on markets (including *Blur: The Speed of Change in the Connected Economy*,[61] coauthored with Stanley M. Davis) says, "It's an eyeball bubble. Investments in tracking-based advertising assume impossibly high values for a customer's attention. The incremental business just won't be that big. And if eyeballs are overvalued, then advertising as a category should crash."[62]

4. **Advertising is something people actually like or can be made to like.** It's not. With a few all-too-rare exceptions (such as Super Bowl ads, which are typical mostly of themselves), advertising is something people tolerate at best and loathe at worst. Improving a pain in the ass does not make it a kiss. Nor does putting a thumbs-up "like" button next to an ad that gets ignored 99.X percent of the time.

5. **The client-server structure of e-commerce will persist unchanged.** It won't. I'll explain why in the next chapter, meanwhile, here's Kynetx CEO Phil Windley: "There are a billion commercial sites on the Web, each with its own selling systems, its own cookies, its own way of dealing with customers, and its own pile of data about each customer. This whole architecture will collapse as soon as customers have their own systems for dealing with sellers, their own piles of data, and their own contexts for interaction."[63]

6. **Companies have to advertise.** In fact, advertising is not an essential function of any company. The difference between an advertiser and an ordinary company is zero. Even if we call advertising an investment, it's on the expense side of the balance sheet and an easy item to cut.

Each of those delusions is a brick in the Chinese wall between the industry's mentality and the larger marketplace outside it. You could call that wall a blind side, but it's more than that. It's a screen on which an industry that smokes its own exhaust has long been projecting its fantasies. It sees those projections rather than the real human beings on the other side. It also fails to see what those human beings might bring to the market's table, beyond cash, credit cards, and coerced "loyalty."

The Fix

Advertising may fund lots of stuff that we take for granted (such as Google's search), but it flourishes in the absence of more efficient and direct demand-supply interactions. The Internet was built to facilitate exactly those kinds of interactions. This it has done since the mid-nineties, but only within a billion different silos, each with its own system for interacting with users, and each with its own asymmetrical power relationship between seller and buyer.[64] This system is old, broken, and long overdue for a fix.

The Internet, meanwhile, has always been a symmetrical system. Its architecture, defined by its founding protocols (which we'll visit in chapter 9) embodies end-to-end principles. Every end on the Net has equal status, whether that end is Amazon.com, the White House, your laptop, or your phone. This architectural fact is a background against which advertising's asymmetries, and its delusional assumptions, have always stood in sharp relief.

SO, THEN

When the backlash is over, and the advertising bubble deflates, advertising will remain an enormous and useful business. We will still need advertising to do what only it can do. What will emerge, however, is a market for what advertising *can't* do. This new market will be defined by *what customers actually want*, rather than guesses about it.

3

Your Choice of Captor

Find out just what any people will quietly submit to and you have the exact
measure of the injustice and wrong which will be imposed on them.

—Frederick Douglass[1]

The term "client-server" was invented because we didn't want to call it
"master-slave."

—Craig Burton[2]

THE ARGUMENT

The World Wide Web has become a World Wide Ranch,
where we serve as calves to Web sites' cows, which feed us
milk and cookies.

The Internet and the Web are not the same things. The Internet is a collection of disparate networks whose differences are transcended by protocols
that put every end at zero functional distance from every other end. The
World Wide Web is one application that runs on the Internet. Others include
e-mail, messaging, file transfer, chat and newsgroups, to name just a few.
But the World Wide Web is the big one—so big that we tend to assume
it's the whole thing, especially since the Web is where we spend most of
our time online and when it has absorbed so many other formerly separate
activities. E-mailing, for example.

Sir Tim Berners-Lee, who invented the Web in 1989, later said it aspired to be "a universal linked information system, in which generality and portability are more important than fancy graphics techniques and complex extra facilities. The aim would be to allow a place to be found for any information or reference which one felt was important, and a way of finding it afterwards."[3] He did not intend to create a vast online shopping mall, an industrial park of advertising mills, or home to a billion-member "social network" owned by one company. But that's what the Web is today. True, somewhere in the midst of all that other stuff, you can still find the simple, linked collection of documents that Sir Tim meant for the Web to be in the first place. But that collection is getting harder and harder to find, mostly because there's little money in it.

Thus, the Web we know today is largely the commercial one that appeared in 1995, when Netscape and Microsoft created the first retailing Web servers along with the first widely used Web browsers. The commercial Web's early retailing successes—notably Amazon and eBay—remain sturdy exemplars of selling online done well. A key to their continued success is personalization, made possible by something called the *cookie*: a small text file, placed in your browser by the Web site, containing information to help you and the site remember where you were the last time you visited.

Those ur-cookies have since evolved branching into many breeds of Trojan marketing files. Variously called "Flash cookies" (based on Adobe's proprietary Flash technology), "tracking bugs," "beacons," and other names, they track your activities as you go about your business on the Web, reporting back what they've found to one or more among thousands of advertising companies, most of which you've never heard of (but some of which we visited in the last chapter).

The online advertising business says the purpose of these tracking methods is to raise the quality of the advertising you get. But most of us care less about that than we do about being followed by companies and processes we don't know and wouldn't like if we did.

While much complaining is correctly addressed to the creepy excesses of the online advertising business, little attention has been paid to the underlying problem, which is the design of the commercial Web itself. That design is *client-server*, which might also be called calf-cow. Clients are the calves. Servers are the cows. Today, there are billions of commercial cows, each mixing invisible cookies into the milk they feed to visiting calves.

Client-server by design is submissive-dominant, meaning it puts servers in the position of full responsibility for defining relationships and maintaining details about those relationships. And, since this is all we've known since 1995, most of the "solutions" we've come up with are more sites and site-based services. In other words, better cows.

What Are Your Names?

Back before computing got personal, and all the computing that mattered was done in enterprises, one of the biggest problems was a proliferation of *namespaces*. (In technical terms, a namespace is an identifier or a directory for them.) Different software systems each had their own namespaces. For the enterprise, this meant an employee, or information about an employee, might be known by different names and attributes, within each of the separate software systems used in human resources, marketing, sales, accounting, and so on. For an employee, this meant maintaining up to dozens of different logins and passwords. For the HR and IT departments, it meant integration hell, or the impossibility of any integration at all. To this day, the namespace problem is one of the most vexing in all of enterprise computing.

Out on the Web, that's solved for sellers, because each tends to have one customer-facing system. But for us customers, it's still a mess, because the old corporate namespace problem is now ours, multiplied by the number of relationships we have on the Web. Thus, we are required to keep track of as many different logins and passwords as there are Web sites requiring them. This makes the problem nearly as big as the sum of all Web sites. At last count (as I write this), there are over 200 million registered domains, about half of which have the commercial *.com* suffix.[4] Since some domains have many retail sites (eBay and Etsy, for example), the total number of commercial sites is much higher. Search for "privacy policy," and Google will tell you it appears on more than a billion Web pages. Even if one login and password might get you to all of eBay and Etsy, we are still talking about hundreds of login-password combinations.[5] Enterprises don't care, because it's not their problem. They care only about their relationship with you. Not about your relationships with every other company. That leaves you and me with an umpty-million (or -billion) namespace problem.

Login Rolling

There are partial workarounds. You can set up browsers to automatically fill out forms and auto-complete commonly typed strings of words and numbers. There are programs that remember passwords for you. But the most popular "single sign-on" (SSO) login methods are provided by grace of your relationship with Facebook, Google, Twitter, or Yahoo. Those ubiquitous "Connect with Facebook" buttons, for example, are the user-facing side of a program called Facebook Connect.

When Facebook announced Facebook Connect in December 2008, Mark Zuckerberg wrote this in the company blog:

> Over the summer we announced an extension of Facebook Platform called Facebook Connect. Facebook Connect makes it easier for you to take your online identity with you all over the Web, share what you do online with your friends and stay updated on what they're doing. You won't have to create separate accounts for every website, just use your Facebook login wherever Connect is available.
>
> Starting today, you'll see prompts for Facebook Connect at websites across the Internet and have the opportunity to take your Facebook profile information, friends and privacy preferences to your favorite sites.[6]

To call your Facebook identity "your online identity" is delusional as well as presumptuous, because none of us interact only with Facebook on the Web. But that by itself isn't the only problem. The larger problem with Facebook Connect is unintended data spillage. For example, what if you don't want to share "what you do online with friends," or if you think you're just taking Facebook's shortcut when you log in for the first time at some other site? In other words, what if you only want Facebook Connect to be what it presents itself as: a simple login option for you at other sites—with no "social" purpose at all? Or, if you do want to be "social," how about being selective about what Facebook data you're willing to share—exposing some data to some sites and different data (or no data at all) to other sites? In other words, what if your "privacy preferences" aren't just the one-set-fits-all selections you've made at Facebook?

The site I Shared What?!? (ISharedWhat.com), created by VRM developer Joe Andrieu, does an excellent job of simulating what you reveal about yourself and others when you use Facebook Connect. Here's what it just told me:

You've just shared: your basic details, your news feed, your friends on Facebook, the activities listed on your profile, the interests listed on your profile, music listed on your profile, books listed on your profile, movies listed on your profile, television shows listed on your profile, all the pages you have 'liked', your shared links.

That's *after* I jiggered my privacy settings in Facebook to reveal as little as possible. The results were the same both times, before and after. I'm no dummy, but—as of this writing—I have no idea how to keep from spilling rivers of personal data when using Facebook Connect. So I just avoid it.

But I'm the exception. As of December 2010, a quarter-billion people were logging into 2 million Web sites using Facebook Connect, with 10,000 more Web sites being added every day.[7]

Privacy is the marquee issue here, but the deeper problem is control. Right now you don't have much control over your identity on the Web. Kim Cameron, father of the cross-platform Identity Metasystem when he was an Architect at Microsoft, says your "natural identity"—who you are and how you wish to be known to others—gets no respect on the commercial Web.[8] Every cow thinks you are its calf, "branded" almost literally. In the World Wide Dairy, all of us walk around with a brand for every Web site that gives us milk and cookies. Our virtual hides are crowded with more logos than a NASCAR racer.

Who you are to the other cows is not of much interest to any one cow, unless they "federate" your identity with other cows. Think of federation as "large companies having safe sex with customer data." That's what I called it in a keynote I gave at Digital ID World in the early 2000s. It still applies.

Tough Teats

A similar problem comes up when you have multiple accounts with one site or service, and therefore multiple namespaces, each with its own login and password. For example, I use four different Flickr accounts, each with its own photo directory:

1. Doc Searls—http://www.flickr.com/photos/docsearls/

2. *Linux Journal*—http://www.flickr.com/photos/linuxjournal/

3. Berkman Center—http://www.flickr.com/photos/berkmancenter/

4. Infrastructure—http://www.flickr.com/photos/infrastructure/

The first is mine alone. The second I share with other people at *Linux Journal*. The third I share with other people at the Berkman Center. The fourth I share with other people who also write for the same blog.

Flickr in each case calls me by the second person singular "you" and does not federate the four. To them, I am four different individuals: one cow, four calves. (Never mind that three of those sites have many people uploading pictures, each pretending to be the same calf.) My only choice for dealing with this absurdity is deciding which kind of four-headed calf I wish to be. Either I use one browser with four different logins and passwords, or I use four different browsers, each with its own jar of cookies. Both choices are awful, but it's best to choose one. So I take the second option and use one browser per account—on just one laptop. When I use other laptops, or my iPhone, my Android, or the family Nokia N900, iPod Touch, or iPad, I'm usually the first kind of calf, using one browser to log in and log out every time I post pictures to a different account. Which I mostly don't do at all, because it's one big pain in my many asses.

Crazy as all this is, it hardly matters from the cow side of the calf-cow relationship. In fact, the condition is generally considered desirable. After all, the World Wide Ranch is a real marketplace: one where cows compete for calves. Hey, what could be more natural?

The media, even online, are no help either. Business publications, both online and off, love to cover what I call "vendor sports," in which customers are prizes for corporate trophy cases. That's why business writers often regard "owning" customers as a desirable thing. For example, in "Rim, Carriers Fight Over Digital Wallet," from the March 18, 2011, *Wall Street Journal*, Phred Dvorak and Stuart Weinberg write, "RIM and carriers like Rogers Communications Inc. in Canada, and AT&T Inc and T-Mobile in the U.S., disagree over exactly where on the phone the credentials should reside—and thus *who will control the customers*, revenue and applications that grow out of mobile payments."[9] The italics are mine.

In the dairy farm model of the marketplace, captive customers are more valuable than free ones. Since this has been an ethos of mass marketing for a century and a half, the milk-and-cookies system of customer control has proven appealing to businesses outside the online world as well as within it. As of today, both worlds are worse off for it as well.

SO, THEN

For free markets to mean more than "your choice of captor," we need new systems that operate on the principle that free customers are more valuable—to both sellers and themselves—than captive ones.

Improving slavery does not make people free. We need full emancipation. That's the only way we'll get free markets worthy of the name.

4

Lopsided Law

The law will never make men free. It is men that have got to make the law free.

—Henry David Thoreau[1]

THE ARGUMENT

We've lived so long without *freedom of contract* that we've forgotten what it is and why it's good for everybody. Our heads are now so accustomed to shrink wrap, click wrap, and other one-sided "agreements" that we can hardly imagine anything else in the networked world.

On January 8, 2011, Deepa Praveen was adding tags to photos on her Flickr account when a digital trap door opened and she found herself dropped onto a page with a strangely existential message: "User no longer exists."[2] Everything she had created at Flickr, including her own identity there, was gone. So she sent an e-mail to Flickr's help desk. On January 9, she received a response saying her issue had been escalated to a senior representative. After hearing nothing for two days, she created a new account and put up a photo of a sunset with this copy written on it in white:

MIGHT IS RIGHT (?).

More than 1000 days.
more than 10,000 man hours.

more than 600 photos.
more than 6,000 mails from
more than 600 contacts
more than 2000 called for a contact,
more than 20,000 fvts for her photos,
more than 35,000 comments,
more than 250,000 views ...
Everything is gone in [one] second.
It says "user no longer exists."
For "them" that was just another
PRO ACCOUNT

Don't I deserve a reason before they pressed the DEL key?

Deepa Praveen
Another victim of Flickr account deletion...

That same day, Thomas Hawk, a well-known photographer with one of the largest and most familiar portfolios on Flickr, ran Deepa's photo as a blog post, without remark.[3] Many comments and blog postings followed, including a post of my own titled, "What if Flickr fails?"[4] That one alone gathered 110 comments.

On January 12, Deepa received a blank e-mail from Flickr. Confused, she wrote back and got what appeared to be an automated reply:

In joining Flickr, our members agree to abide by the Yahoo!
Terms of Service and the Flickr Community Guidelines:

http://www.flickr.com/guidelines.gne
http://www.flickr.com/terms.gne

Your account was brought to our attention through Report Abuse. Upon review, we determined that your content and/or behavior was in violation and your account was terminated.

Deepa was not an ordinary Flickr user. Hers was a pro account, meaning that she paid for benefits beyond those given to eyeballs that Flicker's parent, Yahoo, sells to advertisers. (One pro-level benefit at Flickr is seeing no advertising.)

Naturally, many Flickr users were freaked, and more account-deletion stories surfaced. As things heated up in the comment thread under my own post, I invited Flickr officials to join the discussion. On January 14, two did: Blake Irving and Zack Sheppard (executive vice president, chief product officer, Yahoo, and senior community manager at Flickr, their signatures said). Their comments, one apiece, were friendly and cordial, but not much help. Wrote Zack, "In regards to account deletions, we don't comment on specific members except to the account owner themselves, however it's important to note that we do give a warning to educate the member before deleting in most cases."

On January 27, Deepa finally got a message from Flickr about why her account was terminated:

> Hi there,
>
> Like I said before, we saw behavior in your account that went against our guidelines and required us to take action—which was to delete your account. Our guidelines apply to any and all content you post on Flickr— photos you upload, comments you make, group discussions you participate in, etc.
>
> I am afraid I cannot give you any more specific information than this.
>
> Thank you for your understanding,
>
> Cathryn

The next day, Deepa wrote to tell me she had not been a member of any group (at least not recently), could not recall making any comments that might be offensive, had not knowingly violated anyone's copyright, and had not posted any images that might be offensive. "What I requested is a reason," she wrote. "A specific reason for deleting my account."

Others following her story said they also had no clues about reasons, since Deepa's photos were artistic and noncontroversial. That's the case with photos she posted on her new Flickr account, some of which Flickr's parent, Yahoo, had featured on one of its other sites. In her e-mail, she added,

> If they are taking an action of termination of the legal contract and thereby terminating the service offered, I can accept it. Fair enough. But as a fair procedure do I need a reasonable explanation from them before deleting the service they offered to me in the first place? They are bound to give an answer to all those services they terminated. Don't we deserve a fair procedure? As a party to the contract, do I deserve a right to be heard?

It Gets Sticky

Ethically, the answer is yes. Legally, it's no. That's because Flickr's is a *contract of adhesion*. According to *West's Encyclopedia of American Law*, an adhesion contract is:

> A type of contract, a legally binding agreement between two parties to do a certain thing, in which one side has all the bargaining power and uses it to write the contract primarily to his or her advantage.
>
> An example of an adhesion contract is a standardized contract form that offers goods or services to consumers on essentially a "take it or leave it" basis without giving consumers realistic opportunities to negotiate terms that would benefit their interests. When this occurs, the consumer cannot obtain the desired product or service unless he or she acquiesces to the form contract.[5]

Adhesive contracts, also known as *boilerplate* and *standard form* contracts, are the most common in business and comprise nearly all the contracts that users encounter on the Web. Sites call these "agreements," "click wrap," "terms of service," and similar names. Lawyers also call them "click wrap" and "browse wrap." (Both of those are online names for the "shrink wrap" licenses that came with boxed software in the days before software was downloaded or lived in "the cloud.")

What makes these contracts adhesive is that they nail down the submissive party while the dominant party is free to change whatever it wants. Friedrich Kessler, who popularized "contracts of adhesion" in a landmark article by that name in the July 1943 edition of the *Columbia Law Review*, explains how these contracts came to be:[6]

> The development of large scale enterprise with its mass production and mass distribution made a new type of contract inevitable— the standardized mass contract. A standardized contract, once its contents have been formulated by a business firm, is used in every bargain dealing with the same product or service. The individuality of the parties which so frequently gave color to the old type contract has disappeared. The stereotyped contract of today reflects the impersonality of the market ... Once the usefulness of these contracts was discovered and perfected in the transportation, insurance, and banking business, their use spread into all other fields of large scale enterprise, into international as well as national trade, and into labor relations.[7]

Half a century later, that same perfection spread across the commercial Web as well.

Let's look at a couple of examples, starting with Google Accounts (which includes Gmail, personalized Web history, iGoogle, and Google Checkout):[8]

2. Accepting the Terms

2.1 In order to use the Services, you must first agree to the Terms. You may not use the Services if you do not accept the Terms.

2.2 *You can accept the Terms by*:

(A) clicking to accept or agree to the Terms, where this option is made available to you by Google in the user interface for any Service; or

(B) *by actually using the Services. In this case, you understand and agree that Google will treat your use of the Services as acceptance of the Terms from that point onwards.*

I've italicized the part that matters. It translates to *use = agreement.*

Then, there is this, also from Google:

19. Changes to the Terms

19.1 Google may make changes to the Universal Terms or Additional Terms from time to time. When these changes are made, Google will make a new copy of the Universal Terms available at http://www. google.com/accounts/TOS?hl=en and any new Additional Terms will be made available to you from within, or through, the affected Services.

19.2 You understand and agree that if you use the Services after the date on which the Universal Terms or Additional Terms have changed, Google will treat your use as acceptance of the updated Universal Terms or Additional Terms.

I call this the "Vogon clause." In Douglas Adams's *The Hitchhiker's Guide to the Galaxy*, Earth is destroyed without warning by Vogons (an ugly species of alien bureaucrats) to make way for a hyperspace express route, the plans for which, the Vogons explain, have been available for the last fifty years at the local planning department on Alpha Centauri.[9]

Adhesion contracts are also absurd in a more basic way: the dominant party—the one providing all the terms—can change terms whenever it pleases, while the submissive party has no choice but to acquiesce or go away. Thus, the contract is Velcro for the vendor and Super Glue for the customer. This is why, for example, Apple can change its fifty-five-page Terms of Use for iPhones every few weeks, and customers' only choice is to click "accept." And, since use = agreement, there's no reason for the customer to look at the agreement, unless doing without the service is a legitimate option. For most customers, it isn't.

And so far, we're just talking about terms of service. Privacy policies are just as bad, if not worse.

The PR in Privacy

For nearly all Web sites and their services, privacy policies are ass-coverage for the company and PR for the customer or user. For example, Linden Lab's privacy statement, titled "Protection and Disclosure of Your Information," "requires" the new entity to follow the old privacy policy; in the next sentence, it says your personal information can be used in ways "contrary" to the policy, provided you receive prior notice.[10] One assumes that would be on the Vogon model.[11]

Here is why *West's Encyclopedia of American Law* says all this fudging is okay:

> There is nothing unenforceable or even wrong about adhesion
> contracts. In fact, most businesses would never conclude their
> volume of transactions if it were necessary to negotiate all the
> terms ... [12]

In the Internet Age, that reason has been reduced to an excuse. But it's an excuse that works, as long as *we* continue to believe there are no alternatives.

The "old type contract," Kessler says, "reflects a proud spirit of individualism and of laissez faire. Contracts were constructed to manifest "genuineness and reality of consent," which harmonized with the ethics and ideals of "small enterprisers, individual merchants and independent craftsmen, dedicated to free enterprise."[13] He adds,

> With the decline of the free enterprise system due to the innate
> trend of competitive capitalism towards monopoly, the meaning of
> contract has changed radically.[14]

In other words, "genuineness and reality of consent" doesn't scale, and stopped scaling as soon as mass manufacture, mass sales, and mass marketing became pro forma for big business—more than a century ago. Explains Renee Lloyd, an attorney and alumnus fellow of Harvard's Berkman Center,

The industrial revolution introduced a new conundrum for contract law, because the business model of mass–everything required an efficient and standard legal mechanism to support it. So we got Kessler's *contracts of adhesion*—not because they were good, but because they were the only thing that worked. In other words, we had to abandon some of contract's core principles, just to get along in the industrialized world, where a successful company might have thousands or millions of customers.[15]

Adhesion contracts-as-laws should be deeply offensive to everybody, as they were to Kessler. But they are also deeply normative. This was the situation that Kessler addressed in 1943. Once power became concentrated in large companies, so did one-sided and coercive contracts that were free in name only.

And yet, Kessler said, the problem by 1943 was even more subtle and pernicious than that:

> Society, by proclaiming freedom of contract, guarantees that it will not interfere with the exercise of power by contract. Freedom of contract enables enterprisers to legislate by contract and ... in a substantially authoritarian manner without using the appearance of authoritarian forms.
>
> Standard contracts in particular could thus become effective instruments in the hands of powerful industrial and commercial overlords enabling them to impose a new feudal order of their own making upon a vast host of vassals.[16]

And vassals we are.

Still, our acquiescence to *contracts of adhesion* doesn't mean that all adhesive contracts stand up in court. Says *West's Encyclopedia of American Law*, "Many adhesion contracts are unconscionable; they are so unfair to the weaker party that a court will refuse to enforce them."[17]

This has not happened yet on the commercial Web. In fact, *contracts of adhesion* got a big thumbs-up in *ProCD v. Zeidenberg*, which was decided by Judge Frank H. Easterbrook in 1995.[18] In this case, ProCD sued Matthew Zeidenberg for breach of its shrink-wrap contract, which restricted sale of ProCD information. It argued that while Zeidenberg did not "manifest assent" by clicking a statement to agree with the contract terms, the information about the proposed license agreement appeared in three places: the outside of the package, the text of the license itself, and the text that displayed each time the software was loaded. Based on these facts, Easterbrook concluded that Zeidenberg was bound by the terms of the license. The court further held,

> Shrinkwrap licenses are enforceable unless their terms are
> objectionable on grounds applicable to contracts in general
> (for example, if they violate a rule of positive law, or if they are
> unconscionable). Because no one argued that the terms of the license
> at issue here are troublesome, we remand with instructions to enter
> judgment for the plaintiff.[19]

Thus, ProCD validated *contracts of adhesion* in electronic transactions. For better and worse, it also paved a smooth legal path for e-commerce as we know it today.

Matters of Unconscience

So, was Flickr behaving in an unconscionable way toward Deepa Praveen? Here are Flickr's terms:[20]

5. FLICKR'S RESERVATION OF RIGHTS

Flickr expressly reserves the right to immediately modify, delete content from, suspend or terminate your account and refuse current or future use of any Yahoo! service, including Flickr pro, if Flickr, in its sole discretion believes you have: (i) violated or tried to violate the rights of others; or (ii) acted inconsistently with the spirit or letter of the TOS, the Community Guidelines or these Additional Terms. In such event, your Flickr pro account may be suspended or cancelled immediately in our discretion, all the information and content contained within it deleted permanently and you will not be entitled to any refund of any of the amounts you've paid for such account. Flickr accepts no liability for information or content that is deleted.

6. INDEMNITY

You agree to indemnify and hold harmless Flickr, and its subsidiaries, affiliates, officers, agents, or other partners, and employees, from any claim or demand, including reasonable attorneys' fees, made by any third party due to or arising out of your use of and access to Flickr pro, your violation of the TOS, these

Additional Terms or the Community Guidelines, your violation
of any rights of another person or entity, or your violation of any
applicable laws or regulations.

These terms might be considered unconscionable on their face if they
were uttered by, say, a neighborhood camera store. But the situation is different for a company hosting more than 5 billion photographs for 51 million registered users,[21] and accumulating 3,000 new photos every minute.[22]
A company operating on that scale isn't built for holding customers' hands,
much less for making judgment calls on every uploaded photo. As a big
company with deep pockets, Yahoo is also a fat target for lawsuits. So, given
the immensity of the company's exposure risk, being able to delete accounts
quickly and thoroughly seems like a prudent stance to take, even in the face
of peeved customers.

So, you might think, even if that's a good excuse for Yahoo, it shouldn't
be for smaller companies. Yet clearly it is, because *contracts of adhesion* are
now pro forma for companies of all sizes operating on the Web. I've looked
at dozens of these things, and colleagues of mine (including many lawyers
and law professors) have looked at thousands. The terms are all pretty much
the same. Since searches for "privacy policy" now bring up more than a billion results, we're talking about a maximally entrenched problem—and one
that relatively few have bothered to challenge, in court or anywhere else.[23]
The Electronic Frontier Foundation in February 2011 listed just twenty-
five such cases.[24] None of them would encourage Deepa—or anybody—to
become number twenty-six.

It's pointless to challenge these contracts so long as three conditions persist: (1) only one side gets to write the agreements, (2) the agreements need
to cover all conceivable possibilities, and (3) the other side's only choice is to
agree or walk away, which is nearly impossible in a networked world.

It's No Context

The scope of a contract is contained by its context. When we're at home,
that's a context. When we're at work, that's a context. When we're shopping, that's a context. When we're driving, that's a context. When we rent a
canoe, a tuxedo, or a ladder, those are contexts. That's why most contracts
in the physical world are straightforward, easy to understand, and not built
to screw one party or the other. Take a typical equipment rental agreement.
It says who is responsible for what and covers such basics as who pays, how

much, and when and where the equipment should be returned. In contexts like these, freedom of contract is still alive and well.

In mass markets, however, the context is needing to sell the largest quantity of products to the largest number of customers. Here it is easier and safer for company lawyers to write contracts that equate use with agreement, dump all conceivable risk and liability on the user or customer, release the vendor from all but the most obvious and unavoidable responsibilities, reserve the right to change any term at any time, and to post notice of the change on a Web page almost nobody watches.

Thus, the context-less nature of mass markets in the physical world finds an ideal match in the context-less nature of the Web. This is why nearly all the boilerplate contracts of adhesion for Web-based companies and services look pretty much like what I said in the last paragraph, regardless of a company's size.

But the story doesn't end there. Networked markets are massive only in their geometries. Activity within them is still end-to-end, any-to-any, involving millions of separate and distinct individuals. And the Net is open to boundless new developments as well. So there is nothing to stop individuals from acquiring more tools and more power, including the ability to assert their own terms, as equals with sellers. In fact, those tools are in the works right now, and we'll visit progress in chapter 20.

SO, THEN

While freedom of contract has been set back farther on the Web than it was already in mass markets, almost all markets are now becoming networked at the individual level. With that come countless openings to new means for freedom's ends.

5

Asymmetrical Relations

CRM … moved from having been brought in as a platform for driving improvements in the customer experience, to being run as a platform for cost cutting and for risk management … in many cases all it did was move the waste/inefficiency on to the customer.

—Iain Henderson[1]

THE ARGUMENT

Relationships are two-way. They require consenting parties, absence of coercion, respect, commitment, and other properties that have been largely absent from big business and CRM for the duration. We will not have real relationships between vendors and customers until customers come fully equipped to engage; that is, until there are VRM tools and systems to match the CRM ones.

CRM came into vogue as a label in the mid-1990s, after sales force automation (SFA) met the Internet. SFA began as database marketing in the 1980s, but began to take off in a big way when Tom Siebel and Rebecca House founded Siebel Systems (now Oracle CRM) in 1993. Gartner projects $13.1 billion in sales for CRM vendors in 2012. That's up from $8.9 billion in 2008.[2] According to the research firm Trefis, the "Global Customer Relationship Management (CRM) Software Market has increased from $6.6 billion in 2006 to about $10 billion in 2009," and has steady projected growth to $22 billion by 2017.[3]

Gartner, the giant analyst sometimes credited with coining the term CRM, continues to make a distinction between SFA and CRM, with the former as a subset of the latter.[4] Currently, it ranks Salesforce at the top of both.[5] Here's what Salesforce says about CRM on its home page:

> Customer relationship management (CRM) is all about managing the relationships you have with your customers. CRM combines business processes, people, and technology to achieve this single goal: getting and keeping customers. It's an overall strategy to help you learn more about their behavior so you can develop stronger, lasting relationships that will benefit both of you. It's very hard to run a successful business without a strong focus on CRM, as well as adding elements of social media and making the transition to a social enterprise to connect with customers in new ways.

The second person "you" and "your" are Salesforce's corporate customers. Each of them has its own ways of relating to customers. So, while Toyota, Siemens, Starbucks, and Dell all use Salesforce to relate to their customers, as a customer of those four companies, you don't have a single way to change your address or phone number with all of them at once. You have to do that separately with each. Multiply that work times all the different companies that see you as their customer alone and you meet a problem that CRM does not yet solve.

As a result, satisfaction with CRM's work is not especially high at our end of the supply chain. In October 2010, Michael Maoz, vice president and distinguished analyst with Gartner, wrote,

> Over the past ten years the level of customer satisfaction has edged up only slightly—for most industries in the vicinity of 3–5 percent. Considering that over US $75 billion was spent on CRM-related business applications in that time period, and triple that sum on process improvement, and hundreds of books written, you might expect better ... [6]

Yet this is not all CRM's fault. CRM bears the full relationship burden because there are no corresponding tools on your side that allow you to manage many vendors in the same way vendors manage many of you. Those tools are coming, with VRM, for vendor relationship management. We'll get to those in part III. Meanwhile, let's take a closer look at where CRM is now, and where it's going, on the way to meeting VRM.

Wasting Ways

Iain Henderson, who labored many years in the CRM business, characterizes CRM-based relations as "islands of success surrounded by seas of guesswork and waste." In relationships, the islands and seas look those in table 5-1, going through time from top to bottom (seas of guesswork and waste are in upper-case type).

The lowercase items in "What both do" and "What the vendor does" are all in the lingo of CRM, which has developed many ways of minimizing actual contact with customers and normalizing service around a minimized set of variables. This involves even more guesswork and waste than we can depict here—again, on both sides.

As a customer, you typically encounter this when your problem is not one of the few the call center provides when it says, "Press 4 for (whatever)."

In summarizing his research on CRM effectiveness for different kinds of companies, Iain rates CRM performance with different data types, which he gives green, yellow, or red markings. Green is good, yellow is blah, and red is bad. I've turned his graphics into a table with values: 1 for good, 0 for blah, and –1 for bad (see table 5-2).

TABLE 5-1

CRM-based relationships

What the customer does	What both do	What the vendor does
Articulate need	GUESS	Articulate product/service
Search	GUESS	Target
Find (engage)	GUESS	Enquiry management
Negotiate	Begin to RELATE	Negotiate
Transact	Transact	Transact
WASTE	Welcome	WASTE
WASTE	Relationship servicing	WASTE
WASTE	Relationship development	WASTE
WASTE	Manage problems	WASTE
WASTE	Manage exits	WASTE
WASTE	Reengagement	WASTE

TABLE 5-2

CRM effectiveness for various companies

Data type	Retail bank	Global publisher	Luxury carmaker	Manufacturer
Customer or prospect	1	0	0	1
Association		0		0
Relationship	0			0
Household	0			
Postcode	1			1
Location		0	0	
Address	1	0	1	1
Contact detail				1
Internal hierarchy		−1	−1	
Named contact	0	0	0	
Medium	−1			−1
Other personal data	0			1
Permissions	1	−1	0	1
Appearance	−1			−1
Advertisement	0			
Customer interaction	−1			−1
Outlet	−1	−1	−1	−1
Campaign	1	1	−1	1
Product offer	0	−1	−1	
Product	1	0	0	1
Competitor product	0	−1	−1	1
Ad hoc group	−1	0	0	1
Account	1	0	0	1
Customer product	1	−1	0	0
External data		0	0	
Additional data	−1	−1	−1	−1
Status	1	0	0	0

TABLE 5-2

CRM effectiveness for various companies

Data type	Retail bank	Global publisher	Luxury carmaker	Manufacturer
Follow-up	−1	−1	−1	1
Payment	0	−1	−1	1
Billing document	0	−1	−1	−1
Total	2	−9	−8	7

Not all the companies studied had the same data types, and the data types have different weights, but this gives a good picture of how poorly CRM actually works.

Customer Disservice

Have you noticed how extra-friendly and concerned call-center people have become? Here's the script-guided verbal handshake:

"Hello, my name is Bill. How are you today?"

"I'm fine. How are you?"

"Thank you for asking. I'm fine. How can I help you today?"

"My X is F'd."

"I'm sorry you're having that problem."

They always ask how you are, thank you for asking how they are, and are sorry you have a problem. After loading Adobe's latest suite of apps on one of my laptops, almost all my Adobe apps stopped working, including prior generations of the same suite. I spent *three days* on the phone with Adobe, unscrewing all the problems. I lost count of the number of people I spoke to. Except for the last call—the ultimately successful one—all the calls began with an exchange like the one recounted and ended by being dropped. And, in each case, the next service person at the call center said that the last person I spoke to marked down my problem as "solved."

They even talk like that in chat sessions. A while back I had four chat sessions in a row with different agents of Charter Communications, the cable company that provides Internet service at a relative's house. The sessions took place on a laptop in the crawl space below, where Charter's equipment was located. Every chat was comically absurd and involved no institutional memory of the prior chat. The clear message that ran through the whole exchange was, *We're just here to give you a slow-mo dose of futility, and hope you figure out your problem in the meantime.*

And many of us do. In fact, lots of us take up the slack where company support is absent or dysfunctional. In "Customer Service? Ask a Volunteer," Steve Lohr of the *New York Times* writes about "an emerging corps of Web-savvy helpers that large corporations, start-up companies and venture capitalists are betting will transform the field of customer service."[7] He cites the work of enjoyment-motivated volunteers "known as lead users, or super-users" who have made unpaid contributions to product development in a diversity of fields, from skateboarding to open-source software. Then he asks, "But can this same kind of economy of social rewards develop in the realm of customer service? It is, after all, a field that companies typically regard as a costly nuisance and that consumers often view as a source of frustration."

This is all part of a larger trend my wife calls "outsourcing customer service to the customer." For evidence, she cites ATMs, self-service gas stations, self-service checkout in grocery stores, call-center mazes that send customers to Web sites, and Web sites that bury or refuse to reveal information (such as addresses and phone numbers) that would help a customer contact human beings at a company directly.

At its best, this kind of outsourcing falls into a creative category that Eric von Hippel, professor of technological innovation in the MIT Sloan School of Management, calls *Democratizing Innovation* (also the name of his best-known book).[8] Demand and supply join hands and help each other out, in full respect for what the other side is best equipped to bring to the table both share. At its worst, you get customers wandering around in futility, occasionally venting on public forums, in faint hope that somebody else out there might be able to help solve a problem.

That was my own experience after a complete breakdown in communications with Sprint. The saga began when I got a "courtesy call from Sprint in July 2009, offering to "work out" a bill for more than $500, racked up, allegedly, when I went past the 5Gb per month usage limit on my laptop's Sprint EvDO data card in June. I not only didn't know Sprint had imposed a data limit, but had chosen Sprint as a mobile data vendor precisely because it *didn't* have a data limit. And yet I was sure that my usual monthly usage was far less than 5Gb, and I hadn't done anything that special in June. Surely there was a mistake somewhere. But the courtesy caller couldn't look into that. All she could do was "work" with me. "What would you be willing to pay?" she asked. "Nothing," I replied. The $59.99 per month I already paid was all the "work" I was willing to do.

Which wasn't quite true. I had to find out what went wrong and fix it. So I called various numbers at Sprint and, at length, got exactly nowhere. So I put up a blog post titled, "What's 10,241,704.22kb between ex-friends?" and hoped that exposing the problem to thousands of readers might get me somewhere.

It didn't. Several months went by, Sprint cut me off, and then began to threaten action to collect the overage charge. So I tweeted an appeal to @Sprint-Cares on Twitter, with a pointer back to my blog post. Somebody from Sprint then got in touch with me, checked back on my usage history and payment record, saw that the oddball month was a complete anomaly, and dropped the charges. (At this writing, Sprint is back to offering unlimited data again.)

Getting Social

I doubt that @SprintCares was part of whatever Sprint at the time had for a CRM system, and I suspect it still isn't, more than two years later. But @SprintCares is considered part of a new CRM breed, called sCRM, for social CRM. Think of sCRM as a way for "social customers" to interact with companies, not as a new CRM offering. Not officially, anyway.

During the time I consulted for BT in the U.K., I watched sCRM start with one person solving problems for customers on Twitter using the handle @BTcare. This turned into a whole staff of customer service people, as @BTcare began working 24/7 to deal with customers engaging BT through Twitter, rather than through the company's call center. Facilitating that move was J. P. Rangaswami, then the chief scientist at BT. He now holds the same title with Salesforce.

And, as a social customer myself, I have found sCRM very handy. For example, @CZ, a Verizon employee, has helped with my Verizon FiOS account. I've also had good luck engaging with other companies, as a journalist, by knocking first on the @CompanyName door. And, last but far from least, there's my social experience with @Microsoft. Specifically, Microsoft Word for Macintosh 2011. Word is pro forma in publishing these days, and it's what I'm using to write and edit this book. When something went wrong with the manuscript (I'll spare you the gory details), I appealed to @Microsoft on Twitter and got help directly from the Word development team. Still, would everybody tweeting to @Microsoft get the same level of help? Kinda doubtful.

So there's a huge gap here.

CRM vendors are addressing the issue with new "social" offerings for their customers, which are the companies that sell stuff to you and me.

In *CRM at the Speed of Light*, Paul Greenberg says we are now in "the era of the social customer," that "the customer has taken control of the conversation," and that the social transformation happening around CRM is much bigger than the one happening within CRM, or within business itself.[9]

No doubt that's true. But CRM companies are pushing social hard now. In August 2011, Salesforce introduced The Social Enterprise, which aims to turn the company's customers—businesses—into "social enterprises." This means three things:

1. Connect the company to social networks, including Facebook, Twitter, and LinkedIn.

2. Create internal corporate social networks that work the same way.

3. Make the company's enterprise applications more social.

These are all good, but don't cover the full range of what it means for individuals to be social in the networked world:

1. Many customers are not on social networks, and never will be.

2. Many customers on social networks wish to be social with companies only when there's trouble, and don't want to be contacted or pitched to at other times.

3. Direct interactions between customers and companies are personal, not social.

4. sCRM is so unlike the rest of CRM that integrating it is likely to take a lot of work and time.

For an example of how far the industry needs to travel on this new path, Greenberg contrasts the success of Bill Gerth—better known as @comcastcares on Twitter—with Comcast's bottom-tier reputation for customer service. The latter is exemplified by the oft-told story of Mona Shaw, the Virginia grandmother who snapped after one too many mistreatments by her local Comcast office, trashed the place with a hammer, and got hit with only a small fine by a sympathetic court.

SO, THEN

The C in CRM stands for *customer*, not *customers*. It's personal, not social. What doesn't work with CRM won't be fixed until personal tools for relating are developed on the customer side. Those will be VRM tools. Thus, VRM+CRM will work much better than CRM alone. You can read about VRM in part III and VRM+CRM in chapter 24.

6

Dysloyalty

The lady across the hall tried to rob a department store with a pricing
gun. She said, "Give me all of the money in the vault, or I'm marking down
everything in the store."

—Stephen Wright[1]

Honesty is the best policy. If you can fake that, you've got it made.

—George Burns[2]

THE ARGUMENT

In retailing today, loyalty is more claim than fact.

Some viruses can move from one species to another. Rabies, swine flu, and
HIV are three examples. The name for this transfer is *zoonosis*.

The same thing can happen with marketplaces, where both good and
bad ideas can "go viral." In the last decade and a half, we've seen zoonosis
happening between the commercial Web and the brick-and-mortar world,
as new ideas for capturing customers have moved virally from the former
to the latter.

Capturing customers has always been a fantasy of vendors in any case,
so the offline marketplace was ready to listen to the virtual voice that said
something like, "Hey, forcing people to become voluntary slaves to Web
sites seems like a good idea; and consumers don't seem to mind logging
in all over the place, rather than just showing up. So let's coerce loyalty

by making our customers carry around cards and key tags. We'll post discount prices just for card-carrying customers, and overcharge everybody else for the same stuff. We can track customers and their purchases by the data we gather, increase their switching costs, and personalize our promotions."

And here we are, carrying around a mess of loyalty cards and key tags, so we can get rewards and discounts everywhere we shop.

My own car key ring goes with our 2000 Volkswagen Passat, which has 162,000 miles on it. The key itself is a proprietary Volkswagen one, designed so only Volkswagen can replace it. Long ago, the key fell apart, but we keep it in one piece with a rubber band, because Volkswagen charges its captive customers hundreds of dollars to replace it.

On the key's ring are tags for Shaw's and Stop & Shop, two grocery stores I sometimes visit. (My wife, a foodie, prefers to shop at Trader Joe's. I explain why in Chapter 25.) I don't carry any cards or tags in my wallet, but we do have a pile of them in the armrest of the car. My wife also has a separate wallet for loyalty cards in her purse. It may be the heaviest thing in there.

They're all a pain in the butt.

Loyalty programs of many kinds have been around since the 1800s (the biggest press run in history was the 1966 Green Stamps catalog), but the spread of retailers' loyalty card systems in the late 1990s and early 2000s clearly suggests that the cookie-based commercial Web model has spread offline as well.[3] The offline equivalent of cookies are magnetic strips and bar codes.

Obviously, it's fair to assume that the programs work pretty well or are at least rationalized well enough to continue justifying them. But so far, I've found no research on the customer side that starts from the premise that maybe we don't need these programs at all—or that it makes sense to base our understanding of loyalty on what customers actually feel.

So I decided to do some research on my own, based on my own feelings and my own experience, just with retailers whose loyalty cards I carry around. I'm just one customer, but I think my experience is revealing.

Mass Markets

We'll start with Shaw's, a New England grocery store chain. I shop at Shaw's in the Boston area for three things I've seen in too few other stores: (1) La Brea Bakery bread, (2) Cholula Hot Sauce, and (3) pork sausage. (The first two are tastes I acquired in California. The third is one I acquired in North Carolina.) I usually pick up other staples when I'm at Shaw's: eggs, milk, fruit, vegetables, meat, and so on. But I wouldn't bother if it didn't have those three slightly unusual items.

The "discount" prices for Shaw's card-carrying customers are about even with other stores that have no loyalty programs, such as Market Basket and Trader Joe's (e.g., $1.99 for a dozen large eggs). The "normal" prices at Shaw's are so much higher (e.g., $2.99 for the same eggs) that I assume it overcharges customers who don't carry the cards.[4] Thus, the only "benefit" of my Shaw's card is a weekly e-mail that has not once attracted me back to the store for anything. The subject line for the latest of these says, "David, Use this Email-Only Soft Drinks Coupon." (My real name is David. Only relatives, old friends, and robotic acquaintances use it.) The body of the e-mail is a mess of small graphic elements, all but one of which load in my e-mail client. It has "Handpicked Savings Just For You," including an e-mail-only coupon for $1.00 off Coca-Cola products, and $.30 off Hood milk. I never buy Coke, and don't care much for bottled drinks. But I do buy a lot of milk, which I use to make yogurt. So I wonder, *Is Hood the expensive name-brand milk, or the house brand that's always cheaper?* (Answer: the former.) And, *What do the phrases "effective with the Card" and "No Rewards Card Required" mean? Do I need to print this out? Do I need to click on the "Add to my list" button? Will it know when I check out that I've got this discount?* The answers don't matter, because $.30 is no deal maker and worth less than the time I've already wasted thinking about it.

As for the weekly e-mail-only offers, I'd never bother with those either, but for research's sake, I hit "download." This opens a new browser tab with a pdf of a coupon sheet. None of the items makes me want to print out the whole sheet, which would also waste the fresh ink I paid almost $80 for at Staples last week. (Both my printers are free Epsons that came with laptops I bought. They're good printers, but ink tends to be gone after a few dozen pages. I just calculated the cost of owning these printers at hundreds of dollars per year, and more than $.12 per page. I bring this up because that's what it costs for me to print out junk mail from Shaw's.)

Of course, I'm far from typical and haven't been a coupon clipper since I was last unemployed, many decades ago. But maybe Shaw's has plenty of customers who love this kind of stuff. Maybe those customers use "my recipe box" and "my shopping list."[5] But I doubt it. What I assume instead is that Shaw's, like every other chain store, is just trying to keep up with retail technology fashion, which is currently in thrall of "personalizing" everything electronically while depersonalizing the face-to-face side of the business.

For a case in point, here's another Shaw's story. A couple years back, the store installed some of those now-ubiquitous self-checkout systems. Our kid loves the things, because they involve bar-code scanning, one of the cheap thrills in his life. Alas, the system failed to give us our members-only prices. After failing to solve the problem with technology, the nice woman behind the service counter gave us a generous credit toward future purchases. She also gave us some interesting intelligence about the loyalty system itself. While this is not a verbatim quote, it's the gist of what she said: "We hate those things. We have checkout professionals here. They know how to scan and bag your purchases. They are friendly and like interacting with customers. Too often customers make mistakes with self-service, and we have to go help them out, which defeats the whole purpose. The loyalty cards don't do much, as far as we can tell, besides slow things down for everybody. We have to maintain two prices for everything, and the cards don't keep people from shopping elsewhere. I think we'd be better off without the whole thing."

Or, maybe not.

John Deighton, the Harold M. Brierley Professor of Business Administration at Harvard Business School, is one of the world's leading authorities on this kind of thing. One day over lunch, when I told him that Shaw's story, he dismissed it as an exception and assured me that these programs work very well for stores that are inventive and execute well. As an example, he singled out Stop & Shop. Since Stop & Shop is on our beaten path, I shop there much more often than at Shaw's.

Lately (as I write this), Stop & Shop has added a system called Scan It!, which gives customers handheld gizmos to scan bar codes, obtain promotional discounts, and follow running tallies of what's in the cart. So I've experimented with it, shooting pictures of the gizmo screen with my phone, so I could remember later what happened.

The first coupon to come up on my first trip with the gizmo was, "Save 75¢ when you buy TWO (2) of any Old El Paso products. Limit 1." So I bought two packets of Old El Paso taco seasoning and a can of Old El Paso non-fat refried beans. The gizmo then suggested lots of other stuff, most of which were not interesting, so I ignored them. But the system worked quite well, as far as it went, which was actually quite far:

- Sophisticated (and potentially informative) devices for customers to carry around

- New carts, with holders for the new devices

- New tech at the self-checkout lines

- (I'm assuming) new CRM, inventory management, IT, and other back-end adjustments, to make the whole system work

That's a lot. Yet I found myself thinking, *Why can't I use my own device here—like, my smartphone?* Sure enough, a little postcard-sized circular at checkout said, "Introducing the Stop & Shop app for iPhone and Android." Here's the copy:

Your circular just went mobile!

- View it on your mobile device
- Access your online account
  - Track your Gas Rewards points
  - View your savings
  - View online exclusive offers
- Find the nearest store on the go

I took the card home with me, got on the laptop, registered on the Stop & Shop site (using the member number on the key tag), installed the app on my iPhone, fired it up, and logged in. After what seemed like about 10,000 keystrokes and pokes on the phone, I could see my account. Racked up already were 108 "gas points," which (I saw when I clicked on the link) entitled me to a discount of $.10 per gallon, though I didn't yet know where. The Weekly Ad link went a screen titled, "Weekly Circular for Store #0776." Below that were the categories shown in table 6-1.

TABLE 6-1

Weekly ad categories

Dry goods	22
Bakery	10
Beverages	26
Canned foods	5
Condiments, spices, baking	26
Dairy	35
Deli	11
Floral	3

(Continued)

TABLE 6-1 *(Continued)*

Weekly ad categories

Frozen foods	26
Household products	19
Pet supplies	11
Snacks and desserts	27
Produce	24
Infant care	5
Meat, seafood, and poultry	47
Health, beauty, pharmacy	37
General merchandise	1

While I suppose this is a huge improvement over print, it's still old ink in new bottles and useless except in this one store.

Again, credit where due: Stop & Shop is a pioneering retailer and a Jones for other grocery stores to keep up with. I salute that. Yet I also want a loyalty system of my own: one that can work with any store willing to cooperate. I'd like Stop & Shop to salute that too, when I show up with it.

Gas Down

A few weeks after my first experience with Stop & Shop's gizmo and phone app, I pulled into a Shell station to buy some gas and found it festooned with Stop & Shop promotional postings. There was a big banner under the Shell sign by the roadside, a stand-alone sign next to that one, another glued to the side of the pump, another hanging from the gas hose, and another next to the pump's card reader and key pad. They all promised savings of up to $.30 or more per gallon.

On a sticker next to the display on the pump, it said,

BEFORE inserting payment:

- Enter number found on the back or your key tag
- Or insert large Stop & Shop Card

I had thrown away my large (credit card size) Stop & Shop card long before this encounter, because I figured all I needed was the key tag. (After all, that's what works at the store.) I didn't have my reading glasses there at the pump, so I held the tag at arm's length, carefully punched in the tiny thirteen-digit number, and hit Enter. Two messages came back. The first was, "You have no Stop & Shop discounts." The second was, "Apply for the new Shell Drive for Five SM Card today and save 5 cents per gallon."

After I finished pumping my full-price gas, I went in the gas station, where one of the many Stop & Shop promo signs told me I could find a brochure for the program. I found a stack and took one home. The rules for reward points and gas price eligibility were both highly detailed and woefully complex. The back panel also featured Shell promotion for *five* different cards you can use at the station.

I see only two reasons why customers would be willing to do all the work required to get these discounts and make them count for much. One is that they buy groceries only from Stop & Shop and gas only from Shell stations. The other is that they are junkies for promotional gimmicks.

SO, THEN

Loyalty programs today are still normative to the extreme and likely to stay that way until means for showing and leveraging *real* loyalty come along.

7

Big Data

I've just read that I am dead. Don't forget to delete me from
your list of subscribers.

—Rudyard Kipling[1]

THE ARGUMENT

Producing and integrating data sets of all sizes can be a good
and useful thing—especially if customers get to do it too, with
their own data.

In the digital world today, we leave clues about our lives all over the place.
This is why there is a big business in "data integration." Acxiom, for example, maintains billions of records on hundreds of millions of individuals,
with up to a thousand "identity elements" per individual. These are built of
data from all the following and more:

- Telephone directories

- Fishing, hunting, boating, and pilot licenses

- Property file and assessor records for more than 100 million
  properties

- Voter registration

- Proprietary files from multiple industries

- Numerous proprietary data sets

- Criminal files

- Professional licenses

- More than 40 million businesses (including, we assume, retailers)[2]

Then there are businesses that put tracking files in your browser to report on your movements around the Web, or that follow crumb trails left by the "location services" in your smartphone. Wouldn't all that intelligence paint a pretty clear picture of who you are, what you like to buy, and much more—including, for example, where you are now, where you'll go next, and what kind of credit and money you're carrying?

Not in my case, and I suspect not in yours, either.

First, you could take all the available data in the world about me and still not know the three things I go to Shaw's for. (And I'll bet, now that it's in a book, retailers *still* won't know. There's also a good chance my tastes will change anyway.)

Second, I'm not involved in all this data crunching. At best, my input to data integration services is minimal.

Case in point: Rapleaf. According to the *Wall Street Journal* (in its What They Know series, mentioned earlier), Rapleaf is the biggest player in the new personalization game. Here's what Rapleaf says about itself on the company's Web site:

> Rapleaf is a San Francisco-based startup with an ambitious
> vision: we want every person to have a meaningful, personalized
> experience—whether online or offline. We want you to see the right
> content at the right time, every time. We want you to get better,
> more personalized service. To achieve this, we help Fortune 2000
> companies gain insight into their customers, engage them more
> meaningfully, and deliver the right message at the right time. We also
> help consumers understand their online footprint.[3]

Not to brag, but I have a large online footprint. I've lived on the Web since 1995. I've disclosed a great deal about my life through my blog, since 1999, to millions of readers. I surf the Web all day, almost every day, on two laptops, a phone, an iPad, and more different browsers than I'll bother to count. My phone contains hundreds of apps, many of which are reporting personal information to advertisers and third parties. I've put up thousands of tweets for more than fifteen thousand followers on Twitter. I have many hundreds of friends on Facebook and a CV on LinkedIn that is filled out in great detail. And then there are those fifty thousand photos on four Flickr accounts I talked about back in chapter 4. So I figured Rapleaf should know a boatload of juicy stuff about me.

To find out, I went to Rapleaf's site in January 2011, registered, and checked my profile. What I found there was (drum roll ...) not much.[4] Table 7-1 shows what I copied and pasted from its page about me:

The zip code it had was wrong, so I removed it. (The only choice other than leaving it wrong, oddly.) Its guess of our household income was also wrong (it was on the high side). I removed that too (which I would have done in any case). The rest I left as you see in the table. There's not much to say about it, because it doesn't say much.

Six months later, in June 2011, nine of the sixteen categories still had wrong information, including the ten-year-old zip code I had removed in the last visit.

In December 2010, two months after Rapleaf got raked over the coals by the *Wall Street Journal* ("A Web Pioneer Profiles Users by Name," "Thousands

TABLE 7-1

Rapleaf profile

Your interests:	Your demographics:
Entertainment	Age: 55–64
Entertainment > music	Gender: Male
News and current events	Location: Santa Barbara, California, United States
News and current events > online news	Zip: -
Shopping	Influencer Score: 91–100
Shopping > auctions	Education: -
Shopping > mass merchants and department stores	Occupation: -
Shopping > online shopping	Children in the household: Yes
Sports and recreation	Household income –
Sports and recreation > basketball	Marital status: Married
Technology > blogging	Home owner status: Own
Technology > online journals	
Technology > social networks	
Travel	

of Web Users Delete Profiles From RapLeaf," "Privacy Advocate Withdraws from RapLeaf Advisory Board," "How to Get Out of Rapleaf's System," "RapLeaf's Founder on Privacy, Business"), the Rapleaf company blog ran a series titled "The 12 Days of Personalization."[5] Day 12 begins,

> As we know by Day 12, personalization is all about companies giving you what you want, when you want it. Companies can utilize personalization in their email marketing campaigns to create valued relationships between their customers and brands ...
>
> Bringing targeted, high-value purchase opportunities directly to a viewer greatly increases the chances that a browser will become a buyer. And they will thank you for it.[6]

This is fantasy. Twelve years have passed since Christopher Locke joked in *The Cluetrain Manifesto* about marketers' wacky wish to turn the Internet into "TV with a buy button," and here's Rapleaf, calling us "viewers" and imagining that we'll thank them for yet another annoyance—only now a personal one.[7]

Eat your spinnage

In recent years, business publications have become thick with stories about Big Data, and how crunching that data is going to be the Big Thing for Big Business and lots of start-ups. The assumption by writers and their sources is that Big Data needs Big Clouds (from the companies selling products and services for both). I just looked up "big data" (with the quotes) in Google News. Top stories include:

- "CIOs Jump Into Clouds for Big Data Sharing." *Internet Evolution*

- "Forrester Research Analyst Advocates Integration of Big Data ..." TMC

- "Big Data's Integration Hurdles." *IT Business Edge (blog)*

- "Startup Aims to Create Big Apps for Big Data." *GigaOM*

- "Time to Analyze All That Big Data." *IT Business Edge (blog)*

No doubt every store with a loyalty program is already being pitched "solutions" of the sort pumped in those news stories. In the last bulleted item, writer Mike Vizard points toward a McKinsey report titled, "Big Data: The next frontier for innovation, competition and productivity."[8]

It's thick with juicy facts and findings, artfully organized, and addressed to McKinsey's constituency: large companies and governments. But here's one paragraph that speaks directly to where we live (or go):

> Geo-targeted mobile advertising is one of the most common ways organizations can create value from the use of personal location data. For example, consumers who choose to receive geo-targeted ads might have a personalized advertisement for a favorite store pop up on their smartphone when they are close to that store. Or a smartphone user meeting with friends at a bar or restaurant might receive a coupon offer for drinks or food from that establishment … Compared with more traditional forms of advertising such as TV or print, geo-targeted campaigns appear to have higher relevance to the consumer at the moment when a purchase decision is likely to be made and therefore boost the potential for an actual sale. Advertisers certainly seem to believe this to be the case, and they are paying increased rates for this service compared with advertising without geo-targeting.[9]

Not bad, I suppose. But also not good enough, because the customer—the one enjoying the "consumer surplus"—is still a calf to cows producing Big Data fortified milk (and, of course, cookies).

My vote for the best authority on totally personalized data goes to Jeff Jonas, chief scientist, IBM Entity Analytics Group, and IBM distinguished engineer. He came to IBM through acquisition of Systems Research and Development (SRD), which he founded in 1984. In addition to assisting the United States in national security and counterterrorism efforts, SRD worked for Las Vegas casinos, designing and developing methods for spotting cheaters and cheating patterns. Jeff's work has been featured in movies and many TV shows, as well as in academic and business journals.

On August 16, 2009, Jeff put up a landmark blog post titled, "Your Movements Speak for Themselves: Space-Time Travel Data is Analytic Super-Food!"[10] Here are the money paragraphs:

> Mobile devices in America are generating something like 600 billion geo-spatially tagged transactions per day. Every call, text message, email and data transfer handled by your mobile device creates a transaction with your space-time coordinate (to roughly 60 meters accuracy if there are three cell towers in range), whether you have GPS or not. Got a Blackberry? Every few minutes, it sends a heartbeat, creating a transaction whether you are using the phone or

not. If the device is GPS-enabled and you're using a location-based service your location is accurate to somewhere between 10 and 30 meters. Using Wi-Fi? It is accurate below 10 meters ...

With the data out and specialized analytics emerging, this infant industry is already doing some pretty amazing work. Your space-time-travel data makes where you live and where you work self-evident, and it reveals your most frequent, periodic, infrequent and rare destinations ... information certainly useful to attentive direct marketing folks.

This kind of thing sets off privacy alarms all over the place, naturally. And, in the absence of conscience by companies doing the collecting and crunching—plus a near-complete absence of control tools for users— privacy advocates turn toward government for help. And they're getting results, sort of.

One is the "Do-Not-Track Online Act of 2011," sponsored by Senator Jay Rockefeller.[11] It would require the FTC "to prescribe regulations regarding the collection and use of personal information obtained by the tracking of online activity of an individual, and for other purposes." Around that same time, an FTC staff report made clear that the commission would rather not do that, preferring guidelines, principles, and "educating business" options.[12] A Commerce Department "green paper" on the same topic is packed with buzzword compounds like "Bolstering Consumer Trust Online Through 21st Century Fair Information Practice Principles."[13]

I could cite many more of the same, none of which give "consumers" any hope of rescue by the Feds.

SO, THEN

We wouldn't need to be tracked if we weren't being cattle. And we won't solve the privacy problem until customers appear to vendors in human form.

8

Complications

Virgo: You will take the first hellish step down a dark path from which there can be no return when you agree to get updates on Carnival Cruise specials and discounts.

—*The Onion*[1]

THE ARGUMENT

We have made business—especially retailing—too complicated, and we've done that by distancing business from human beings, especially customers.

In October 2000, I had the good luck to be joined at lunch at a retail conference by one of the other speakers there: Lee Scott, then the CEO of Walmart. One of the questions I asked him was, "What happened to Kmart?" His answer, in a word, was, "Coupons." As Lee explained it, Kmart overdid it with coupons, which became too big a hunk of its overhead, while also narrowing its customer base toward coupon clippers. It had other problems, he said, but that was a big one. By contrast, Walmart minimized that kind of thing, focusing instead on promising "everyday low prices," which was a line of Sam Walton's from way back. The overhead for that policy rounded to zero.

Walmart also succeeded, Lee said, because its basic approaches were simple. At heart, it was still the old Walton family five-and-dime, no matter how complicated the business got as it grew.

Still, retailing is complicated. If you're working an operation more sophisticated than a lemonade stand, you're dealing with banks, government red tape (local, state, federal), lawyers, insurance companies, landlords (and/or tenants), employees, shippers, computer and network issues, customers, and all the complexities of acquiring, paying for, selling, and backing your goods and services. Why make it harder than it has to be?

Easy: because *market* is a verb and not just a noun. You *market* to create demand, differentiate your goods and services from everybody else's, and make the shopping "experience" more interesting, compelling, and so on.

Which is all fine, as far as it goes. Problem is, it tends to go away from the customer.

Setting the Stage

Back in the early 1990s, when I was making a good living as a marketing consultant, I asked my wife—a successful businesswoman and a retailing veteran—why it was that heads of corporate sales and marketing departments were always from sales people and not from marketing people. Her answer: "Simple: Sales is real. Marketing is bullshit."

When I asked her to explain that, she said this wasn't marketing's fault. The problem was the role marketing was forced to play. "See, sales touches the customer; but marketing can't, because that's sales's job. So marketing has to be 'strategic.'" She put air quotes around "strategic." She acknowledged that this was an oversimplification and not fair to all the good people in marketing (such as myself) who were trying to do right by customers. But her remark spoke to the need to distinguish between what's real and what's not, and to dig deeper into why the latter has become such an enormous part of the way we do business.

Most of what a customer sees of marketing is the advertising and promotional stuff we've been talking about for the last few chapters. But there's more going on behind the scenes. *Much* more.

Here's a list of arcane phrases, just from the patois of retailer-supplier interactions, back up in the supply chain:

- **Advertising allowances.** Flat fees or percentages of wholesale purchase prices, paid to the retailer by suppliers to help defray the retailer's advertising costs.

- **Buyback allowances.** Provisions that allow the retailer to return old or unsold products to suppliers.

- **Contests and prizes.** Enticements offered by suppliers to retailers.

- **Conventions and association meetings.** Settings where suppliers and retailers meet to discuss new products or product lines along with promotional plans for them; where authoritative speakers talk about new industry fashions, trends, or concepts; where retailers can be trained by experts or by suppliers; and where the industry talks to itself, face to face.

- **Co-op advertising.** A form of reimbursement to a retailer by a supplier for advertising the supplier's goods, using the supplier's logo (or whole prepared ads), and for meeting other requirements of the supplier.

- **Dealer premiums** are prizes or gifts from suppliers to retailers and their salespeople when sales goals or other benchmarks are reached.

- **Display allowances.** Fees that retailers charge their suppliers for shelf and floor space where displays, counter stands, floor stands, racks, and shelf signs can be set up.

- **Diverting.** Purchasing by a retailer in volume from a supplier at a discount in one region, and then shipping the goods to another region where there is no discount.

- **Forward-buying.** Stocking up by retailers of products, usually when offered by the manufacturer in volume at a discount, in anticipation of a "sale" on the goods in the store, or of actual demand by customers.

- **Push money or spiffs.** Incentive money paid to retail salespeople for pushing particular products, product lines, or brands.

- **Slotting fees.** Also known as "pay-to-stay" fees or "allowances," these are sums paid by suppliers to retailers for shelf or floor space.

- **Trade deals.** Short-term discounts and other incentives that suppliers provide retailers for "sales" and "specials."

- **Variable trade spending.** Discounts and allowances by suppliers to retailers that create enticing price differentials between the suppliers' products and those of competitors. These may be tied to sales volume and used to maintain that volume with a low price on the shelf.

Not all those things fall under the heading of marketing, but all of them are caused or influenced by marketing imperatives, mostly of the "strategic" sort.

Here's another way to look at that list: *customers asked for none of it.* True, some customers like contests and enjoy playing the games retailers entice them to play—enough to justify the TLC Network's "Extreme Couponing" show. ("Twelve of the best extreme couponers go cart-to-cart in a face-off to determine who takes home the title of America's Biggest Super Saver," says one promo.[2]) But what kind of store wants only Super Savers? Not even Walmart, as Lee Scott made clear above.

Computer programmers have a name for accumulated clutter that stays in code but has outlived its original purpose, which may not have been fully legitimate in the first place. The word is "cruft." Within the narrow scope of marketing-as-usual, the list above might look fine; but within the scope of the whole relationship with customers, or the larger marketplace, a lot of it is cruft. Even if it plays on TV.

Needs versus Wants

One of the earliest bits of wisdom I learned about shopping for groceries is that most of what you need for staying alive is out along the walls, not in the aisles. It's on the perimeter that you find the fresh produce, vegetables, cheeses, meats, and dairy products. The aisles are for the more durable stuff in bags, cans, bottles, and boxes: potato chips, boxed cereals, disposable diapers, soft drinks, light bulbs, and so on. Of the fifteen thousand to sixty thousand SKUs (stock-keeping units—distinct products) carried in American supermarkets, most are in the aisles.[3] And many (if not most) of those are complicated by the promotional gambits I just listed.

The distinction between need-to-buy and might-want-to-buy is one that helps tease markets apart from marketing. Grocery stores don't need to create demand for their goods. Humans need to eat, and in the civilized world, grocery stores are where humans go to buy food they can serve to themselves. But grocery stores want to make more money than selling need-to-buy goods alone can provide, so they've created sophisticated and complex ways of offering a mind-blowing variety of stuff, some of which is good-to-get (say, spices, soap, and toilet paper) and most of which you may not want or need (say, jars of pickles or floor wax).

The result is cognitive overload out the wazoo—for stores as well as for their customers. What are the costs of that overload? Is it even worthwhile to measure them, if the biggest question is still "Which complication works best?" Whatever the answer, it should be clear that we need less of it.

SO, THEN

Marketing won't be bullshit when customers make clear that bullshit won't work anymore. Fortunately, there are many more ways for customers to do that in networked markets than in the industrial ones when customers had no choice but to play along with marketing's games.

PART II

The Networked Marketplace

A powerful global conversation has begun. Through the Internet, people are discovering and inventing new ways to share relevant knowledge with blinding speed. As a direct result, markets are getting smarter—and getting smarter faster than most companies.

—*The Cluetrain Manifesto*

9

Net Pains

The Web is a mess, as organized as an orgy.

—David Weinberger[1]

THE ARGUMENT

For the Intention Economy to emerge, the Internet needs to support maximized economic activity, driven by copious signals from individual customers and users, and responses to those by vendors. How well that happens depends on how well we understand the Net itself and its generative properties—and keep those properties alive and well.

One night not long ago, my son Jeffrey (then fourteen) and I watched *Blade Runner* on Netflix. Here we were, in the year 2011, watching a *future* noir classic about the year 2019 that was shot in 1982. We enjoyed the movie, but we couldn't help marveling at its prophetic hits and misses.

In *Blade Runner*'s future, Los Angeles has become a grimy dystopia where office buildings the size of mountains rise from a landscape of oil refineries and crowded urban streets. Haze hangs everywhere, especially indoors, where smoking is pro forma. Antigravity cop cars zip through the sky, while blimp-shaped billboards float above streets, displaying video ads for off-world vacations. Manufactured humans called *replicants* are indistinguishable from the real thing—except to professional sleuths called "blade runners" (such as Harrison Ford, the star of the movie).

Since *Blade Runner*'s guesses about the future weren't implausible in the fullness of time, it was easy to suspend disbelief and enjoy the show. But science fiction from the past runs aground when its guesses are proven wrong in the present; so *Blade Runner* gave us plenty of goofs to savor, too. The most common ones were promotional "product placements"—a movie-funding convention that *Blade Runner* pioneered. Logos for at least thirty companies appear in the movie.[2] Some brands, such as Coca-Cola, are still around, but many of the others, including TDK, the Bell System, Atari, and RCA, have faded or disappeared. (The kid asked, "What's RCA?") But the technical goofs stood out more. Computers in the movie still have vacuum-tube displays, and when Harrison Ford's character needs to make an urgent call, he uses a pay phone. The Internet is nowhere in sight.

Now imagine you're back in 1982. Somebody tells you that in twelve years, the world will adopt a new communications system that nobody owns, everybody can use, and anybody can improve. The system will be all-digital and will provide ways for anybody to communicate with anybody, anywhere in the world, and to copy and share anything that can be digitized—including mail, print publications, music, radio streams, TV programs, and movies—at costs that approach zero. Would you believe it? Or would it sound as far-fetched as antigravity cars?

How about if you were also told that the same system would end the livelihoods of many journalists and recording artists, undermine media businesses of all kinds, expose millions of diplomatic communications to the world, provide new ways for bad people as well as good to collaborate in secret, and undermine civilization as we know it?

Both forecasts would be true.

My point: the Net is more than a new development, more than a game changer. It is a new environment for business, culture, and human interactions of all kinds. It is also a perfect example of how the miraculous becomes mundane. The Internet is now so common, so ordinary, that we hardly pause to get perspective on how radically it has changed nearly everything it connects. Nor do we pause to contemplate its progress toward (and away from) end states good and bad—or how we may be slowing progress in either or both directions.

So, for a rough measure of progress so far, here are two more family stories, both starring Jeffrey at an earlier age.

Story #1. It's 2002, and the Jeffrey is seven. As always, he's full of questions. As sometimes happens, I don't have an answer. But this time, he comes back with a simple demand:

"Look it up," he says.

"I can't. I'm driving."

"Look it up anyway."

"I need a computer for that."

"Why?"

Story #2. It's 2007, and we are staying overnight in the house of an old family friend. In a guest bedroom is a small portable 1970s-vintage black-and-white TV. On the front of the TV are a volume control and two tuning dials: one for channels 2 through 13, the other for 14 through 83. Jeffrey examines the device for a minute or two and says, "What is this?" I say it's a TV. He points at the two dials and asks, "Then what are *these* for?"

Progress is how the miraculous becomes mundane. The beauty of stars would be legend, Emerson said, if they only showed through the clouds but once every thousand years. What would he have made of commercial aviation, a system by which millions of people fly all over the globe, every day, leaping continents and oceans in just a few hours, while complaining of bad food and slow service, and shutting their windows to block light from the clouds below so they can watch a third-rate movie with bad sound on a tiny screen?

The Internet is a sky of stars we've made for ourselves (and *of* ourselves), all just a few clicks away. I recently found that Searls.com, which has been hosted at Rackspace.com since that company was a side project by some students in Texas, is actually in Virginia. Over the years *Linux Journal's* servers have been in many places: Seattle, Amsterdam, Costa Rica, Texas ... [3] In Paris last summer, my wife had countless live Skype sessions with her company in Los Angeles, many using video, with little apparent delay. No doubt there were costs somewhere. But Skype operates profitably, somehow. So, presumably, do the Internet service providers (ISPs) in L.A. and Paris. We take these things for granted as well.

These days, Jeffrey no longer relies much on parents (or anybody, actually) for answers. He just goes to the Net over a laptop, a smartphone, or a tablet, each connected wirelessly. True, these options are still luxuries (or absent) in most of the world, but we can see two vectors of progress in the way one kid takes the Net for granted. One points to the end of centrally controlled media. The other points to what Bob Frankston, coinventor of spreadsheet software, calls *ambient connectivity*.[4]

Two roadblocks currently stand athwart progress toward those ends. One is that there is no agreed-upon understanding of what the Internet is. The other is that phone and cable companies—along with compliant legislators and regulators—insist on maintaining those legacy businesses at all costs. Those costs include boundless opportunities in a networked world they are best positioned to help create. Both are slowing the Internet's evolution and growth, and the economic benefits that will follow.

What It Isn't

Look up "The Internet is" (with the quotes) on Google, and check the results. Here are the top answers, as of the day I'm writing this, in order:[5]

... *terrible (theinternetisterrible.com)*

... *a copy machine (kk.org/thetechnium)*

... *a global system of interconnected computer networks that use the standard Internet Protocol Suite (TCP/IP) (Wikipedia)*

...*for porn (a 2005 video uploaded by Evilhoof and Flayed)*

... *expanding (a 2006 video uploaded by Chocolate Tampon)*

... *shit (theinternetisshit.com)*

... *made of cats (rathergood.com/cats)*

... *affecting traditional journalism (mashable.com)*

... *now sufficiently embedded in society (David Clark)*

... *dead (Prince)*

... *an agreement (Doc Searls and David Weinberger in* World Of Ends.*com)*

... *changing us (Nicholas Carr in his book* The Shallows*)*

The answers are all over the place because the Internet is not a *thing*, even though it can support just about *anything*. So, because it can support anything, it is understood in any number of different ways. Like the universe, there are no other examples of it, and all our understandings of it are incomplete.

But, being human, we must proceed from what we do understand, starting with its *protocols*. These are agreements among computers and other devices about how data moves between physical networks. The Internet's base protocols are the *Transmission Control Protocol* and the *Internet Protocol* (combined as TCP/IP). These are about as minimal as protocols can be, defining in simple terms how anything can connect to anything else, at any distance, over any available paths, and pass packets between those ends on a "best effort" basis.

By TCP/IP's design, the Net has no single purpose—or any purpose at all—other than to move packets of data from any one end to any other end. This pushes toward zero the functional distance between those ends and minimizes the efforts required to find paths for data between them. While those efforts do have costs, the Internet itself has no interest in those costs. It has no agenda for creating or protecting scarcities, because it is not a business and therefore has no business model. It is as elemental as oxygen or a pine tree. Those have no business models, either, but are highly useful to business. So, thanks to its any-purpose design and absent business model, the Net supports trillions of dollars in business activity, much of which would not exist if the Net were not there.

Yet little in that last paragraph is obvious to most people. Instead, what's obvious to people is that they get billed for something called "broadband" or "high-speed Internet" by their ISP, which in nearly all cases (at least in North America) is a phone or a cable TV company. Those companies don't define the Net the same way as TCP/IP does, even though they use those protocols. Instead, ISPs define the Net as one among three services they sell as a "triple play." The other two are telephony and cable TV.

Between those very different views, a battle line has been drawn.

Any versus Only

To simplify things a bit, look at the Net's future as a battleground where *any* and *only* fight it out. On the side of *any* are the Net's protocols. On the side of *only* are governments and businesses with interests in restricting and controlling access to the Net, and thwarting many purposes to which the Net might be put. This battle also happens inside our own heads, because we tend to view the Net both ways. Ironies abound.

For example, the Internet is often called a "network of networks," yet the Net was designed to transcend the connections it employs and is therefore not reducible to them. It is not comprised of wiring and is not a "service," even though it's called one by ISPs.

So let's look at the sides here. On the *any* side, "net-heads" (yes, they call themselves that) frame their understanding of the Net in terms of its protocols and those protocols' virtues. On the *only* side, "bell-heads" (yes, they call themselves that, too) frame their understanding of the Net in terms of wiring infrastructure and billing systems.

To net-heads, the Internet is a vast new virtual space with qualities such as *neutrality* and *generativity*. To maximize economic opportunity and vitality, those virtues need to be maximized, even if phone and cable TV businesses don't wish to acknowledge or support those virtues.

To bell-heads, the Internet's "network of networks" is a collection of mostly private properties, with which owners should be free to do what they please. So, if what pleases them is throttling certain kinds of data traffic to maximize QoS (quality of service), too bad. They are The Market, which will grow best if they act in their own economic self-interest. Hey, look at all the good they've done already. (Want dial-up again, anyone?) And look at the robust competition between cable and phone companies. Isn't that producing enough economic benefits for everybody?

Since net-heads tend to make social arguments, while bell-heads tend to make economic ones, net-heads get positioned on the left and bell-heads on the right. Between the two are boundless technical arguments that aren't worth getting into here.

I'm a net-head, but one who wants both sides to recognize that the Net's original design is encompassing and beneficial for economies and societies everywhere. That is, I believe the argument for the Net is the same as the one for gravity, sunlight, the periodic table, and pine trees: that it is part of nature itself. What makes the Net different from all those other products of nature is that humans made the Net for themselves.

The Net's nature—its essential purpose—is to support everything that uses it, just as the essential purpose of a clock is to tell time. So, while the Net today relies on phone and cable connections, its support-everything purpose should not be subordinated to legacy phone and cable TV businesses. The Internet, in the neutral and generative form defined by its protocols, is a far larger and more interesting market environment than the one defined by the parochial and limited interests of phone and cable companies, both of which are desperately trying to hold on to their legacy businesses and would be better served by embracing all the opportunities the Internet opens up, for everybody.

We're going to evolve past those old businesses anyway. Phone and cable company engineers know that, and so do many of the business leaders in those companies, even as they fight to protect their legacy businesses at all costs.

As a pro-business guy, I sympathize with phone and cable companies, which are cursed by the need to maintain margins in existing businesses while building out infrastructures that obsolete those businesses. These companies get little credit (especially from net-heads) for their genuine innovations and for their ability to innovate more. We do need them, whether we like them or not.

Likewise I sympathize with old-school ISPs: the original and surviving Internet service providers, which went into the business of doing everything the Internet Protocol encouraged, and dealing in the process with the real-world limits of wiring, spectrum, regulatory complications, and political game playing at every level. These companies never wanted to be in the TV or phone businesses, and they get little (if any) love from either side in business and policy battles.

But mostly I respect the nature of the Net as an environment that is profoundly supportive of everything that depends on it, including every kind of business that requires a data connection to the world. And I don't think letting the carriers (or the governments) run the whole show will get us the fully market-supportive Internet we need.

Opportunity Knocking

The worldwide economy has a virtual Internet of its own, in the mesh of protocols by which sellers and buyers do business. This is one reason why business and the Internet get along so well and why the Web we know today is largely a commercial one.

Realizing that both the Internet and business are protocol-based helps us see how the Net liberates economic activities and how important it is to free the Net from the single-purpose businesses that own its "last mile." Even phone and cable companies need to see how much business is prevented by subordinating the all-purpose Internet to their single-purpose systems—and how much more opportunity will open up for them if they help build out any-purpose Net infrastructure.

My own perspective on Net-based opportunity is anchored in the summer of 1976. I was still in my twenties, married, the father of two kids, and a former journalist and radio personality living in a small rural enclave outside Chapel Hill, North Carolina. I say *former* because I couldn't get a job in journalism or radio. I had been laid off by one local radio station and turned down by the rest of them. There were no job openings at any of the area newspapers or magazines, and efforts to sell my work to publishers in New York and elsewhere had also failed. I still made a few bucks freelancing, but not enough to support my family. So I fell into working odd jobs. I even worked off rent at my landlord's sawmill. While I eventually did well in other professions, I gave up my ambitions in journalism and radio, simply because opportunities in those fields had run out.

My view toward those opportunities was bounded by geography and employment options in North Carolina—boundaries the Internet later obliterated. I could see that obliteration coming when I first started learning about the Net in the 1980s. I experienced it firsthand when Phil Hughes, the publisher of *Linux Journal*, hired me to write for that magazine and a companion publication called *Websmith*, in 1996. That was my first job as a journalist in more than twenty years. In the decade and a half since then, I've continued working as an editor at *Linux Journal*, always following the Net closely, never ceasing to marvel at the casual geekery that made this miraculous thing possible. I've also been exasperated at how we mistake phone and cable company means for the Net's actual ends.

Those ends are endless, because the Net's capacity expands with every new protocol added to the Net's suite of them—and because these protocols are generally compliant with the "end-to-end principle," which was first described by Jerome H. Saltzer, David P. Reed, and David D. Clark in the 1981 paper "End-to-End Arguments in System Design."[6] Put simply, the end-to-end principle says the intelligence that matters most exists in boundless variety at the ends of a network, rather than with the mediating systems that sit in the middle. Therefore, they said, network protocols should be designed primarily as means for those ends, rather than to serve the parochial interests of intermediary operators, such as phone and cable companies.

In May 1997, David Isenberg, then working for AT&T, self-published a paper titled, "The Rise of the Stupid Network"—his own end-to-end argument against AT&T's cherished belief that a network should be smart, in the sense that it needed a big all-knowing, all-doing, all-thinking company like AT&T in the middle, doing the important stuff. David wrote, "Powerful leading indicators of the Stupid Network began arriving when entrepreneurs who had no vested interest in maintaining telephone company assumptions begin to offer profitable, affordable, widely available data services."[7] By then, Amazon.com and eBay were two big examples. Now we have Wikipedia, Skype, Google, Twitter, Facebook, LinkedIn, and all of e-commerce.

AT&T was no doubt a smart company, and so was every other phone and cable TV company in the world. But none could begin to contemplate, much less support, any of the new and amazing things that are born and grow on the stupid Internet, every day. Why is it not obvious to everybody that the stupid Internet hosts a whole new world of opportunities?

The simple answer is that we don't understand it. The more complex answer is that we understand it too many different ways.

Frames

We understand everything metaphorically. That is, we think and talk about everything in terms of something else. That something else is a *conceptual metaphor*, or what cognitive linguists also call a *frame*.

For example, the most common frame for time is money. That's why we *save, waste, lose, invest,* and *set aside* time. So, think of each frame as a box of words for one subject that we borrow from when we talk about something else. Thus, we borrow the vocabulary of money when we talk about time.

Another example: life. The most common frame for life is travel. Borrowing from the travel frame, we say birth is *arrival*, death is *departure*, choices are *crossroads*, and careers are *paths*. We also say we get *stuck in a rut, fall off the wagon, get lost in the woods, take the fast lane, cross that bridge when we come to it,* and *win the race*.

The irony of metaphors is that they're right while they're wrong. In fact, time is not money, and life is not travel. Time is a measuring system. Life is a self-sustaining process. But, as living beings, we experience time as something valuable. We experience life as directed motion. So we talk about time in terms of money and life in terms of travel.

This goes even for our moral systems. We say *good is up* and *bad is down* because we walk upright. We say *good is light* and *bad is dark* because we are diurnal: daylight animals. If owls could talk, they might say *good is dark* and *bad is up*.[8]

I bring us down this digressive path because there are some concepts— time and life among them—that are so general and encompassing that we will never explain them perfectly, no matter how well we know them from experience. Such is the case with the Internet, which is cursed by being like nothing at all. Or, like everything.

Thus, the challenge of defining the Internet always reminds me of an old joke essay question: "Define the universe, and give three examples."

Ending at Zero

In *Small Pieces Loosely Joined*, David Weinberger writes,[9]

> Suppose—just suppose—that the Web is a new world that we are just beginning to inhabit. We're like the earlier European settlers in the United States, living on the edge of the forest ... Of course, while the settlers may not have known what the geography of the New World was going to be, they at least knew that there was a geography. The Web, on the other hand, has no geography, no landscape. It has no distance. It has nothing natural in it. It has few rules of behavior and fewer lines of authority. Common Sense doesn't hold there, and uncommon sense hasn't emerged ... We don't even know how to talk about a place that has no soil, no boundaries, no near or far.[10]

Craig Burton, Senior Analyst with Kuppinger Cole, combines these three ideas we've visited so far—*end-to-end*, *stupid*, and *a new world*—by describing the Internet as a vast hollow sphere, comprised entirely of ends:

> I see the Net as a world we might see as a bubble. A sphere. It's growing larger and larger, and yet inside, every point in that sphere is visible to every other one. That's the architecture of a sphere. Nothing stands between any two points. That's its virtue: it's empty in the middle. The distance between any two points is functionally zero, and not just because they can see each other, but because nothing interferes with operation between any two points. There's a word I like for what's going on here: *terraform*. It's the verb for creating a world. That's what we're making here: a new world.[11]

I think of Craig's hollow sphere as a giant three-dimensional zero. Thanks to that zero, I sat in Paris in July 2010, listening to an English language broadcast of the World Cup, from WDNC: the same North Carolina radio station whose transmitter I used to run on weekends in 1974. The cost of this wasn't zero, just like the cost of water from a spigot isn't zero. But the cost was low enough to ignore, and that's a big part of what makes the Internet so appealing and useful.

Back when I worked at WDNC, we were proud that our signal reached dozens of counties in North Carolina and Virginia. It still does, but the station also reaches the whole world over the Internet, without worrying much about anybody extracting tariffs or fees between the station at one end and the listeners at many others. Thanks to the same protocol suite, I can write a blog post anywhere, put it up on a server in Cambridge, Massachusetts, and have it read by countless people all over the world, many of whom have been notified by RSS—Really Simple Syndication—without any of us belonging to any publisher's managed syndicate.

RSS as we know it today was designed and defined by Dave Winer, who also pioneered blogging and podcasting. Today, if you look up RSS on Google, you'll get more than 12 billion results.[12] That's because Dave has always tried to obey one of his favorite sayings: "Ask not what the Net can do for you; ask what you can do for the Net."[13] (He sometimes substitutes Web for Net. Both make the same point.) The authors of other Internet protocols obey the same imperative. At this writing, Wikipedia lists forty-three protocols in its Internet protocol suite entry, and that's not counting "more" in each of its four protocol categories.[14]

TCP/IP was proposed in 1974. Some protocols, such as FTP (File Transfer Protocol) are older. Others, such as HTTP (Hypertext Transfer Protocol), came along later. Most are as ownerless as a handshake or a dance move. None are encumbered by intellectual property claims, even if intellectual property is involved. Instead the Internet's protocols embody principles that are abbreviated as "NEA." They mean:

- Nobody owns it.

- Everybody can use it.

- Anybody can improve it.

While one could argue that the first ideal overstates or misrepresents facts, it isn't an issue. For example, it doesn't matter for the rest of us that somebody owns Ethernet's patents. Those patent holders decided long ago to set Ethernet free,[15] for zero-cost use and improvement by anybody (exemplifying the other two letters in NEA). One result is that almost nobody outside the networking world remembers IBM's token ring, which competed with Ethernet back in the days when both were young and hot. Even today, some techies still regard token ring as the superior technology. But IBM wanted to sell token ring to customers, while Ethernet's owners (Xerox, Intel, and Digital Equipment Corporation) and patent holders (notably Bob Metcalfe, widely considered the father of the protocol) wanted to make it useful to everybody, and thereby create whole new markets. So they gave it away.

The difference was between two prepositions: *with* and *because*. IBM wanted to make money *with* token ring, while Xerox, Intel, and Digital wanted to make money *because* Ethernet was free. The result was a big win for everybody, including IBM, thanks to Ethernet's free and open nature.

Back in the late 1980s, when Craig Burton was Executive VP Corporate Marketing at Novell, I found out from a friend who worked at a component supplier that Novell was actually the world's largest maker of Ethernet interface boards. This was when nearly everybody in business used PC clones, few of which came with Ethernet installed. That left open a market for Ethernet interface cards. Those cards then cost about a thousand dollars apiece. It was widely assumed at the time that 3Com was the king of Ethernet cards, but here I was learning that Novell was the real title holder. So I asked Craig why Novell didn't make a big deal about its position in the Ethernet interface card market. He replied, "Because it's going to be a zero-dollar business. In a few years, Ethernet will be a standard jack on the back of every computer." And so it was, and still is.

Today, Craig says the same thing about Internet service. The first cost of the Net is like the first cost of Ethernet. It's $0, or close enough. Yes, ISPs are good to have, but their model should be roads, electric service, or water distribution, not telephony or cable television. (Although they should be free to sell those services.) Your road department doesn't say whether your driveway should be concrete or gravel. Your water department is not also your "plumbing service provider." Yes, there are understandings about how and where you connect what's yours to what's theirs. But few if any of those say what you can do on your side of the relationship.

What we need here is what J. P. Rangaswami (chief scientist at Salesforce) and I call "because effects," and economists call positive externalities. J. P. and I coined "because effects" because they are easy to explain this way: you make money *because* of them, rather than *with* them. The total "because effect" of the Internet is incalculable. The Net has become a rising tide of capacity for connection that lifts all boats—economic, social, and otherwise. That capacity rises as the inverse of the Net's own movement toward zero in the ease and cost of connectivity.

The third NEA ideal—*Anybody can improve it*—is what makes the Internet such an adaptive form of infrastructure. It is also why the Net constantly improves as a marketplace, becoming more and more useful and efficient for everybody and everything that relies on it. So, while the Net can support seller-built inconveniences that limit customer choices, it can also provide customers with ways of working around those limitations.

SO, THEN

The Net's capacity to support limitless economic activity and growth will win in the long run because it will prove out in the very marketplaces it supports. But there will be a great deal of resistance along the way, as the narrow interests of both Big Government and Big Business try to contain the Net's potential within the scope of their own ambitions. Still, the evolutionary direction of the Net is toward ambient connectivity. Whatever that looks and feels like, it won't resemble either the phone system or cable TV. Rather it will look like everything, together.

10

The Live Web

Urge and urge and urge …
Always the procreant urge of the world …
Out of the dimness opposite equals advance …
Always substance and increase …
Always a knit of identity …
Always distinction …
Always a breed of life.

—Walt Whitman[1]

The network is the urban site before us, an invitation to design and
construct the City of Bits (capital of the twenty-first century), just as, so long
ago, a narrow peninsula beside the Meander became the place for Miletos.

—William J. Mitchell[2]

THE ARGUMENT

The Live Web isn't just real time. It's real place as well. And
the best real-world model for that place is the city.

In 2003, my son Allen and I were talking about the future evolution of the
Internet and the Web in particular. As he saw it then, the Web we knew
was mostly static. Sites changed constantly, but not so fast that Google and
other search engines couldn't index everything on the whole Web every few
days. But search engines didn't show what was happening right now, in

real time. That's because nearly every Web site in those days was more of a construction project than a venue for live events. Allen didn't see this as a problem so much as an early limitation that would be overcome when anybody and anything could engage each other in real time. He called that future environment "the Live Web."

Blogs were the earliest, widespread Live Web life form. What makes a blog live is syndication. When a blog post (or a news story) goes up, it notifies the world of that fact through an RSS feed. This fact came in handy when David Sifry and I were working together on a story about blogging for *Linux Journal* in November 2002. To help us do the research required, David invented Technorati, which went on to become what he called a "Live Web" search engine, borrowing Allen's term.

Both Allen and David turned out to be ahead of their time, which began to arrive in a big way when Twitter and Facebook made the live nature of the Web obvious to everybody.

For me, the most dramatic example of the Live Web at work came when my daughter called me in Boston one afternoon from her home in Baltimore. "We just had an earthquake!" she said. "It feels just like it did back in California. Everybody rushed outside and started yelling, 'Are you okay?' to each other. Have you heard anything?" I looked for #earthquake on Twitter. The first results were from Virginia, D.C., Maryland, then Philadelphia, then New York. "It must be coming from somewhere south of you," I said. Then our house began to rock. "Wow! I'm feeling it here now," I said, and watched fresh tweets from others in Boston.

But here's the important thing: Twitter and Facebook are just early versions of far more evolved species. They are as prototypical of the future Live Web as AOL and Compuserve were for the Static Web. They are also companies and therefore single points of failure. They will die. That means we can't depend on them or any other company alone to give us the Live Web. To imagine our way to the Live Web, we need to look past Silicon Valley, Wall Street, and the natural environment we see outside of humanity: the forests, jungles, and oceans of the world. Instead, we need to look at cities.

How We Live

The human population of Earth passed seven billion while I was writing this book. Already by 2006, over half our population lived in cities. (In the

United States, we've now passed 82 percent.) From now until 2050, over a million people per week will be added to cities. While these are interesting facts that can lead in many directions, the most pertinent one for us here is mortality in business. That's because cities live while businesses die off—as do people and other living things. What do cities do that companies and other living systems don't?

Geoffrey West has an answer. West is a theoretical physicist who enjoyed a long and distinguished career in his field before he and some colleagues began seeking a scientific model of cities. In the course of that work, they also studied companies. What they found was that cities continue to grow in size and vitality while plants, animals, and companies grow only to the point when they can't any more. "It's very hard to kill a city," West says. "You can drop an atomic bomb on a city and thirty years later, it's surviving. Very few cities fail. All companies die."[3]

That's because cities scale in a *superlinear* way, while plants, animals, and companies scale in a *sublinear* way. In mathematical terms, the leverage of growth is greater than one for cities and less than one for plants, animals, and companies. So, as a city grows, it needs *less* energy to keep growing, while a company needs *more*. Hence, a city has no inherent burdens of size, while an organism does. As my wife likes to say, "Trees don't grow to the sky." Sublinear scaling is the reason. The typical path of sublinear growth is sigmoidal: after it hockey-sticks up a steep growth slope, it bends right toward the horizontal. West and his colleagues studied twenty-three thousand companies and found that "they all start by looking like hockey sticks, they all bend over, and they all die like you and me."[4]

Yes, companies can renew themselves. They can invent new products and services that hockey-stick toward the sky at the speed of a start-up. Yet each success makes the company bigger again, and bigness has costs that can only be offset by constant innovation and even greater growth. This simply doesn't happen beyond a certain level of hugeness, unless the company breaks into smaller pieces that all grow independently. But then it's not one company anymore. By dividing into separate pieces, the original company dies.

Cities, on the other hand, are by nature arrangements of many living things. All those things die individually, while the city lives on as a collective system with benefits that transcend the mortalities of everything that comprises it. West says this works because *cities are networks*.

Worldwide City

"All of life is controlled by networks," West says. But when you contain that network inside a single entity, it is mortal. When you combine those living networks with others of the same and related kinds, the economies of scale bring increasing returns. "The bigger you are, the more you have, per capita." For example, "higher wages, more super-creative people, more patents ..."[5] You also get more crime, disease, and other downsides as well. But cities also increase hope for solving those things, because the sources of solutions are networked.

What the Internet does is give all of connected civilization the benefits—at least online—of living in a city. By connecting each of us to all of us, the Internet is the biggest city of all.

SO, THEN

Cities are generative. They foster invention, innovation, enterprise, adaptation, and proliferation. They also have the properties of commons and are the natural habitats of markets. Indeed, cities have always grown around marketplaces and connections to commerce, especially shipping. (It's no coincidence that the Internet's undersea fiber optic cables connect to cities and countries at "landing points.")

Most of all, cities are collections of customers. And the best customers have full agency.

11

Agency

Trust thyself: every heart vibrates to that iron string.

—Ralph Waldo Emerson[1]

THE ARGUMENT

Agency is personal. It is the source of confidence behind all intention. By its nature, the networked marketplace welcomes full agency for customers. So, because the best vendors are customer-driven, there will be many more ways for both vendors and customers to thrive in the networked marketplace and, therefore, in the Intention Economy as well.

When we use the word *agency* these days, we usually mean a party that acts on behalf of another one—such as an advertising, PR, real estate, talent, or literary agency. But the deeper original meanings of agency are about *acting for one's self*. Here are the *Oxford English Dictionary*'s relevant definitions of *agent*:

1. a. One who ... acts or exerts power.

2. He who operates in a particular direction, who produces an effect.

3. a. Of persons: One who does the actual work of anything, as distinguished from the instigator or employer; hence, one who acts for another, a deputy, steward, factor, substitute, representative, or emissary.[2]

In the Intention Economy, liberated customers enjoy full *agency* for themselves and employ *agents* who respect and apply the powers that customers grant them.

Work

The age of industry began in shipping and trade. Under the OED's fourth definition, the earliest examples of *agency* refer to activities in distant places. The dictionary cites Jonathan Swift (1745), whose character would rather not be "at the charge of exchange and agencies," and a document from 1800 referring to "foreign houses of agency." The next definition, "An establishment for the purpose of doing business for another, usually at a distance," cites examples starting with Reuters Agency in 1861. The first agency of government comes two decades later.

Business in the industrial world is complicated. Nobody can do everything, and that's one reason markets work. Opportunity appears where something can be done that others are not doing or are not doing well enough. Many of those opportunities are representational in the sense that agency, in the form of work, is handed off. We hire agents to work as extensions of ourselves.

Democracies too are representational arrangements. Democratic governments are agencies of their people. That these agencies should also have agencies makes sense.

But agency is personal in the first place. Having agency makes us effective in the world, which includes the marketplace. This raises some interesting questions. What does it mean for a customer to have full agency in the marketplace? Is it just to show up with sufficient cash and credit? Is it enough to be known as a good customer only within the scope of a company's CRM system? That's the current default assumption, and it's woefully limiting.

Take, for example, my agency as a customer in the airline business. Most years, I fly more than a hundred thousand miles. I bring to the market a portfolio of knowledge, expertise, and *intent* (that is, agency) that should be valuable to me and valuable to the companies I might deal with. I know a lot about the science and history of aviation; about many airlines old and new; about many airports and their cities; and about geography, geology, weather, astronomy, and other relevant sciences. I'm a photographer whose work is known within some aviation circles and to a small degree adds value to flying in general. I am also a fairly easy passenger to please. I require no assistance, have no dietary restrictions, show up early, and don't trouble airline personnel with rookie questions. I prefer certain seats but don't freak out if I don't get them, and I'm often one of the first to trade seats if it helps a couple or a family sit together on a plane. I am also willing to pay for certain privileges. Yet, only the first item—miles flown—is of serious interest to the airline I usually fly, which is United. That I'm a million-mile flyer with United is unknown and uninteresting to all but that one airline.

Thus, I have a measure of agency only within United's system and somewhat less than that with other members of the Star Alliance, to which United belongs. My self-actualization as a passenger is not my own, but that of a "1K" (100,000 miles per year) or whatever it says on my United Mileage Plus membership card in a given year. I am a high-value calf in their well-tended corral. It's nice that my one-company status gets me some privileges with other airlines in the Star Alliance. But, since the IT systems of Star Alliance member airlines are not entirely communicative, those privileges are spotty. Asking any Star Alliance airline to be a cow for the calves of other airlines makes each of them groan.

The other airlines don't know what they're missing because they *can't* know what they're missing. All their heuristics are confined to their own CRM systems, plus whatever speculative "personalized" jive they buy from data mills. None of that milled data comes directly from you or me. If Delta buys data about me from, say, Acxiom, my agency is nowhere to be found. All of the agency is Acxiom's, and it is not even acting as *an* agency for me in the representational sense of the word. I've offloaded no work on it at all, but it is doing work on my behalf, sort of.[3]

We can only do better if agency is ours and not theirs.

Self-Actualization

To consider what self-actualization means in the marketplace, it helps to examine the business sections of bookstores and libraries. They are full of books about self-actualization for companies and their employees, but there are few if any books for customers. There is nothing, yet, about what it means for you and me to be self-actualized as customers. If there were, what would it say?

In *A Theory of Human Motivation*, psychologist Abraham Maslow placed "the need for self-actualization" at the top of the list of human motivations—above survival, safety, love, and esteem.[4] Specifically,

> Even if all these needs are satisfied, we may still often (if not always) expect that a new discontent and restlessness will soon develop, unless the individual is doing what he is fitted for. A musician must make music, an artist must paint, a poet must write, if he is to be ultimately happy. What a man can be, he must be. This need we may call self-actualization.
>
> This term, first coined by Kurt Goldstein, is being used in this paper in a much more specific and limited fashion. It refers to the desire for self-fulfillment, namely, to the tendency for him to become actualized in what he is potentially. This tendency might be phrased as the desire to become more and more what one is, to become everything that one is capable of becoming.[5]

Let's forget for now that Maslow wrote this in 1943, that he later revised it, and that others take issue with it. Let's just recognize that Maslow helps us understand a few things about what human beings wish to be.

Being customers is part-time work for most of us (even for shopping addicts). Yet, we bring more to market than fits into the scope of any seller's current systems, which accept only a small range of signals from customers. How much more can customers bring, and vendors embrace, if the range of signals and actions on the customer side are freed up? We don't yet know, but we're starting to find out.

In *Here Comes Everybody: The Power of Organizing Without Organizations*, author Clay Shirky examines the effects of social networking tools, a disruptive fact of marketplace life for which the business world reached maximum thrall in 2011. (And with good reason: Facebook alone boasted 750 million users.) "None of the absolute advantages of institutions like businesses or schools or governments have disappeared. Instead...most of the relative advantages of those institutions have disappeared—relative, that is to the direct effort of the people they represent."[6]

While Clay's focus is on the social, the personal remains more than implicit. Each of us has far more agency in the networked market than we could possibly enjoy in the industrialized marketplace. Since the two are becoming one, our agency will become valuable to industry.

SO, THEN

When you limit what customers can bring to markets, you limit what can happen in those markets.

In the rest of Part II (chapters 12 to 15), we look at ways those limits will end and opportunities for personal agency will open up.

12

Free and Open

We hackers were actively aiming to create new kinds of conversations outside of traditional institutions … This wasn't an accidental byproduct of doing neat techie stuff; it was an explicit goal for many of us as far back as the 1970s. We intended this revolution.

—Eric S. Raymond[1]

THE ARGUMENT

Free markets on the Internet depend on FOSS (free and open source software) code and development methods. Therefore it pays to understand both.

No question matters more to reporters than "What's the story here?" If the reporter doesn't ask that question him- or herself, some managing editor will.

Yet the story format is incapable of containing the full truth behind whatever subject the reporter might cover. That's because stories, by design, require conflict or struggle. Whether the topic is politics, the weather, fashion, or sports, you need some kind of trouble or the reader moves on. The cheapest metaphors for trouble—the ones with the biggest boxes of words to work with—are war and sports. Thus, when writing about technology, the easiest stories to write are product versus product, company versus company, CEO versus CEO. But not everything that matters can be found on battlefields and arenas, imagined or real. Such is the case with FOSS.

While a zillion "Windows versus Linux" and "Bill versus Linus" stories ran in the 1990s and the 2000s, there never was much of a fight, because Bill Gates, Linus Torvalds, and their respective projects were driven by different motivations, and they labored in different ways in different organizations toward goals that were only superficially similar and competitive. Yes, Windows and Linux were both operating systems and, in some cases, competed. But Windows had to make money for Microsoft, while Linux just had to make things work. That deeper difference is far more important than the superficial similarities between the two operating systems and the markets they serve.

Here's another way to look at it: Microsoft had a story, while Linux didn't. While Microsoft needed to succeed in the commercial marketplace, Linux simply needed to succeed as a useful blob of code.

The dull story-free fact of Linux's life is that its only job is being the best possible operating system for the widest variety of applications. All other FOSS projects also have the same kind of mundane and straightforward purposes. Thus, they succeed simply by working and being used. Asking Linux, Perl, or Python for their business model is like asking the same of granite or sunlight.

It might have made great copy if Torvalds, the creator of Linux, were a Filippo Brunelleschi or a Christopher Wren, and if Linux's programmers were building a great cathedral. But Linus came up with Linux "just for fun" (also the title of his book about it[2]), and that's what keeps him going as Linux's alpha maintainer. Rather than sculpting fine works of art, Linux programmers "submit patches." When asked specific questions about what Linux actually does in the world, Linus answers, "That's user space. I only do kernel space."[3] That's not the kind of thing Brunelleschi or Wren would have said.

Yet, the results of work by Linux programmers are beyond profound. Today, most of the sites and services we enjoy on the Net and the Web (including nearly all of Google, Yahoo, Amazon, Facebook, Twitter, and Wikipedia) are built on top of Linux or its close relatives, plus Apache, another FOSS code base, which serves about 60 percent of all the Web's pages.[4] Both Linux and Apache have the charisma of pavement. And they're just two among millions of other dull but essential FOSS code bases.

The total number of FOSS projects may never be known. At the current growth rate, GitHub will probably soon pass 2.5 million code repositories for over a million programmers, if it hasn't already by the time you read this. SourceForge will pass 300,000, and who knows how many more will be using Google Code (it doesn't post numbers). All those code bases were created by and for intelligent minds at the Internet's ends. Nearly all of them began with one individual's work. And all of them grow by accretion of unique contributions by other individuals, all contributed by way of the Net.

Active and useful FOSS code is social as well as personal, in the sense that the writers of free and open code need to cooperate with each other. Yochai Benkler explains this in both "Coase's Penguin, or Linux and the Nature of the Firm" and *The Wealth of Networks*. In "Coase's Penguin," he writes,

> The central organizing principle is that the software remains free of most constraints on copying and use common to proprietary materials. No one "owns" the software in the traditional sense of being able to command how it is used or developed, or to control its disposition ...
>
> I suggest that we are seeing ... the broad and deep emergence of a new, third mode of production in the digitally networked environment. I call this mode "commons-based peer-production," to distinguish it from the property- and contract-based models of firms and markets. Its central characteristic is that groups of individuals successfully collaborate on large-scale projects following a diverse cluster of motivational drives and social signals, rather than either market prices or managerial commands.[5]

Thus, while commons-based peer production may be better for producing code than "property- and contract-based models," smart firms are also advantaged by adapting to the open source code production model, rather than by fighting it.

IBM offers a good example of adaptation. In the late 1990s, while other companies fought the adoption of Linux by their customers and their own engineers and IT departments, IBM took to heart the lessons of token ring's loss to Ethernet. Upon discovering the extent of Linux development going on inside the company, IBM decided not only to adopt Linux, but to brag about investing a billion dollars in it.[6] All that noise made IBM's effort seem much easier than it really was. Dan Frye, vice president for open systems development at the IBM Systems and Technology Group, told me it took a number of years before IBM management learned that it couldn't tell its Linux developers what to do—but that instead the reverse was true: Linux developers were the ones taking the lead. Here is how Andrew

Morton, one of the top maintainers of the Linux kernel, explained the relationship between wise companies and open source developers:

> Look for example at the IBM engineers that do work on the kernel. They understand (how it works) now. They are no longer IBM engineers that work on the kernel. They're kernel developers that work for IBM. My theory here is that if IBM management came up to one of the kernel developers and said "Look, we need to do that," the IBM engineer would not say, "Oh, the kernel team won't accept that." He'd say, "WE won't accept that." Because now they get it. Now they understand the overarching concern we have for the coherency and longevity of the code base.
>
> Given that now these companies have been at it sufficiently long, they understand what our concerns are about the kernel code base.[7]

Andrew now works for Google.[8]

Best Intentions

Commons-based peer production has also proven useful for spreading ideas, including open source itself. Search Google for "open source" (with the quotes), and you'll get results in many dozens of millions. Yet, the term has been in wide use only since February 8, 1998. That's when Eric S. Raymond (known for maintaining the Jargon File and editing *The New Hacker's Dictionary*, among other things) issued a bulletin to the programming community titled, "'Goodbye, 'free software'; hello, 'open source.'"[9] It set out, with a fine degree of calculation, to establish open source as a common and well-understood concept.[10]

The strategy worked just about perfectly, thanks in large measure to the charismatic personality and polemical genius of Eric, whom Christopher Locke calls "a rhetorician of the first water."[11] What rocks here—and is easy to forget—is that "open source" was *intentional*. As Eric explained in *The Cluetrain Manifesto* (and as I quoted at the start of this chapter), "We intended this revolution."

Eric's efforts also took advantage of a movement that was already well underway. That movement started in 1983, when Richard Stallman announced the GNU Project. The GNU Manifesto, the Free Software Definition, the Free Software Foundation, and the GNU General Public License (GPL) followed. Said the GNU Manifesto, "'Free software' is a matter of liberty, not price. To understand the concept, you should think of 'free' as in 'free speech,' not as in 'free beer.' Free software is a matter of the users' freedom to run, copy, distribute, study, change and improve the software."[12] So, while Eric and friends correctly recognized problems with "free software" as a label, the founding importance of freedom was not diminished by the Open Source Initiative's rebranding effort.

SO, THEN

Freedom, liberty, and openness and independence persist as values—not only in FOSS code, but also in how they support construction of organizations, businesses, and goods in the connected world.

What you and I bring to the marketplace also needs to embody those same values. We need to contribute our own patches to the Live Web we share. Few of us can do that today, and this too exposes an opportunity. We can see that opportunity open up if we understand the raw materials we'll be working with. In a word, those are bits.

13

Bits Mean Business

Bits behave strangely. They travel almost simultaneously, and they take almost no space to store. We have to use physical metaphors to make them understandable …

The Internet was designed just to handle just bits, not emails or attachments, which are inventions of software engineers. We couldn't live without those more intuitive concepts, but they are artifices. Underneath, it's all just bits.

—Hal Abelson, Ken Ledeen, and Harry Lewis[1]

THE ARGUMENT

Abundant data is neither a problem nor a solution. It's an opportunity. But we do have problems to solve along the way.

The Internet makes data productive, abundant, and—in many ways— priceless. Yet data has no natural scarcity and therefore costs as little as sunlight and gravity. Data also yearns toward abundance by proliferating in ways that gravity and sunlight cannot. "The Internet is a copy machine," Kevin Kelly says.[2] This amplifies a problem that Thomas Jefferson saw two hundred years ago when he argued against regarding ideas as property. In a letter to Isaac MacPherson in 1813, Jefferson wrote,

> He who receives an idea from me, receives instruction himself without lessening mine; as he who lights his taper at mine, receives light without darkening me.

That ideas should freely spread from one to another over the globe, for the moral and mutual instruction of man, and improvement of his condition, seems to have been peculiarly and benevolently designed by nature, when she made them, like fire, expansible over all space, without lessening their density in any point, and like the air in which we breathe, move, and have our physical being, incapable of confinement or exclusive appropriation. Inventions then cannot, in nature, be a subject of property.

Data has the same combustive and light-giving power as ideas. In *Code and Other Laws of Cyberspace*, Harvard Law School professor Lawrence Lessig summarizes a seminal effect of this:

Born in a research project in the Defense Department, cyberspace too arose from the unplanned displacement of a certain architecture of control. The tolled, single-purpose network of telephones was displaced by the untolled and multipurpose network of packet-switched data. And thus the old one-to-many architectures of publishing (television, radio, newspapers, books) were complemented by a world in which anyone could become a publisher. People could communicate and associate in ways that they had never done before. The space seemed to promise a kind of society that real space would never allow—freedom without anarchy, control without government, consensus without power. In the words of a manifesto that defined this ideal: "We reject: kings, presidents and voting. We believe in: rough consensus and running code."[3]

The words Lessig quotes were spoken in 1992 by David Clark, one of the three authors of "End to End Arguments in System Design," and a leading figure in the Internet Engineering Task Force (IETF), which has produced many of the Internet's defining protocols.[4]

Some other Internet protocols, however—notably those the phone and cable companies use for data transmission—are not defined by the IETF. Nor do they express the ethos of "rough consensus and running code." If your Net connection is ADSL (usually abbreviated as just DSL) or over a fiber-optic connection from a phone company, it's using protocols defined by the International Telecommunications Union, or ITU, which began as the International Telegraph Union in 1865.[5] If your connection to the Net is over a cable TV system, the standards employed are DOCSIS, which is an ITU standard maintained by CableLabs, a cable TV industry association.[6]

For the last hundred years or more, the ITU has been mostly a phone company institution, and it remains so. Thus, its interest in supporting new economies is compromised by its interest in sustaining old ones—and also by the interests of governments that are involved in the process. Government interests include imposition of tariffs and taxes, protection of domestic industries, politically or security-motivated censorship, and worse. In other words, the ITU cares less about the Net's economic leverage beyond what it does for what in the trade are called "operators": phone and cable companies. In a speech at the Techonomy conference in August 2010, Reinhard Scholl of the ITU spoke glowingly about the networked future, but did not once utter the word *Internet*.[7] Instead, he talked up *broadband*, an old telco term that puts a gloss over the operators' plans for shaping the Internet to fit their business models and growth plans.

Since then the rhetorical divide between net-head and bell-head has become wider, and the distinction between the Internet and broadband has become sharper—at least to the degree that the two words are used by each group. For example, in December 2011, Susan Crawford, a law professor and leading net-head, wrote an opinion piece for the *New York Times* titled "The New Digital Divide." A sample:

> While we still talk about "the" Internet, we increasingly have two separate access marketplaces: high-speed wired and second-class wireless. High-speed access is a superhighway for those who can afford it, while racial minorities and poorer and rural Americans must make do with a bike path.

Note that she says "high-speed access" rather than "broadband."[8]

She also uses the word "Internet" twenty-six times in the piece. On the bell-head side, Verizon CEO Ivan G. Seidenberg wrote back a letter to the editor that used the word "broadband" six times and "Internet" just once, because he couldn't avoid it if he wanted to say (as he did) "The 2011 World Economic Forum global survey ranks the United States first in Internet competition."[9]

The prior month, at another Techonomy conference, ITU Secretary General Hamadoun Touré talked up broadband again. According to a *Forbes'* report, Hamadoun "explained why his agency's Broadband Commission two weeks ago declared broadband communications a basic universal human right—on the list now with the right to food, health, and housing." The report continues,

> Universal broadband access is a crucial step to achieving the
> Millennium Development Goals to eradicate global poverty by 2015 ...
>
> The key to achieving global broadband access, he said, is public-
> private partnership. Having joined the ITU from a career in the
> satellite communications industry, Touré calls himself "a private
> sector guy," and has succeeded in securing the involvement of more
> than 700 companies in the ITU initiative to extend broadband
> access.[10]

No doubt this is a worthy effort in many ways; but it is also a paint
job on the body-snatch "broadband" is doing on "Internet." It's one more
way the ITU and its constituents try to stuff the Internet genie back in the
pre-1984 bottle.[11]

In some ways we already live inside that bottle. Take, for example, the
mobile phone data services that are branded 3G or 4G. Those are short
nicknames for the ITU's standards for third- and fourth-generation mobile
data communications.[12] The biggest problem for both (as it was for 1G
and 2G) is that they stop at national boundaries that the Internet was built
to ignore.

This is why, even though you might be able to use your 3G devices in
another country, you also risk bills of many hundreds or thousands of dollars
(or pounds, or euros) for "roaming"—even if you're connecting through the
same mobile phone company (say, Orange, Vodafone, or T-Mobile). To the
ITU and the operators, roaming charges are a feature, not a bug. National
boundaries not only bring bonus payments to phone companies, but tariff
payments to governments. They also flourish in a fog of complicated telco
company offerings and policies that Scott Adams, creator of the *Dilbert*
comic strip, calls a "confusopoly":

> A confusopoly is any group of companies in a particular industry
> that intentionally confuses customers about their pricing plans
> and products. Confusopolies do this so customers don't know
> which one of them is offering the best value. That way every
> company gets a fair share of the confused customers and the
> industry doesn't need to compete on price. The classic examples
> of confusopolies are phone companies, insurance companies, and
> banks.[13]

Ryan Singel of *Wired* summarizes this problem in "Wireless Oligopoly Is
Smother of Invention":

Imagine if the wireless carriers controlled your wired broadband connection or your television set. You'd have to buy your television from your cable company, with a two-year contract, and when that ended, you'd have to ask them to unlock it so you could take it to another provider.

If the wireless company ran your ISP, you'd have to use a computer they approved, and if you wanted to use a different one, you'd pay more. Want Wi-Fi in your house? That'll be an extra $30 a month and $150 to buy an approved but functionally limited Wi-Fi device.[14]

So, on the net-head side, we have open protocols and open software creating open infrastructure that supports boundless opportunities for every economic, social, governmental, or you-name-it entity. On the bell-head side, we have phone companies selling you packaged and metered "data services" that work almost exclusively to the economic benefit of those companies and their partners in government and the "content" business. Which side will win?

In the long run, both, but only when the carriers and their technologies subordinate their legacy businesses to the Internet and its imperatives, which support limitless business opportunities for which the carriers will enjoy first-mover, real estate, and geographical proximity advantages. Maybe Verizon and the ITU will help with that. But not whole-heartedly, to say the least.

As we said in chapter 9, this is a fight between *any* and *only*. And there are far more opportunities on the *any* side.

Prethinking the Impossible

One of the first to see these opportunities was Reese Jones. In the late 1980s, Jones was a graduate student doing brain research at UC Berkeley, and a cofounder of the local Macintosh users group. It was in that second capacity that Jones saw an opportunity: running a computer network over ordinary phone wires. At the time, Apple used a robust protocol it named AppleTalk, which would allow connecting any number of computers together using Apple's proprietary wiring. Jones saw that Apple's wiring was basically nothing more than what's called "twisted pair." More importantly, Jones saw abundant twisted pairs in existing phone wiring in most homes and businesses. That's because most phones and phone systems used only two wires rather than four. The "dry pair" could therefore be used to connect computers. All they needed was a little dongle to bridge between the connector in the back of a computer and a standard RJ-11 phone plug. Jones invented that dongle, called it a PhoneNet connector, and started a company called Farallon Computing to sell it.

PhoneNet connectors allowed users to string together reliable do-it-yourself networks of nearly any size. As a plug-and-play system, PhoneNet relieved customers of the need to buy expensive proprietary Apple wiring. PhoneNet also helped Apple to succeed in spite of itself. (This was during the Steve Jobs interregnum, when Apple was clueless compared to the company Jobs rebuilt after returning in 1998.) PhoneNet also brought telephony and computing together in a casual way for the first time. This was intentional. Jones actually liked telephony, which he saw as a business that had worked out many problems already, chief among which was support for the most basic of human needs: to talk with one another.

As it happened, the late 1980s was filled with computer industry buzz around "groupware" and "workgroup computing"—much as there is today around "the cloud" and "social computing." Jones didn't buy it. "People don't compute in groups for the same reason they don't talk at once in groups," he said. "What they do is converse. Two at a time. See, at any one time the human brain can only pay full attention to what one other person says. Even when one person speaks to a large group, the relationship is still one-to-one, speaker to listener. Conversation is the bottom line. If computing isn't about conversation, it won't go anywhere."[15]

So, even though Farallon was a PC business, Jones said his long-term ambition was to make "software for telephones." He saw telephones as more proven and personal than PCs, and ideal platforms for a boundless variety of applications, all of which would thrive on smart devices optimized for conversations between individuals but hardly limited to that alone.

It took another twenty years, but we have those now with smartphones. Nokia delivered the first, around the turn of the millennium, but Nokia was crippled by its partnerships with mobile phone companies. I remember comparing my Nokia E62 smartphone with a friend's E61 over beers in Brussels in the spring of 2007. Her E61 had a wi-fi connection. My E62 did not. When I asked the folks who loaned me the phone (one of the benefits of being a journalist for a tech magazine is getting these kinds of things) why the E62 lacked E61 features, they explained that the American carriers (mine was AT&T) didn't want those features.

I wasn't surprised. A few years earlier, I had attended a meeting hosted by Nokia. After listening to innovators from a dozen companies—ranging from start-ups to giants—explain the amazing new things they were doing, and how these things might work on phones and other handhelds, one of Nokia's top engineers explained that the phone industry differed from the computer industry in this fundamental way: OEMs (the name for gear makers like Nokia) knew their road maps, going years out into the future, and so did the operators, who were "partners" in those plans. Listening to this guy talk, I felt like the year was 1450 and I was sitting in on a briefing for plans cooked up between the Medici bank and the Vatican.

He then explained that he already knew what would be going into Nokia's phones, feature by feature, years in advance. Also, that he could hardly imagine adding the kinds of things we were talking about. The clear message: nobody was going to tell Nokia what to do. Except, of course, the operators. That was why, if AT&T didn't want wi-fi on a Nokia E62, it wasn't going to be there.

World Wide Marketplace

As marketplaces go, the Internet is the biggest one of all. It favors nobody and supports everybody, everywhere it works in the world. But the opportunities the Net provides cannot be seen in full if we look at it only through lenses provided by phone companies and governments. Bob Frankston, who co-invented spreadsheet software with Dan Bricklin, does his best to reveal this opportunity in an essay titled "FSM—The First Square Mile, Our Neighborhood":

> Words have a way of reflecting and reinforcing our mental models. We think of telecommunications in terms of content being delivered (as with TV) so we often hear about the "last mile" or even the "first mile." We should think about connectivity within our neighborhoods—the first square mile to contrast with the first mile traveled ...
>
> The problem with today's telecommunications industry is that is a service industry in which the providers' incentive is to increase their profit by selling us more services. "Internet" ... is a recent addition to the product mix. The more Internet access they provide the less valuable the services are because we can create our own solutions. The other problem with the Internet is that bits are simply

bits and they can take any path. I compare trying to make money selling bits with trying to operate a canal across an ocean. In other words the carriers must limit us to using narrow paths across the sea of bits. This is why we are laying fibers along all our highways but only a tiny fraction of fiber is actually lit up and even then only a small portion of the potential capacity is available.

We're trapped in the Regulatorium—that is, the FCC's regulatory system that was established during the great depression in 1934 when the marketplace was not to be trusted. Changing legislation requires a political consensus but you can't get that consensus until you have an agreed-upon alternative. This is difficult when we lack examples and when the very premises that define the Regulatorium are threatened by the idea that networking is something we do ourselves. It's like asking the railroad regulators to tolerate unregulated car driving.[16]

Think of cars as VRM tools, which they are. They provide independence for customers and ways of engaging with vendors. To engage with customers with cars, businesses provide parking lots and drive-through lanes. Often government helps, with road improvements, parking spaces on streets, and public parking lots.

The popularity of cars is what caused the paving of roads, the building of highways, the spread of suburbs, and the growth of businesses at intersections and highway exits everywhere. In the evolution of Internet infrastructure, we are today about where roads and parking lots were in 1900, when railroads still ruled the commercial transportation world—but it was beginning to become clear that cars were going to become the first option for people who wanted to shop in places farther than walking distance away.

On the Internet's sea of bits, laptops and smartphones give us ways to see, hear, and be present in any number of other places, anywhere in the world, at the same time. In this sense their apparent functions are closer to teleportation than to transport. But transport of bits is involved, and the car metaphor does apply—especially around implications.

Look at what the car does for both customers and businesses, and you'll see hints toward how much more the Internet will do for both.

To see the difference between the Net's possibilities and the more limited ones of broadband, consider two contexts: "the cloud" and the Live Web.

With the cloud your data can be anywhere. And since your data is bound to get big, you'll need maximized capacities for transporting that data back and forth between locations. Today's broadband connections are still highly asymmetrical: fast down, slow up. The main reason for this in the first place was television, which is mostly downstream. But the percentage of data movement devoted to what used to be television is going to go down over time, even if it continues upward in the short run. The growth in Net use and the nature of the cloud both guarantee that.

With the Live Web, you need to be moving data back and forth constantly between your devices and both APIs and cloud services. This too requires maximized data traffic capacities, and minimized interference by carrier restrictions or government blockages.

How much business opportunity will we find on the Net's world wide dance floor? The best answer might be this question, asked in 1900: How much business would the car bring in the twentieth century?

SO, THEN

The Internet is better for business than broadband, because the Internet is a public marketplace while broadband is a private business providing controlled access to that marketplace. The difference will become clearer as customers become more independent, and the full implications of the cloud and the Live Web become manifest.

14

Vertical and Horizontal

So then Apple is the ultimate unGoogle. Right? Not so fast.

—Jeff Jarvis[1]

THE ARGUMENT

Markets grow in at least two dimensions. It doesn't make sense to argue that one axis is better than another when both together are doing the job.

The smartphone business was invented by Nokia and RIM around the turn of the millennium and then royally disrupted by Apple and Google a few years later. Today, Apple and Google define the smartphone business, together, though not always in direct competition. It is important to understand how this works, because the two companies' directions are orthogonal: ninety degrees off from each other. And because they do that, the market for both—and for everybody else as well—is huge.

Apple's punch to the smartphone market was vertical. It came up from below like a volcano and went straight toward the sky. With the iPhone, Apple showed how much invention and innovation the old original equipment manufacturer (OEM)–operator marriage had locked out of the smartphone marketplace, completely redefining the smartphone as a pocket computer that also worked as a phone.[2] iPhones were beautiful, easy to use, and open to a zillion applications that were easy for programmers to write and for users to install.

The Google punch was horizontal. It came from the side, spreading its open Android platform toward the far horizons. As a platform, Android supported everything Apple's iOS did—and more, because it was open to anybody, making it more like geology than a foundation. The old cartels could still build vertical silos on Android, but anybody could build just about anything, anywhere.[3]

So, while Apple shows how high one can pile up features and services inside one big beautiful high-rise of a silo, Google provides a way not only to match or beat Apple's portfolio, but to show how broad and rich the open marketplace can be.

We need innovation in both directions, but we can't see how complementary these vectors are if we cast the companies innovating in both directions as competitors for just one space. So, while it's true that Apple phones compete with Android-based phones straight up, it's also true that Apple makes phones and Google doesn't.[4] And, while it's true that iOS and Android compete for developers, iOS only runs on Apple devices; there is no limit to the number and variety of devices that run on Android. In the larger picture here, Apple and Google are stretching the market in orthogonal directions. The result is a bigger marketplace for both and for everybody else who depends on smartphones.

Chief among those are users. There are now many more users of smartphones than of laptops, just as there are many more users of pockets than of cars. What smartphones do for users—specifically, for *customers*—is provide a box of tools customers can use to engage vendors in the marketplace. Liberated customers will rely on smartphones more than on any other single device. In other words, no device will be more essential to the development and growth of the Intention Economy than smartphones.

To understand what will make the Intention Economy spring forth from customers' purses and pockets, let's look at the orthogonal directions in which Apple and Google are taking us.

Steve Being Steve

To understand the iPhone, one must understand Apple, and to understand Apple, one must understand Steve Jobs. This is hard, because Apple is like Steve and Steve was unlike anybody. As a result, both are examples only of themselves: unique to a near-absolute degree. This is why it makes little or no sense to "be like Apple." It can't be done, except in some of the exemplary ways that Apple does what every other company ought to do, but too often neglects—such as customer service. But no company can do the one thing Apple does best, which is transform industries by opening up whole new markets, over and over again. That was what Steve did, and it's not something any other company has ever done so well, and for so long—or is ever likely to do again.

Case in point: not long after Steve returned to Apple, one of the first things he did was kill off Apple's clones. Naturally, a great cry of outrage went up. One response to the outrage was an e-mail I wrote to Dave Winer, which he published, on September 4, 1997:

> So Steve Jobs just shot the cloners in the head, indirectly doing the same to the growing percentage of Mac users who preferred cloned Mac systems to Apple's own. So his message to everybody was no different than it was at Day One: all I want from the rest of you is your money and your appreciation for my Art.
>
> It was a nasty move, but bless his ass: Steve's art has always been first class, and priced accordingly. There was nothing ordinary about it. The Mac "ecosystem" Steve talks about is one that rises from that Art, not from market demand or other more obvious forces. And that art has no more to do with developers, customers and users than Van Gogh's has to do with Sotheby's, Christie's and art collectors …
>
> The simple fact is that Apple always was Steve's company, even when he wasn't there. The force that allowed Apple to survive more than a decade of bad leadership, cluelessness and constant mistakes was the legacy of Steve's original Art. That legacy was not just an OS that was 10 years ahead of the rest of the world, but a Cause that induced a righteousness of purpose centered around a will to innovate—to perpetuate the original artistic achievements …
>
> Now Steve is back, and gradually renovating his old company. He'll do it his way, and it will once again express his Art.
>
> These things I can guarantee about whatever Apple makes from this point forward:
>
> 1. It will be original.
>
> 2. It will be innovative.
>
> 3. It will be exclusive.
>
> 4. It will be expensive.
>
> 5. Its aesthetics will be impeccable.

> The influence of developers, even influential developers like you, will be minimal. The influence of customers and users will be held in even higher contempt.
>
> The influence of fellow business artisans such as Larry Ellison (and even Larry's nemesis, Bill Gates) will be significant, though secondary at best to Steve's own muse.[5]

I share this because I think we need at least *some* of what Steve did best, and what nearly all CEOs simply can't do at all: create markets while proving out ideas in a contained vertical space that the founding vendor alone controls. While Apple's controlling nature rubs my FOSS fur the wrong way, I cut Steve and his company some slack, because constructive creation is a good thing, and great artists can't help wanting to control things.

Back in the mid 2000s, I was catching up with Tony Fadell on the phone. Tony at the time was vice president of engineering at Apple and involved in many successes there, starting with the iPod. (He resigned in 2008, but stayed on as a special adviser until 2010.) I've known Tony since the mid-nineties and found him exceptionally good at providing helpful intelligence about Apple while revealing absolutely nothing about the company's secrets. On this call, he said, "If you want to understand Steve, don't look at Apple, look at Pixar." His points, from bulleted notes I took at the time:

- As few products as possible.

- Every product is original (nothing derivative).

- Every product is delightful, beautiful, successful, and profitable.

- Every product breaks new ground and moves both technology and art forward.

At that time, Apple Stores were still new, and few. Tony pointed out that there was nothing in the history of retailing that would encourage anybody to try starting another computer store. The smoking ruins of similar efforts by ComputerLand, Radio Shack, CompUSA, Circuit City, Gateway, and Sony all gave unanimously dire warnings. Meanwhile Dell and many other companies were kicking butt selling directly to individual customers or to the enterprise market. Yet Steve wanted to build out this new retail channel and knew it would succeed. And it did.

Likewise with the iPhone.

This is where another of Steve's motivations comes in. He liked to fix product categories that are stuck or broken. That's what the Macintosh did for personal computing in 1984, with its graphical user interface and simple industrial design. It's what the iPod did for digital audio players in 2001.

Smartphones in the mid-2000s were so stuck in unholy alliances between operators and OEMs that little that was promising or cool had happened there—or would ever happen, if progress were left up to just those two parties. Apple broke that logjam by making its own phone: one that embodied all the numbered and bulleted points listed in my notes. Apple also eliminated billing complexity for mobile data, with the original, unlimited $25 per month data plan with AT&T.[6] (Similar simplicities for phone call billing were beyond Apple's reach.) This was huge, and would never have happened without inspired work on Apple's part.

Then, in the summer of 2007, Apple opened the iTunes app store and introduced the iPhone 3G. The market for apps on smartphones exploded. This changed the handheld data device market forever, just as the Macintosh changed the PC market forever in 1984. The difference this time was that the iPhone became wildly popular, while the original Mac served mostly as a prototype.

But, even though the smartphone and app booms were huge, their dimensions were those of Apple's vertical monopoly. The whole thing was contained within Apple's silo. In order to grow, the smartphone and app markets needed to spread horizontally. That's where Google and Android came in.

Google's World

If Apple's philosophy is Think Different, Google's orthogonal corollary would be Think Same—by creating a big, wide open, and new market space, where lots of similar things could grow, outside of anybody's silo.

That probably flatters Google a bit too much, because it's not all-open and has its silos, too. (Plus other problems, some of which we've visited already and others of which we'll tackle later.)

See, Google is a net-head company. In a deep and abiding way, it *gets* the Net and what the Net does for the connected world. Thus, Jeff Jarvis's book, *What Would Google Do?*, might as well have been titled, *What Would the Net Do?* In Jeff's words, the Net "commodifies everything."[7] Google and the Net do this to obtain *because effects*. Rather than make money *with* Android, Google wants to make money *because of* it. And it doesn't mind lots of other companies making money because of it, too. In fact, that's exactly what Google wants.

So, like Apple, Google wants to fix slow, damaged, or broken markets. But unlike Apple, Google wants to fix those markets by making them freer and more open for everybody—and therefore much larger as well. That is, to grow markets horizontally.

Google also likes to explore and demonstrate what can be done with a new idea, new code, new hardware technologies, new apps, new forms of infrastructure, and new ways of doing business. Google is also committed to open source and understands in its bones how open source works, which is horizontally rather than vertically. Those bones, by the way, are comprised of engineers: thousands of them, including the company's two founders.

Open source building materials and designs are ideal for creating foundations of broad new markets. That was the idea behind Android, and that's why Android succeeded. Thanks to Android, customers have a choice of more than one true smartphone and countless new, smart, handheld devices. No one hardware OEM can control those markets anymore, and developers have a choice of platforms other than Apple's closed one.

True, there are problems with Android for developers, just as there are problems with Apple's iOS. The biggest one with Android is too many target devices and too many feature differences among them. Developers had the same problem with RIM's BlackBerry and Nokia's smartphones, which have used several different operating systems and had radically different versions for different operators. The difference with Android is that there are still hundreds of thousands of applications working on Android devices and more coming out all the time, in spite of the complicated terrain there.

Generativity

In *The Future of the Internet and How to Stop It*, Jonathan Zittrain borrows a word from biology to label the capacity of an enabling technology or standard to encourage boundless growth, in hardware, software, and usage. The word is *generativity*.

JZ (as he is known to friends) illustrates generativity with an hourglass.[8] At the waist of the hourglass is the generative technology. Below the waist is all the hardware it invites, enables, and runs on. Above the waist is all the software and uses the technology invites and supports. His point: generative standards (such as the Internet) and technologies (such as generic PCs and mobile devices) invite, run on, and support a boundless variety of

TABLE 14-1

Seven hourglasses of generativity

Software	Anything	Anything	Anything	Anything	Anything	Anything Apple approves and sells
Generative technology or standard	Internet (TCP/IP)	Linux	Android	Microsoft Windows	Apple OS X	Apple iOS
Hardware	Anything	Anything	Anything	Any Microsoft-licensed hardware	Apple hardware	Apple hardware

other standards, technologies, and uses, for both hardware and software. So, while platforms support only what runs on top of them, generative standards facilitate development below them as well as above.

Look at table 14-1 as seven hourglasses. Note that, for software, nearly anything runs on all seven standards (the Net) and technologies (popular computer and mobile operating systems). For hardware, the Net, Linux, and Android run on any hardware, while Windows runs only on licensed hardware (though there is a lot of that), while Apple's operating systems run only on Apple's hardware.

But there are advantages to vertical integration, and to control by one company. Apple's products are famously beautiful, easy to use, backed by good customer service, and so brilliantly marketed that they often establish and define whole product categories. This is not something any company can do.

In all these respects Apple makes what Regis McKenna, Geoffrey Moore, and other marketing gurus call a *whole product*. That is, one that provides everything both customers and third parties need.

With Android, Google does not make a whole product—and doesn't want to. Instead, it makes a purposely partial non-product that device makers, mobile service companies, and customers are free to complete in the form of their own products. In this way Google expands public markets horizontally—for everybody—at least as well as Apple expands private markets vertically. The difference is the one between a high-rise office building and the rest of the city. It is also the difference between the industrial and the information ages.

While Apple tries to build an all-encompassing company, Google equips everybody with a way to make an all-encompassing city that will be good for many companies.

At this early stage in the growth of smart mobile devices, progress in both directions has been dramatic. Apple's iPhone continues to lead both in innovation and in customer entrapment. Android leads in opening opportunities for everybody on the World Live Web. Thus, Android became the world's top-selling smartphone by the end of 2010 and will continue to lead until something even more live and open comes along.[9]

Closed Frontiers

Meanwhile, the problem today for both Apple and Android is that mobile operators still own the frontier, and they don't like the mobile equivalent of "white box" (generic, functionally identical) computers. Not if those devices are going to connect to the Net over cellular phone and data systems, both of which are controlled by mobile operators—and by national laws that go back to the dawn of telephony.

My first encounter with this problem came in the summer of 2010, when I took a new Google Nexus One smartphone (intentionally a generic, white-box Android device, made for Google by HTC) to France for a few weeks, where I incorrectly assumed it would enjoy some of Bob Frankston's ambient connectivity. After all, for years Europe has been way ahead of the United States in mobile telephony. I figured the same would be true of mobile data.

Not so. Outside the wi-fi zone in our rented apartment, the Nexus One failed completely as a data device, through no fault of its own. My chosen provider, Orange, sold me two data plans in a row that the phone burned through in a matter of minutes. The reason was that reasonable rates were available only with two-year contracts, and by French law those were available only to those holding French bank accounts. Unreasonable rates were what you got with prepaid plans. These rates were so high that not one of the four Orange stores I dealt with could tell me what they were. "Just don't use data," was the final advice of the last salesperson I bothered with the problem. So, after spending €75 and a week of troubleshooting failure, I gave up on data over mobile telephony outside the United States—at least until I could find a work-around.

"No problem can be solved from the same level of consciousness that created it," Einstein said.[10] This is why the carriers' plans to turn the Internet into a big phone system will fail. End-to-end is simply a better way to get ambient connectivity than by endlessly improving the old phone system. But it's impossible to see that future as long as we're stuck in the framework of telephony's past. That's what we have with 3G, 4G, and all the bells and whistles of "high speed" mobile data service from phone companies.

The Net Rules

Every technology, every domain of science, has what are called *boundary conditions* between levels of an operational hierarchy. Take, for example, a mechanical clock. You can understand the clock at a number of levels. At the bottom level, the clock depends on the laws of chemistry and physics. Without good materials, you can't make the clock. Above that, you have laws of mechanics. These depend on the laws of chemistry and physics but cannot be reduced to them. This is because chemistry and physics have a boundary above which they have nothing to say. Even if you know every-thing about chemistry and physics, you can't explain mechanics with them. Likewise, the laws of mechanics are harnessed by the purpose of the clock, but you can't use mechanics alone to explain the clock because the clock's purpose is above the upper boundary of mechanics. If you were to disassem-ble the clock and lay out all its gears and other parts, you wouldn't know what to make of them unless you understood that these make up a clock. In fact, the clock itself would make no sense unless you knew its purpose was to tell time. Thus, we have this hierarchy of domains, each of which has an upper and lower boundary.

In this sense, the Internet is about telling time, not about maintaining the mechanics for doing that. The mechanics of the Net are endlessly varied and substitutable. The Internet Protocol itself simply requires that a best effort be made to find a path from one end of the Net to the other. John Gill-more, civil libertarian and co-founder of the Electronic Frontier Foundation (EFF), famously said, "The Net interprets censorship as damage and routes around it."[11]

This is an intentional design feature of the Internet and not just an acci-dental property. And this feature comes, at least in part, from study of the phone system by the Internet's founding geeks. The phone system used what's called "circuit switching," which was ideal for billing everything that could possibly be billed. The Internet uses "packet switching," which very pointedly does *not* care about billing. In fact, it was invented to relieve the world of a need for billing on networks.

That's why the Internet is good for business, but not *its own* business. Business protocols—ceremonies of relationship, conversation, and transaction—are supported almost perfectly by the technical protocols of packet switching and best-effort data transport. And the cost of moving bits is not high, once the capacity is installed. Since fiber-optic cabling is capable of carrying enormous sums of data traffic, while disturbing the physical environment remarkably little (especially when compared to the easement and build-out requirements of electricity, gas, water, roads, waste treatment, and other public utilities), business should have a great deal of interest in seeing Internet infrastructure completed everywhere. But it can't feel or express that interest if it can't understand what the Internet is, or at least settle on one metaphor that makes clear how something so huge and stupid as the core of the Earth can be good for business.

A Frame for Business

We frame the Internet in many ways, but the most common three are *transport*, *place*, and *publishing*.

When we call the Internet a *medium* through which *content* can be *uploaded*, *downloaded*, and *delivered* to *consumers* through *pipes*, we're thinking and talking inside the *transport* frame. We find it in the tech language as well. The Net's core protocol pair, TCP/IP, stands for Transmission Control Protocol and Internetworking Protocol (together generalized as the Internet Protocol), and concerns itself with *packets* in the *transport layer*. The File Transport Protocol (FTP) and all the mail protocols also use transport language and framing.

When we speak of *sites* with *domains* and *locations* that we *architect*, *design*, *build*, and *construct* for *visitors* and *traffic*, we employ the language and framing of real estate, or *place*. We do the same when we speak of going *on* the Net, and when we call it a *world*, a *sphere*, a *space*, and an *environment* and *ecology*.

When we say we *author*, *edit*, *put up*, *post*, and *syndicate* things called *pages*, we employ the language and framing of *publishing*. When Dave Winer improved its technology and practices with RSS, the Web became even more of a publishing platform.[12]

We can't help using all three frames, but the one that works best for *all* business (and not just those in transport, such as phone and cable companies) is *place*. That's because it's beginning to dawn on business that the worldwide marketplace we call the Internet is indeed a place, and that we're leaving a lot of money on the table if both demand and supply are not sitting there, facing each other and dealing as equals. Personally. Anywhere. Even if the two are not in the same country or continent.

Wide Wins

Cities also grow in vertical and horizontal dimensions. Prosperous companies (and ones that just like to show off) build skyscrapers, while less vertical companies build their businesses on streets and crossroads where customers live and travel. For most of the last millennium, the biggest buildings at the centers of cities were churches or seats of government. Then, in the industrial age, the biggest buildings were retailing establishments and corporate headquarters, such as the Woolworth and Chrysler buildings in New York, and the Home Insurance Building in Chicago.

Today, Chrysler no longer owns or runs the building that bears its name. The Hancock name still resides on a pair of skyscrapers in Chicago and Boston, but the company that built them has since been absorbed into the Canadian company Manulife Financial, which may be called something else by the time you read this. The Sears Tower in Chicago now called Willis is also sure to be renamed again and again before it comes down.

Most major league sports fields and stadiums are now named after companies that pay for the privilege. Why build something when you can just buy "naming rights"? (Perhaps not coincidentally, the failure rate for buyers of naming rights for ball fields is rather high. Air Canada, CMGI, Enron, 3Com, PSINet, Adelphia, and Trans World have all been hit with what has come to be called the "stadium curse."[13])

No doubt the most beautiful building in California will be the new one Apple builds, according to a design led by Steve Jobs and approved by the Cupertino City Council after a pitch by the Man Himself in his last public appearance as CEO and less than two months before he died. Even more certainly, Apple will follow Steve to the grave. Unless it adapts.

This is an open question. What if companies open up, turn their silos inside out (see chapter 22), interact productively with everybody and everything, and become more citylike in the way they work in the world? Is that adaptive enough for them to survive?

Whether or not the answers are yes, the symbiosis between vertical and horizontal economic, social, and political entities will be better understood, especially after the amount of signaling explodes and far more—and better—research can be done.

SO, THEN

Nothing in the old phone and cable company captive-market models begins to contemplate the Net as a generative place. But the rest of us can, and we have a good working model for it.

15

The Comity of the Commons

The Web changes everything (Everything = Everything).
Embrace it. Totally. Or else.

—Tom Peters[1]

THE ARGUMENT

The Internet is a commons. This is good for business.

If the Internet is a place, what kind of place is it? Remember: (1) all metaphors are wrong, and (2) we have to use them, because we understand everything metaphorically. So let's be clear with ourselves that the Internet is not *really* a place. (Nor is it a printing press, plumbing, a theater, a shipping system, or any other frame we use to think and talk about the Net.) But if we choose to prefer *place* to other metaphors, what kind of real-world *place* would we prefer?

How about a market?

Well, most of what we call markets aren't places either. We use the term *market* when we mean categories ("the home improvement market"), demographics ("the upscale market"), regions ("the New York market"), appetites ("the market for candy"), or a virtual place for selling ("these jewels are on the market") or for buying ("we're in the market for a car"). We also say "the market" or "the marketplace" when we mean the whole of business—especially when posed apart from government. The phrase "neither the state nor the market" appears in hundreds of books.[2]

In respect to the Internet as a place, the term *commons* has come into popular use. Search for *commons* on Google, and the top results will be for Creative Commons, Wikipedia articles, and Wikimedia Commons, a repository for media files that are either in the public domain or available with usage-friendly Creative Commons licenses. But not all things called *commons* are free and open. Also among the top results in a search for *commons* is eRA Commons, with the address *commons.era.nih.gov*, at the National Institutes of Health. At the bottom of that page, it says,

WARNING

> You are accessing a U.S. Government web site which may contain information that must be protected under the U.S. Privacy Act or other sensitive information and is intended for Government-authorized use only. Unauthorized attempts to upload information, change information, or use of this web site may result in ...

Why would something called a "commons" have such a stinted proviso? The short answer is, *because all commons are stinted*. The idea that the commons is a purely open, common pool resource is wrong—one might even say, tragically.

A Tragic Dilemma

For most of us, the noun *commons* tends to arrive with the adjective *tragic*. For that we can thank Garrett Hardin's "The Tragedy of the Commons," a 1968 essay in *Science* on the subject of population growth.[3] Hardin's main argument was against "the tendency to assume that decisions reached individually will, in fact, be the best decisions for an entire society"—an assumption that derives, of course, from Adam Smith's "invisible hand." Here is Hardin's case, slightly abridged:

> The tragedy of the commons develops in this way. Picture a pasture open to all. It is to be expected that each herdsman will try to keep as many cattle as possible on the commons. Such an arrangement may work reasonably satisfactorily for centuries because tribal wars, poaching, and disease keep the numbers of both man and beast well below the carrying capacity of the land. Finally, however, comes the day of reckoning, that is, the day when the long-desired goal of social stability becomes a reality. At this point, the inherent logic of the commons remorselessly generates tragedy ...

Each man is locked into a system that compels him to increase his herd without limit—in a world that is limited. Ruin is the destination toward which all men rush, each pursuing his own best interest in a society that believes in the freedom of the commons. Freedom in a commons brings ruin to all.[4]

Commons Properties

Lewis Hyde challenges Hardin's assumption that common pool resources and a commons are the same thing.[5] In *Common as Air*, he makes a thoroughly argued case against Hardin's tragedy-prone commons and for something much more complex, subtle, and—I believe—important to understand if we are to make the most of the Internet.

"I take a commons to be a kind of property," Hyde writes, "and I take 'property' to be, by one old dictionary definition, *a right of action*," noting "that ownership rarely consists of the entire set of possible actions." For example, "If I own a house in an American city, I have many rights of action … but not all … I cannot put a herd of cows in my yard; I cannot convert my home into a soap factory …"[6] He continues, "My point is that the idea of property as a right of action suggests … that a commons is a kind of property in which more than one person has rights."

He goes on to unpack what nearly all of us (Hardin included) never learned, or forgot, or ignored, about what a commons was and—more importantly for our purposes—how it served both commerce and culture:

> Traditional English commons were lands held collectively by the residents of a parish or village: the fields, pastures, streams and woods that a number of people … had the right to use in ways organized and regulated by custom. Those who held a common right of *pasturage* could graze their cattle in the fields; those with a common right of *piscary* might fish the streams; those with a common of *turbary* might cut turf to burn for heat; those with a common of *estovers*[7] might take wood necessary to heat, furnish or repair their houses. Everyone, the poor especially, had the right to glean after harvest.[8]

Thus, "The commons are not simply the land but the land plus the rights, customs, and institutions that preserve its communal uses." And, "A true commons is a stinted thing; what Hardin described is not a commons at all but what is nowadays called an "unmanaged common-pool resource.""[9]

Notably, markets too were stinted. For example, there might be only one "market day" per week, and that might be further limited to just one afternoon.

Those who shared the commons also enforced their own rules:

> In general no one could erect barriers to customary common rights, not the lord of the manor, not even the king. In fact, if encroachments appeared, commoners had a right to throw them down. Once a year, commoners would "beat the bound," meaning they would perambulate the public ways and common lands armed with axes, mattocks, and crowbars to demolish any hedge, fence, ditch, stile, gate or building that had been erected without permission.[10]

These types of commons, which had retained their essential qualities since Saxon times, came to a tragic end, destroyed by "enclosure" and similar takings by government and commercial interests. To sum it up, the commons lost when industry won the industrial revolution.

Yet the sense of what a commons is, and what it is for, survives in culture and helps make sense of a common pool resource that is not by nature limited in the manner of Hardin's, yet might still be made tragic by those who would enclose it with contrived finitudes (say, "minutes" or "channels") for their own parochial purposes.[11] This is the risk of subordinating the Internet to telephony and cable television, both of which the Internet transcends and subsumes by design—yet both of which funnel Internet access and contain use within legacy telephone and cable company facilities, provisioning, and business models.

So, how can we respect these manorial companies' need to innovate and cause market growth as only they can, while still protecting the World Wide Commons we mostly access by their grace, and which to some degree they already consider at least partially enclosed for their own purposes? And how might we guide government policy away from encouraging or granting additional rights of enclosure to the same companies?

Hyde answers,

> The commons ... needs some kind of built-in border patrol or annual perambulation, a defense against the undue conversion of use rights into rents or the fencing of open fields into sheep pastures. Almost by definition, the commons needs to stint the market, for if the "free market" is free to convert everything it meets into an exchangeable good, no commons will survive.[12]

This is not the kind of talk that tends to warm a capitalist heart. But let's ponder our own enclosed markets—our captive customers, our loyalty-card-carrying calves that also suckle our Web sites' cows. What will happen when they come to possess tools that make them fully independent in the marketplace? What will happen when they cease to be veal and start beating the bounds of the Web or the Net or the marketplace as a whole—especially when those three things come to coexist and codepend to the degree that they become indistinguishable?

Here's how Hyde, in an interview, described the current situation, not long after *Common as Air* came out:

> The rules are not clear. Then we get these polar camps: amateur anarchists on the one side, who happily believe we need no rules, and old guard "intellectual property" purists madly trying to enforce and sharpen the rules that worked so well back in 1965. What Creative Commons and others are doing is trying to enlarge the middle ground.[13]

The amateur anarchists and intellectual property maximalists will still fight, but customers and vendors are the ones in position to civilize the middle ground. We call that ground, that commons, the marketplace. Both sides will stint it to serve their own common(s) interests, because they will know from growing experience how working together will be good for business and for the culture that surrounds it.

SO, THEN

Connected and well-equipped customers will finish enlarging the Net's ground until it is both a commons and a marketplace, under the feet of us all. The choice for business is to shake hands with customers and work together, or to continue heating up the branding irons.

PART III

The Liberated Customer

Emancipation is the demand of civilization. That is a principle; everything else is an intrigue.

—Ralph Waldo Emerson

Long enough have you dreamed contemptible dreams. Now I wash the gum from your eyes. You must habit yourself to the dazzle of the light and of every moment of your life.

—Walt Whitman

16

Personal Freedom

THE ARGUMENT

We've found captivity too agreeable for too long. But we see freedom coming. And we've seen it coming for a long time.

A lot of what humans do is crazy. Some crazy things we can't seem to stop. Making war and despoiling the planet are two examples.[3] But other crazy things come and go, even if they last for generations. They're popular for fifty or a hundred years, and then the culture wakes up and says, "Gee, that was nuts."

Back in the 1950s, smoking and drunk driving were both standard. There were ashtrays on flat surfaces everywhere. Homes, offices, cars, buses, trains, planes, and restaurants were always thick with smoke. Driving drunk was illegal, but common. In *The Right Stuff*, Tom Wolfe described Florida in the early Space Age as "a paradise of Flying and Drinking and Drinking and Driving." And hey, how else were you going to get home from the bar?

Today, smoking and drunk driving are both marginalized. It matters how that happened, but not for the point of this book. What matters here is that the culture as a whole woke up and realized that smoking and drunk driving had *always* been crazy things to do.

In *Cognitive Surplus*, Clay Shirky gives two more examples. First is the Gin Craze of the early 1700s in urban England: "Gin pushcarts plied the streets of London; if you couldn't afford a whole glass, you could buy a gin-soaked rag, and flop-houses did brisk business renting straw pallets by the hour if you needed to sleep off the effects."[4] Second is our own culture's half-century-long slouch in front of the TV. The Gin Craze Clay credits to industrialization; the TV habit, to a surfeit of free time. But, while the Gin Craze was normative only for unfortunates at the bottom of London's social ladder, nearly all of us became couch potatoes. Writes Clay, "We had so much free time to burn and so few other appealing ways to burn it that every citizen in the developed world took to watching television as if it were a duty … The sitcom has been our gin, an infinitely expandable response to the crisis of social transformation."[5]

Now it's hangover time, though less for liberated couch potatoes than for their baffled farmers. Adds Clay, "The television industry has been shocked to see alternative uses of free time, especially among young people, because the idea that watching TV was the best use of free time, as ratified by the viewers, has been such a stable feature of society for so long."[6]

It should be no surprise that people would dump TV once there were better things to do. We dropped cable TV in our own house once it was clear that we didn't even watch the movies we recorded and that it was easier to watch them on Netflix than over cable's control-freakish distribution system. Then we dumped Netflix too, because we have better things to do with our time. And we're far from alone. "Pure consumption of media was never a sacred tradition," Clay adds. "It was just a set of accumulated accidents, accidents that are being undone as people start hiring new communications tools to do jobs older media simply can't do."[7]

When a norm is crazy, we become sympathetic captives of it, exhibiting a kind of Stockholm syndrome—the paradoxical tendency of hostages to sympathize with their captors after being held for a long time. (It was named after captives of bank robbers in Stockholm who did exactly that.) We were captives of smoking and drunk driving. We were captives of television. And we're still captives of a belief system I'll call *adhesionism*, after Friedrich Kessler's *contracts of adhesion* (see chapter 4), by which submissive parties yield to dominant ones, without a peep or a fight. Here is how adhesionism's canon manifests today:

1. Belief by lawyers that lopsided *contracts of adhesion* are the only ones to write when dealing with large numbers of unknown customers and users.

2. Belief by corporate executives that *limiting customer contact and choice is required* for dealing with large customer populations (or even small ones), "at scale," and that having "users" by the billions is better than having customers by the hundreds, thousands, or millions.

3. Belief by "content" producers and distributors that *"consumers" in their natural state are thieves* and not to be trusted to value or pay fairly for the goods they can also get at no cost.

4. Belief by do-gooders that *customers are so naturally weak that they always need government protection.*

5. Belief by economists that *a free market is one where customers choose captors and the best captors win.*

6. Belief, in sum, that *captive customers are more valuable than free ones.*

Adhesionism has been with us since industry won the industrial revolution, and it isn't going away easily. Nor is it without justification. As Chris Locke wrote in *The Cluetrain Manifesto*, "Mass production, mass marketing, and mass media have constituted the Holy Trinity of American business for at least a hundred years. The payoffs were so huge that the mindset became an addiction, a drug blinding its users to changes that began to erode the old axioms attaching to economies of scale."[8]

Management

Those changes Chris cites were made by the Internet, which *Cluetrain* heralded with the subtitle, "The end of business as usual." The "old axioms" he mentions were first studied, described, and evangelized by Frederick W. Taylor, primarily through his 1911 monograph, *Principles of Scientific Management.* Wrote Taylor, "It is only through *enforced* standardization of methods, *enforced* adoption of the best implements and working conditions, and *enforced* cooperation that this faster work can be assured. And the duty of *enforcing* the adoption of standards and enforcing this cooperation rests with management alone."[9] The italics are his.

Taylor established management as a professional category, and his pedagogy came to instruct every large institution in civilization, including education and government. James O. McKinsey's management consultancy, H. L. Gantt's charts, Hugo Münsterberg's industrial psychology, Karl G. Barth's speed-and-feed calculating slide rules, and degrees in management offered by Harvard, Tufts, and countless other schools all trace back to Taylor. World Wars I and II were fueled and guided by Taylorist obsessions with efficiency and productivity.

Peter Drucker was a one-man counterweight to Taylorism and devoted his seven-decade career to recognizing human concerns in business that Taylor's "scientific management" dismissed: personal knowledge, learning, teamwork, human dignity, and innovations arising from the interests and ideas of employees and customers. Drucker also cared about the common good. In *Management: Tasks, Responsibilities, Practices*, he wrote, "If the managers of our major institutions, and especially of business, do not take responsibility for the common good, no one else can or will."[10]

Yet management is not for institutions alone. We all manage ourselves, and we manage our relationships with others. Our ability to manage depends on our agency: that is, to express intent, with effects. Our ability to manage also relies on our ability to delegate some of our agency to others. Yet in there is an oxymoronic sound to "personal management." It's like saying "personal high-rise." That sound is an adhesionist echo of Taylor's teachings and of compromises our parents and ancestors made when subordinating personal agency was a requirement of civilized life.

We no longer need to do that.

Marching Toward Sanity

The road out of Stockholm is a long one, and we've been on it for a long time. Here are a few landmarks along the way.

1943

At the end of the otherwise depressing "Contracts of Adhesion," Friedrich Kessler offered a glimmer of hope for *freedom of contract*: "Its meaning must change with the social importance of the type of contract and with the degree of monopoly enjoyed by the author of the standardized contract."[11] In other words, *freedom of contract* varies inversely with degree of monopoly. Reduce monopoly and *freedom of contract* has a chance.

1954

In *The Practice of Management*, Peter Drucker introduced the concept of "knowledge-work" and the importance of what he (and most of business) came to call "knowledge workers," contrasting those from Frederick W. Taylor's human cogs.[12] Drucker's entire oeuvre, which accumulated through hundreds of books and essays between 1942 and his death in 2005, was one long harangue against Taylorism and on the ability of workers, managers, and customers to learn things together. In 1999, he wrote, "What gives life to and sustains the corporation resides on the 'outside,' not within its direct control, and the customer is the primary mover of those external realities and forces. It is the prospect of providing a customer with value that gives the corporation purpose, and it is the satisfaction of the customer's requirements that gives it results."[13] Drucker is my greatest business hero.

1956

In *The Organization Man*, William H. Whyte Jr. devoted 446 pages to explaining how white-collar workers in the 1950s traded their souls for membership in "The Organization." Then, in closing, he adds,

> I have been speaking of measures organizations can take. But ultimately any real change will be up to the individual himself ...
>
> He must fight The Organization. Not stupidly, or selfishly, for the defects of individual self-regard are no more to be venerated than the defects of co-operation. But fight he must, for the demands for his surrender are constant and powerful, and the more he has come to like the life of organization the more difficult does he find it to resist these demands, or even to recognize them.[14]

1973

In *The Coming of Post-Industrial Society*, Daniel Bell predicted a shift from manufacturing to service-based economies, a rise of dependence on science, and with that, a rise of technical elites. For the rest of us, he at least gave hope that the industrial age might end.[15]

1980

In *The Third Wave*, Alvin Toffler described

> a genuinely new way of life based on diversified, renewable energy sources; on methods of production that make most factory assembly lines obsolete ... and on radically changed schools and

corporations of the future. The emergent civilization writes a new code of behavior for us and carries us beyond standardization, synchronization, and centralization, beyond the concentration of energy, money, and power ... Above all, as we shall see, Third Wave civilization begins to heal the historic breach between producer and consumer, giving rise to the "prosumer" economics of tomorrow."[16]

1982

In *Megatrends*, John Naisbitt laid out ten shifts in ten chapters that have proved remarkably prophetic. Here are the chapter titles:

1. Industrial Society → Information Society

2. Forced Technology → High Tech/High Touch

3. National Economy → World Economy

4. Short Term → Long Term

5. Centralization → Decentralization

6. Institutional Help → Self-Help

7. Representative Democracy → Participatory Democracy

8. Hierarchies → Networking

9. North → South

10. Either/Or → Multiple Option[17]

Wrote Naisbitt, "Networks restructure the power and communication flow within an organization from the vertical to the horizontal ... A network management style is already in place in several young, successful computer firms."[18] At this point, Apple was five years old and the IBM PC was being born.

1990

In *Powershift*, Alvin Toffler wrote of "the autonomous employee" and the "non-interchangeable person." One sample: "As work grows more differentiated, the bargaining position of individuals with crucial skills is enhanced. Individuals, not only organized groups, can exert clout."[19]

In *Megatrends 2000*, John Naisbitt and Patricia Aburdene devoted their final chapter to "Triumph of the Individual." Speaking of the next decade in the present tense, they wrote, "The 1990's are characterized by a new respect for the individual as the foundation of society and the basic unit of change. 'Mass' movements are a misnomer. The environmental movement, the women's movement, the antinuclear movement were built one consciousness at a time by an individual persuaded of the possibility of a new reality."[20] Under the subhead, "The primacy of the consumer," they added, "When the focus was on the institution, individuals got what suited the institution; everyone got the same thing. No more. With the rise of the individual has come the primacy of the consumer. It has been *said* for many years: The customer is king. Now it is true."[21] Later, they added, "The new responsibility of society is to reward the initiative of the individual."[22]

1991

In *Relationship Marketing: Successful Strategies for the Age of the Customer*, Regis McKenna says "it all starts with the customer," describes *positioning* as a "dynamic" process that revolves around the customer, and advises marketing to shift "from monologue to dialogue."[23] McKenna's next book, in 1997, was *Real Time: Preparing for the Age of the Never Satisfied Customer*.

1993

In *The One to One Future*, Don Peppers and Martha Rogers wrote,

> Today we are passing through a technological discontinuity of epic proportions, and most of us are not even remotely prepared. The old paradigm, a system of mass production, mass media and mass marketing, is being replaced by a totally new paradigm, a one-to-one economic system ... The 1:1 future will be characterized by customized production, individually addressable media, and 1:1 marketing, totally changing the rules of business competition and growth. Instead of market share, the goal of most business competition will be share of customer— one customer at a time.[24]

In chapter 7, "Engage Your Customers in Dialogue," they added,

> On the whole, marketers are much more prepared to talk *to* customers than to hear *from* them. This is mostly because there just aren't any convenient, inexpensive media that allow customers to send messages to marketers, while there are all sorts of mass media available to facilitate one-way, non-addressable communication from marketers to customers ... Stop thinking in terms of audiences and

faceless masses of eyes and ears. Think, instead, of human beings—individual human beings. Instead of reaching your *target* audience, think of having a *conversation* with these *individuals*.[25]

The Internet we know (with browsers and e-mail) came two years after Peppers and Rogers' book hit the shelves. Texting would take another decade. "Friending" and tweeting would take a decade and a half. Still, none of those, even today, are adequate to supply the 1:1 future Don and Martha so clearly saw. We are still in the same long, slow moment, and no less in the grip of the industrial age. There remains a concentration of agency on the side of industry. Even so simple a matter as *relationship*, between customers and vendors, has been in the full control of vendors.

1999

In *Permission Marketing: Turning Strangers Into Friends And Friends Into Customers*, Seth Godin challenged the "noninteractive world" of interruptive, attention-grabbing marketing and suggests a new model of manners: actually talking to customers the old fashioned way and building genuine relationships with them.

The Cluetrain Manifesto appeared on the Web in April 1999, at about the same time as *Permission Marketing* came out. The book version of *Cluetrain* was written in the summer of that year, and published in January 2000. Here's one quote from it that points toward the Intention Economy: "Corporate firewalls have kept smart employees in and smart markets out. It's going to cause real pain to tear those walls down. But the result will be a new kind of conversation. And it will be the most exciting conversation business has ever engaged in."[26]

In *Net Worth: Shaping Markets When Customers Make the Rules*, John Hagel III and Marc Singer wrote about the shift of economic power to individuals, the "death of conventional brands," "a virtuous circle between customers and vendors," and other coming changes. Today John adds, "Where we really plowed new ground was with the notion that for the first time technology was making it feasible for customers to capture information about themselves (including transaction histories and relationships with others) and selectively make it available to vendors in return for more relevant value and the related notion that this created a business opportunity for a new form of customer agent (infomediaries) that would help customers to manage these data profiles and become trusted advisers to help customers connect with more relevant resources and vendors."

2001

In *Free Agent Nation*, Daniel H. Pink recalled "The Whyte stuff" of 1956 in a chapter titled, "Bye Bye, Organization Guy," and writes about "this broad shift of power from the organization to the individual," and "the turn from Taylorism to Tailorism."[27]

2006

In *Wikinomics*, Don Tapscott and Anthony D. Williams devoted a chapter to "prosumers" and wrote about "customers as co-innovators" and "embracing customer power."[28]

2009

In "A Customer Liberation Manifesto," Raymond Fisk, who chairs the Department of Marketing at Texas State University–San Marcos, wrote,

> In my nearly thirty years as a services marketing scholar, I have seen the practice of serving customers advance from benign neglect to active engagement. Customer co-creation of value has rapidly become a popular business logic ... and a major force for new service thinking. I think customer co-creation leads to customer liberation! If service organizations truly adopt the logic of co-creation, they will no longer be able to treat their customers as powerlessly subservient.[29]

In *The Power of Pull*, John Hagel III, John Seely Brown, and Lang Davison wrote, "Going forward, individuals will increasingly reshape institutions rather than vice versa."[30]

In *Pull*, David Siegel wrote, "In the world of pull, you don't own the customer; the customer owns you ... your company's economics are aligned with your customer's ... Companies that focus on results for their customers set the pace. Their systems are tied to their customers' systems, so they can work in real time."[31]

Pull is also the first book to visit VRM in depth:

> With VRM ... you control the data that would normally be in a CRM system, so you can give it to the vendor in the same way vendors pass customer data from one sales rep to another. Using the principle of least privilege, you can give out your data as necessary and terminate the relationship at any time. When a product goes into the "haves" section of your data locker, the warranty record follows automatically. Without knowing your name and address, the company can contact

you if there's a problem, and you can contact the company. You can signal that you are planning to switch vendors, and all vendors will come to you with their offers knowing what you have and what kind of customer you are ... [and] eventually most companies and even the government will agree to account portability, because consumers will demand it ... Once you have your information under your control, you will become an institution of one.[32]

And, in the 10th Anniversary Edition of *The Cluetrain Manifesto*, I wrote, "a better system will come along in which demand drives supply at least as well as supply drives demand. In other words, when the 'intention economy' outperforms the attention economy."[33]

Yet, even after seventy years of optimism toward the end of adhesionism, most of us in business remain believers, and most customers are still stuck in Stockholm. We are still batteries in *The Matrix*. We still await liberation. What's it going to take?

Means to Ends

"Invention is the mother of necessity," Thorstein Veblen said.[34] And he's right. We didn't need a car, a copier, a radio, or a smartphone until we saw one and said to ourselves, "I need that." Without necessity-mothering inventions, we wouldn't have had any form of progress since we first learned to chip rocks into axes and arrowheads.

SO, THEN

Customer liberation requires necessity-mothering inventions. Kessler, Drucker, Bell, Whyte, Toffler, Naisbitt, Peppers, Rogers, McKenna, Pink, Siegel, Hagel, and many others have called for or predicted the rise of individual power and autonomy in the marketplace and the inevitable importance of liberated customers to the future of business.

But we need tools. And for that's what VRM is for.

17

VRM

VRM is not just a "phenomenon" generated by placing cool tools in the hands of users. Yes, of course, we need cool tools (it may not happen without them). But we also need new types of service, and new types of business models to make these new types of service possible. It's about all three, together.

—Alan Mitchell[1]

THE ARGUMENT

VRM is the booster stage of a missile fired into the future. To some degree, it is a guided one.

First, a few words about the Berkman Center for Internet & Society, where ProjectVRM was launched in September 2006. From the center's Web site:

> The Berkman Center's mission is to explore and understand cyberspace; to study its development, dynamics, norms, and standards; and to assess the need or lack thereof for laws and sanctions.
>
> We are a research center, premised on the observation that what we seek to learn is not already recorded. Our method is to build out into cyberspace, record data as we go, self-study, and share. Our mode is entrepreneurial nonprofit.[2]

ProjectVRM veers from that mission in just one respect: it began as a *development* project, rather than as a *research* one. That is, its purpose from the beginning has been to encourage development in an area that had been largely neglected: empowering individuals—especially customers—natively, outside any corporate or organizational framework. So, while we wanted to do research, we needed the development horse to pull the research cart.

In the beginning, ProjectVRM was continuous with my own earlier work on digital identity and work done at the Berkman Center under John Clippinger, then a senior fellow there. It was John who approached me in February 2005 to offer Berkman as a kind of "clubhouse" for the "Identity Gang," which later became the twice-yearly Internet Identity Workshop.

But, while customer empowerment overlaps with digital identity, I saw it as a separate and much larger topic, one that would affect the whole of business once it developed fully. So the purpose of ProjectVRM grew to one that encouraged fresh work in specific development areas such as protocols, standards and databases—and in broad market segments such as retail, law, real estate, government, health care, and communications.

The effort has succeeded, and continues to succeed. By the end of 2011, the ProjectVRM wiki listed dozens of development projects, companies, and organizations. So did the ProjectVRM article in Wikipedia. Any work that provides tools that help make customers both independent of vendors and better able to engage with vendors—in the customer's own ways, and on his or her own terms—is VRM work.

To describe that work, let's look first at VRM purposes and then at the kinds of tools they require.

VRM Purposes

In the "Markets are Relationships" chapter of *The Cluetrain Manifesto*'s 10th Anniversary edition, I listed seven VRM purposes:

1. **Provide tools for individuals to manage relationships with organizations.** These tools are personal. That is, they belong to the individual, in the sense that they are under the individual's control. They can also be social, in the sense that they can connect with others and support group formation and action. But they need to be personal first.

2. **Make individuals the collection centers for their own data,** so that transaction histories, health records, membership details, service contracts, and other forms of personal data are no longer scattered throughout a forest of silos.

3. **Give individuals the ability to share data selectively,** without disclosing more personal information than the individual allows.

4. **Give individuals the ability to control how their data is used by others,** and for how long. At the individual's discretion, this may include agreements requiring others to delete the individual's data when the relationship ends.

5. **Give individuals the ability to assert their own terms of service,** reducing or eliminating the need for organization-written terms of service that nobody reads and everybody has to "accept" anyway.

6. **Give individuals means for expressing demand in the open market,** outside any organizational silo, without disclosing any unnecessary personal information.

7. **Base relationship-managing tools on open standards, open APIs (application program interfaces), and open code.** This will support a rising tide of activity that will lift an infinite variety of business boats, plus other social goods.[3]

To those I would add one more: *Make relationships work both ways.* That is, we need to create or improve tools for that on both sides. Those tools are new on the customer's side. Old tools, such as CRM, need to adapt on the vendor's side. We'll visit that challenge in Part IV.

VRM tools

Even though VRM developments are still in their early stages, there are a few things we can say about VRM tools and what they do. Here's a short list:

1. **VRM tools are personal.** As with hammers, wallets, cars, and mobile phones, people use them as individuals. They are social only in secondary ways.

2. **VRM tools make us independent.** They free us to perform as sovereign and independent actors in the marketplace.

3. **VRM tools help customers express intent.**[4] These include preferences, policies, terms, and means of engagement, authorizations, requests, and anything else that's possible in a free market, outside any one vendor's silo or ranch.

4. **VRM tools help customers engage.** This can be with each other, or with any organization, including (and especially) its CRM system.

5. **VRM tools help customers manage.** This includes both their own data and systems and their relationships with other entities and their systems.

6. **VRM tools are substitutable.** This means no source of VRM tools can lock users in.

While both lists suggest specific kinds of work, they actually outline a category that could hardly be broader.

For example, a plain mobile phone is a VRM tool. So is a car. Both are personal, make us independent, help us express intent, help us engage and manage, and are substitutable.

Not that they are perfectly so. For example, nearly all smartphones today are to some degree locked inside a carrier's walled garden. Apple's iTunes is the cushiest Stockholm ever built by a capturing vendor. Still, we are free to leave it and cope with less fancy alternatives, some of which do their best to support your freedom and independence. One is Ting, a new MVNO (mobile virtual network operator) that wants to provide maximal independence and support to customers. In the words of Elliot Noss, the CEO of Tucows, Ting's parent company, "We have to be a VRM company. If I worked toward anything less, my employees would kill me."[5]

And, in the process, Ting is likely to help carriers and regulators understand why free customers are more valuable than captive ones.

There are many other VRM developers as well, which we'll visit in the next chapter.

SO THEN

It's still early in the day for the intention economy, but sanity is dawning, and we're doing our best to make the sun come up.

18

Development

Users that innovate can develop exactly what they want, rather than relying on manufacturers to act as their (often very imperfect) agents.

—Eric Von Hippel[1]

Those who would adopt or create a distributed innovation system … must be prepared to acknowledge the locus of innovation to be outside the boundaries of the focal organization. And this will require a fundamental reorientation of views about incentives, task structure, management, and intellectual property.

—Karim Lakhani and Jill A. Panetta[2]

THE ARGUMENT

VRM development works because it is distributed. That is, anybody can do it anywhere and build on the work others are also doing.

ProjectVRM was designed to encourage a distributed innovation system outside the project itself. It has been guided by teachings such as those of Eric von Hippel, and Karim Lakhani and Jill Panetta (quoted in the epigraph above), as well as my own experience covering free and open source code development for *Linux Journal*. The result is plenty of what Yochai Benkler calls *commons-based peer production* (see chapter 12) and von Hippel calls *democratized innovation.* So, in respect to the four concerns Karim and Jill raise in their quote, here's the rundown:

- For *incentives*, we trust VRM's mission to orient developers toward payoffs downstream. With two small exceptions (a grant toward development of ListenLog and EmanciPay and a Google Summer of Code student paid directly by Google), we have offered no financial support to developers and have not engaged developers to work for the project itself.

- The project's *task structure* is minimal. We hold our own workshops, but also take advantage of gathering opportunities at various conferences and workshops where VRM as a topic makes sense. The twice-yearly Internet Identity Workshops (IIWs) have been especially accommodating for that. There are also a number of allied organizations, such as Adriana Lukas's VRM Hub in London and the Information Sharing Workgroup at the Kantara Initiative (a collaborative development organization), led by Joe Andrieu, Judi Clarke, and Iain Henderson.

- For *management*, I stick to ProjectVRM itself. I don't manage the peers producing code out on the commons or our committee meetings. (Others, more skilled at operating timepieces and calendars, handle those.) While I'm the main guy associated with VRM, I try to evangelize the mission without hogging the spotlight. In fact, I get much more satisfaction from shining the spotlight on what others are doing.

- ProjectVRM itself has little or no *intellectual property*, beyond the few developments we've led directly. Those are all open source and therefore have few if any IP restrictions. ProjectVRM encourages the development and use of FOSS (free and open source) code and principles, even when doing proprietary commercial work. On the whole, developers have followed those urgings.

The Short List

As I said earlier (and can't stress too much), the list of VRM projects and companies is going to change and will have already changed by the time you read this. But I think it's essential to give credit to pioneers. See table 18-1 for the list as it stands on the ProjectVRM wiki in December 2011.

They are variously headquartered in Austria, Belgium, Chile, Canada, Italy, Netherlands, South Africa, Switzerland, United Kingdom, and across four time zones in the United States—as well as out on the Web and the Net.

Most of these projects are under the mainstream radar. They don't show up in typical "Who's Going to Win?" coverage in tech and business

TABLE 18-1

VRM projects and companies

About.me	Precipit.at
Azigo.com	Privowny
The Banyan Project	Prizzm
Connect.Me	ProjectDanube
Ctrl-SHIFT	Project Nori
dot.UI	QIY
Diaspora	r-button
EmanciPay	RedBeacon
EmanciTerm	Respect Network
Evented APIs	Singly
GRM: Government Relationship Management	Social Nori
Higgins	Getabl
Hover.com	SwitchBook
Hypothes.is	Status.net
Information Sharing Workgroup at Kantara	TAS3
Id3	Telehash
Insidr	Thimbl
KRL	Thumbtack
Kynetx, which also does HoverMe	TiddlyWiki
ListenLog	Ting
MyInfo.CL	TrustFabric
The Locker Project	Tucows
The Mine! Project	Übokia
NewGov.us	UMA
Paoga	VirtualZero
Pegasus	VRM Hub
Personal.com	VRM Labs
Personal Data Ecosystem Consortium (PDEC)	Webfinger
Personal RFP	Zaarly

publications, or in the "What's Hot?" line-up at trade shows. In this respect, they are like Linux, Apache, RSS, Jabber/XMPP, and hundreds of other code bases and protocols that are foundational in the extreme, yet call no promotional attention to themselves. In a post to the Project-VRM list reviewing the early history of Apache, Brian Behlendorf (one of Apache's original authors) wrote, "Apache fortuitously grew to dominance long before dominance mattered."[3] Today, Apache serves about two thirds of the world's Web pages, Yet dominance was never what its developers sought. The same was true of those other foundational code bases and protocols.

The best of today's VRM developments will succeed in the same ways and for the same reasons—and with the same lack of mainstream attention to their importance while they establish themselves.

Instruments of Intention

The Internet (as I reviewed in chapter 9) supports both independence and engagement, by design. So do some of its native applications. Three already qualify as VRM tools and as models for other tools being developed today.

E-mail

The protocols SMTP, POP, and IMAP make e-mail on the Internet possible. Those protocols are NEA, meaning Nobody owns them, Everybody can use them, and Anybody can improve them. (For more on NEA, see chapter 9.)

This means any of us can use whatever e-mail server and e-mail client we like. They are all substitutable. If you want to switch your e-mail from your own server to Gmail or Yahoo mail—or back and forth between those—you are free to do that. You are also free to change your mail client from Outlook to Thunderbird to mutt or pine or SeaMonkey—or use Gmail's, Yahoo's, or Hotmail's clients in your browser.

Before the Internet became widely available, all the major mail platforms were proprietary and closed. In my own case, I had accounts with AOL, AppleLink, Compuserve, MCI, The Well, Prodigy, and others I forget—and all are equally dead today. None of them could send or receive mail from each other, and most of the companies involved considered this incompatibility a virtue.

The Internet's mail protocols made us all free to use whatever we liked and to communicate with anyone we liked, anywhere in the world.

Publishing

WordPress and Drupal are today the two major open source personal publishing and content management code bases. Neither locks you into using any one company's publishing platform. The same goes for Dave Winer's OPML outliner and for RSS, which Dave almost single-handedly drove to ubiquity, and which gives every writer or artist a power that once belonged only to giant publishing companies.

Instant Messaging

XMPP is the most widely used protocol for instant messaging (IM). Before XMPP, IM was as locked up and siloed as e-mail was before its open protocols were adopted. To some degree, this is still the case. (AOL's AIM, Apple's iChat, Windows Live Messenger, and Yahoo Messenger all interoperate in various ways through XMPP, but were designed originally as closed proprietary systems. Google Talk used XMPP from the start.) As with e-mail, you can set up your own XMPP-based IM server if you like.

These tools are native to the Internet's commons because, like that commons, they are nonrivalrous and nonexcludable. (*Nonrivalrous* means use of them by one party does not prevent another party from using them; *nonexcludable* means you can't make them scarce.)

Here are some of purposes addressed by VRM tools from the companies and projects listed earlier:

- Gathering, integrating and managing *your own data.*

- Managing *personal identity.*

- Setting *your own terms, policies, and preferences* within a *freedom-of-contract* framework.

- Establishing and participating in *trust frameworks* and *trust networks* developed primarily for individuals, to maintain their independence from any single company.

- *Self-tracking, self-hacking*, and *personal informatics.*

- *Keeping records* of communications and other interactions.

- Personalizing and improving *search.*

- *Expressing demand*, including *personal RFPs.*

- *Programming rules for actions to follow from events of any kind,* also outside the client-server "calf-cow" framework.

- *Blogging* and *microblogging* on open and substitutable systems.

- *Freely owning and managing your own server.*

- *Interacting with CRM systems.*

- Creating new companies or changing existing ones to serve as *fourth parties*, acting as agents for the customer rather than for second (vendor) or third parties.

Think of the VRM toolbox as one with many drawers, of which the ones listed are the first few. New tools will gradually fill all the drawers. Some tools will be all-in-one. Some will be specialized. Some will be (as with e-mail, IM, and publishing) offered as competitive but substitutable utility services. New drawers will appear as more tools, protocols, services, APIs, and other inventions come into use. Some tools already in use, such as browsers, may become more VRM-ish as time goes on, but it's still not clear at this writing how to bet.

Is a Browser Your Car or Your Shopping Cart?

Among name-brand browsers, the decision to stand with both feet on the individual's side has been made only by Mozilla's Firefox, described by Katherine Noyes of *PCWorld* as the only browser that "has your back."[4] *The State of Mozilla Annual Report* for 2010 says, "Mozilla is unique in that we build Firefox to provide an independent offering focused solely on individual experience and the overall good of the Web."[5] Internet Explorer, Chrome, and Safari, the other three top browsers, are all products of giant companies that can easily subordinate the individual user's intentions to their own commercial ones. While the makers of those browers try not to do that, Mozilla is less conflicted, by design.

The problem, meanwhile, is that the Web has gone mostly commercial, and browsers have become shopping carts. In a long blog post titled, "Enough with browsers. We need cars now," I wrote,

> For independence on the Net and the Web, we need cars, pickup trucks, bikes and motorcycles. Not just shopping carts—which are what browsers have become.

Personal vehicles give us independence. They let us drive and shop all over the place, coming and going as we please. In different stores we use the shopping carts provided for us; but we haul home what we buy in our own vehicles. We also meet sellers in stores at a human level, person-to-person. We can talk …

Cars, trucks, bikes and motorcycles are all substitutable goods. That's why, if we're competent drivers or riders, we can switch between them. It's why we can bring what's ours (our wallets and other personal things) with us in any variety of vehicles, without worrying about whether those personal things are compatible with a maker's proprietary driving system.[6]

Later I added,

Nobody has invented a car for the Net or the Web yet. Browsers could have been cars, but they have remained stuck for sixteen years in the calf-cow slave-master world of the client-server model.

Think about how you feel on your bike, or in your car or truck. That's what we want online. We don't have it yet, so let's invent it.[7]

This got push-back from colleagues in the VRM development community. They maintained, correctly, that browsers have 100 percent penetration on the Web, and that they don't *need* to be shopping carts. We can make them anything we like.

I accept that. But I also want to see the development, and it isn't here yet. Could it be an avatar?

Digital Nativity

In "Human Performance Enhancement in 2032: A Scenario for Military Planners," John Smart uses the term *cybertwin* to represent a virtual agent, or a "bona-fide extension of me."[8] He adds,

Today, we are seeing how the datacosm is leading to the emergence of something even more interesting. With semi-smart avatars representing us on the web, we are creating detailed, quantitative and qualitative records of the choices we make about our lives, both major and minor …

With this new information, our avatars are learning how to look for ways to maximize the future value of our choices, both for us individually and wherever possible, for our associates and for the wider world at the same time ... as extensions of our own and other people's intentions.[9]

Sourcing Smart's work, Venessa Miemis posted this on the ProjectVRM list:

what i imagine is an environment where the walls and silos drop away, and the orientation is shifted to a person-to-person type environment—this "car" that would be our tool of empowerment, independence and engagement, would essentially be a simulated self, or cybertwin ...

the more i operate through my cybertwin, the more i understand myself, and the more *it* is able to function on my behalf without my intervention or guidance. interesting services can be built around that personal agent, making it easier to discover people, products, services, experiences, or whatever, that would be useful and meaningful to me ... and there is a minimum standard of trust and ethics that i will tolerate when considering interacting or transacting with you.[10]

Is a cybertwin an invention that will mother necessity? We don't know yet, because nobody has invented one. There are plenty of avatars inside virtual worlds like Second Life, but none in the open and very real worlds of the Internet and the Web. Yet it's not hard to imagine that a cybertwin could be even more native to the Net than our corporeal selves, yet no less ourselves as human beings.

Certainly, something called a "browser" wouldn't have had much sex appeal in, say, 1993, when the Web was already several years old and only a handful of people knew it existed.

Where We Are

All the VRM work going on today falls in the "innovators" stage of Everett Rogers's *Diffusion of Innovation* model, also known as the technology adoption lifecycle:

1. Innovators

2. Early adopters

3. Early majority

4. Late majority

5. Laggards[11]

Across time, adoption forms a bell curve that peaks at number three, early majority.

The most widely popularized adaptation of Rogers's model is Geoffrey Moore's, which notes a "chasm" in the upward slope of adoption, in the middle of number 2, early adopters, between what he calls "visionaries" and "pragmatists"—at least for "disruptive" innovations.[12]

VRM developments only qualify for the "disruptive" label in the sense that they are new and may disrupt some existing categories (such as advertising); but those may choose to adapt instead, since they're also native to the left side of the curve).

Where We Fit

In general, VRM tools are what Clayton Christensen and Michael Raynor, in *The Innovators' Solution*, call "new-market disruptions." These cause "new value networks" where "it is nonconsumption, not the incumbent, that must be overcome."[13] New value networks also constitute "new contexts of consumption and competition" that may not be disruptive in the boat-rocking sense:

> Although new-market disruptions initially compete against non-consumption in their unique value network, as their performance improves they ultimately become good enough to pull customers out of the original value network into the new one, starting with the least demanding tier. The disruptive innovation doesn't invade the mainstream market; rather, it pulls customers out of the mainstream market into the new one because these customers find it more convenient to use the new product.[14]

This positions VRM's usability challenge. For VRM tools to be used as well as useful, they will need to be as obvious and simple to operate as a wallet, a mobile phone, a bike, or a car.

SO, THEN

We have a long way to go, but we've also invented a lot of ways to get there.

In the next six chapters, we'll review a few of the areas where VRM work is taking place and the expected changes that will follow.

19

The Four-Party System

It takes two to tango, but four to square dance.

—Juston Paskow[1]

THE ARGUMENT

Agents of customers and users are a new business species that
is bound to evolve.

Parties dealing with each other in business have ordinal numbers: *first*, *second*, and *third*. In law, the first two are parties to an agreement. The third party is one that has an interest in the dealings between the first and second parties, but has no legal rights within those dealings (though possibly obligations), unless the third party is recognized by the other two as a beneficiary. First, second, and third parties also map to first, second, and third person voices in speech.

In business, however, the most commonly numbered party is the third one. Credit card companies, for example, perform a third-party service to the first and second parties in a retail transaction and have their own first- or second-party agreements with retailers using their services. Visa itself has what it calls "third-party agents," which include Merchant Servicers, Encryption Support Organizations, Independent Sales Organizations, and other arcane entities.[2] (The uppercase letters are Visa's.) In technology, we are familiar with "third-party developers," who make "third-party apps."

In general, third parties operate on the supply side of the demand-supply divide and therefore serve as accessories to the second party (as seen from the customer's side). So, for example, you may be an iPhone customer using third-party apps, but you deal with those third parties through Apple's store and install those third-party apps through Apple's system. Although third-party app developers are legally separate from Apple and have their own first- and second-party agreements between Apple and themselves, their third-party status to you as a customer is mostly aligned with Apple's second-party one.

As customers employ more tools of their own for dealing with vendors, the need for services that help demand drive supply are bound to appear. Some will just help individuals collect and organize their data. Others (perhaps the same companies) can serve as agents or fiduciaries for customers, on behalf of the customer's first-party role. To help differentiate these new customer-side businesses, we call them *fourth parties*.

Simply put, a *fourth party* is one whose interests are aligned with those of the customer or user or that acts as an agent or fiduciary for the customer or user.

Here are a few characteristics we should expect of fourth parties:

- Substitutability

- Service portability

- Data portability

- Independence

- Accountability (and, in some cases, liability)

There are already a variety of fourth-party services in the world. Don Marti, former editor in chief of *Linux Journal*, lists mail filtering (e.g., SpamAssassin), userscripts (e.g., Greasemonkey), and virtual assistants (some called "concierges"). Buyers' agents in real estate are another. Doctors, lawyers, brokers, and banks also qualify. While each of those last four are paid by individual customers, it is too early in the development of VRM-enabling fourth parties to rule out fourth-party income from the vendors' side. Given how much money is currently being spent on vendor-side guesswork toward driving demand, we should expect plenty of money showing up to help demand drive supply with *actual intentions* toward purchases and relationships.

SO, THEN

As the Intention Economy grows around better signaling, better data flows, and better expression of intention by customers, many businesses old and new will grow and define that economy. *Fourth party* will be the category into which many of them will fall.

20

The Law in Our Own Hands

Companies will have to litigate where people live, instead of people
litigating where companies live.

—Renee Lloyd[1]

THE ARGUMENT

Freedom of contract is best for all parties. For maximized
economic and social benefits, restoring freedom of contract
should be a high-priority goal of reform in practice and law.

To fully grok what we'll be talking about in this chapter, you need to be
familiar with the case we make in chapter 4, where we explore *freedom of
contract* and its long absence from dealings between vendors and customers,
or what in business they call B2C (business to consumer).

Freedom of contract says anybody is free to make agreements with anybody else: essentially to form laws unto themselves. A fun example of a free
contract is this one, between two friends who agree to become kings of Kafiristan, a mythical land in Rudyard Kipling's classic short story, "The Man
Who Would Be King" (which John Huston later made into a perfect movie
by the same title, starring Michael Caine as Peachey and Sean Connery as
Danny):

> *This Contract between me and you persuing witnesseth in the name
> of God—Amen and so forth.*

(One) That me and you will settle this matter together: i.e., to be Kings of Kafiristan.

(Two) That you and me will not while this matter is being settled, look at any Liquor, nor any Woman black, white or brown, so as to get mixed up with one or the other harmful.

(Three) That we conduct ourselves with Dignity and Discretion, and if one of us gets into trouble the other will stay by him.
Signed by you and me this day.
> *Peachey Taliaferro Carnehan.*
> *Daniel Dravot.*
> *Both Gentlemen at Large.*[2]

The contract framed the story, and both men kept their word.

Hope Springs

Friedrich Kessler, who lamented the mass market's need for customer-screwing *contracts of adhesion* also sows hope that *freedom of contract* may defeat that enemy, as it has others before. By contrasting principle and precedent with the prevailing rationalizations of his time (1943, at the height of both World War II and the industrial age), Kessler provides inspiration and guidance for the work going on today. What follow are a series of successive excerpts from Kessler's "Contracts of Adhesion—Some Thoughts About Freedom of Contract," each followed by the help they currently provide.[3]

> Standard contracts ... in the hands of powerful industrial and commercial overlords [enable] them to impose a new feudal order of their own making upon a vast host of vassals.

That's where we are still. The calf-cow model is the Web-based embodiment of that same feudal order.

> ... since not more than a hundred years ago contract ideology had been successfully used to break down the last vestiges of a patriarchal and benevolent feudal order in the field of master and servant. Thus the return back from contract to the status we experience today was greatly facilitated by the fact that the belief in freedom of contract has remained one of the firmest axioms in the whole fabric of the social philosophy of our culture.

In other words, *freedom of contract* prevailed against the feudal system—and we still believe in it, even as companies violate it because they find no other way to operate.

> The role played by contract in the destruction of the institutional framework of capitalistic society is constantly obscured to the lawyer by the still prevailing philosophy of law which neglects to treat contract as the most important source of law.

In other words, lawyers writing boilerplate *contracts of adhesion* are unaware of how little their work resembles what contract was about in the first place or freedom's gravitational attraction toward *freedom of contract's* original value system. Thus, they rationalize their work:

> According to conventional theory contract is only a convenient label for a number of "operative facts" which have the consequences intended by the parties if the law so ordains. In this respect the great philosophers of natural law thought quite differently: society, in proclaiming freedom of contract— according to their teaching—has delegated to individual citizens a piece of sovereignty which enables them to participate constantly in the law making process. Freedom of contract means that the state has no monopoly in the creation of law. The consent of contracting parties creates law also. The law-making process is decentralized. As a result, law is not an order imposed by the state from above upon its citizens; it is rather an order created from below.

So citizens may create law freely through contract and fix what's broken in the marketplace through practice, rather than by waiting for government action:

> In the happy days of free enterprise capitalism the belief that contracting is law making had largely emotional importance. Law making by contract was no threat to the harmony of the democratic system. On the contrary it reaffirmed it. The courts, therefore, representing the community as a whole, could remain neutral in the name of freedom of contract. The deterioration of the social order into the pluralistic society of our days ... was needed to make the wisdom of the contract theory of the natural law philosophers meaningful to us.

Little could be done with that wisdom in 1943, or even in 2011.

> The prevailing dogma, on the other hand, insisting that contract is only a set of operative facts, helps to preserve the illusion that the "law" will protect the public against any abuse of freedom of contract.

And, as we saw earlier, it does a lousy job of that.

> This will not be the case so long as we fail to realize that freedom of contract must mean different things for different types of contracts. Its meaning must change with the social importance of the type of contract and with the degree of monopoly enjoyed by the author of the standardized contract.

Today, the degree of monopoly enjoyed (if that's the right word) by adhesive contract authors verges on absolute. Yet the utility for these contracts has sunk to an all-time low, simply because it is now abundantly clear that these "agreements" are nothing of the sort. They are merely pro forma ceremonies in which the submissive party clicks on a box and hopes for the best. In our Internet age, this "operative fact" has become equally ridiculous and normative.

So, what to do?

Make Law, Not War

It's handy that *freedom of contract* lets us reform both business and law, without waiting for government action. That's twice what could be done with copyright, another legal legacy that too often prevents more business than it protects.[4] Creative Commons, for example, reformed copyright practice during the time two of its founders (Lawrence Lessig and Eric Eldred) were busy fighting a losing battle (*Eldred v. Ashcroft*) in the Supreme Court.[5] Creative Commons did this by releasing at no charge a variety of easy-to-understand (and apply) copyright licenses that gave creators far more control over the use of their works than had ever been contemplated, much less practiced, under the industrialized copyright regime run by publishers and music recording companies.

Thus, Creative Commons achieved in practice what its founders failed to achieve through litigation or through appeals to Congress (which continues to ratchet copyright protections toward forever). This was a remarkable accomplishment, and it is now an excellent model for the VRM community in respect to *freedom of contract*. That is, what Creative Commons modeled for the vendor side of the marketplace (creators), the VRM community can do for *both* sides.

A Level Agreement Field

In *The World is Flat*, Thomas L. Friedman describes the Internet's creation of a new worldwide marketplace:

> When you add this unprecedented new level of people-to-people communication to all these Web-based application-to-application work-flow programs, you end up with a whole new global platform for multiple forms of collaboration. This is the Genesis moment for the flattening of the world ...[6]

That same moment was also Genesis for the cookie, for standard-form "agreements" one "accepted" with a click, and for other instruments by which we were branded like so many calves by countless Web sites.

But the Internet is still there, still flat, and still wider than any corral. Now it's time to do to customer ranching what *freedom of contract* did to the old feudal system. And we'll do it the easy way: by writing straightforward terms for both customers and vendors that both sides (including their faithful machines) can easily understand and agree on (or disagree respectfully)—and are good for both sides.

Coming from Agreements

In early 2011, the start-up Personal.com, which makes a private data vault (among other services), broke new ground with what it called its "Owner Data Agreement." In November 2011:

Summary of Important Terms & Rights for Owners

You own your data

> Under the terms of this Agreement, Owners will own all of their data that they upload to the Personal Service, as well as any data they create while using the Personal Service.

You control who gets access to your data

> Only Owners can grant access to their data that is stored with the Personal Service. Personal will never grant any third party

access to an Owner's data, except strictly in accordance with our Privacy Policy, which is incorporated into and made a part of this Agreement and may be found here, or when specifically required by law.

Data Users are contractually obligated to use Owner data only as authorized by the Owner

Any Data User (as defined below) to whom an Owner elects to grant access to their data stored with the Personal Service will be required to agree to the terms and conditions in this Agreement regarding the use of such data.

Take your data with you

At an Owner's request, Personal will promptly export their data and permanently delete all data that the Owner has stored with the Personal Service.

Summary of Important Terms & Rights for Data Users

Covenants data users must never violate

Data Users may not access, use, store, share or monetize an Owner's Data without explicit consent of the Owner, and must agree to transparency in the usage of Owner Data.[7]

It was a bold and ground-breaking move by Personal.com to call users "owners," especially at a time when there was much debate about whether data could be "owned" at all. (Also, recall the Jefferson quote in chapter 13, about how ideas, like flames, duplicate easily, and make for problematic property.) To my knowledge, Personal's terms had no precedent and modeled a new legal position, both for vendors and for intermediaries.

An agreement like Personal.com's at this writing is the best any vendor or intermediary can do in the absence of full agency on the individual's side. With full agency, however, an individual can say, in the first person voice, "*I* own my data, *I* control who gets access to it, and *I* specify what I wish to happen under what conditions." In the latter category, those wishes might include:

- Don't track my activities outside of this site.

- Don't put cookies in my browser for anything other than helping us remember each other and where we were.

- Make data collected about me available in a standard, open format.

- Please meet my fourth-party agent, Personal.com (or whomever).

These are *EmanciTerms*, and there will be corresponding ones on the vendor's side. Once they are made simple and straightforward enough, they should become normative to the point where they serve as de facto standards, in practice.

Since the terms should be agreeable and can be expressed in text that code can parse, the process of arriving at agreements can be automated.

For example, when using a public wi-fi access point, a person's EmanciTerms might say, "I will not knowingly hog this shared resource, for example, by watching high-def video on it," or "I will not engage in illegal activities here." If the provider of the access point has a VRM-ready service that is willing to deal with the user on his or her own EmanciTerms as well as those of the provider, it should be possible to automate the formalities and let the user bypass the usual "read and accept our agreement" ritual.

Customer Commons is working this same territory, providing sets of terms for both buyers and sellers that can be easily understood by both parties and matched electronically as well as by individuals (including lawyers, but not always requiring them). Because these terms work only for emancipated individuals (and organizations open to dealing with them), we group them together under the heading EmanciTerm.

Customer Commons will also provide a place where lawyers and ordinary folks can examine and review any company's existing terms and privacy policies. The main difference between this and Personal.com's agreement is between first- and second-person voices. Where Personal.com says *you* own your own data (speaking in the second-person voice), Customer Commons uses the first-person voice: *I* own my data, *I* control who gets access to it, and *I* specify what happens under what conditions.

Creative Commons pioneered the idea of asserting terms that make quick and easy sense to lawyers, machines, and ordinary folks. With EmanciTerm, your terms can be matched easily—preferably automatically, in the background—with those of vendors. That's why EmanciTerm includes terms for *both* sides.

Customer Commons is also not working alone on this front. The Information Sharing Workgroup at Kantara has developed an information sharing agreement that deals in detail with the many kinds of personal data that may reside in a personal data store (its term for Personal.com's vault), the many kinds of uses to which that data might be put, and the kinds of controls an individual or other agent may exercise in an agreement with another party.[8]

SO, THEN

We don't need to change laws. Not yet, anyway. Freedom of contract is already embedded in standing law, and all we need now are tools that will cause practice to change. We've started to make those.

21

Small Data

Personal data—digital data created by and about people—represents a new economic "asset class," touching all aspects of society.

—World Economic Forum[1]

The right to be left alone is the most comprehensive of rights, and the right most valued by a free people.

—Louis Brandeis[2]

THE ARGUMENT

We need ways of gathering, organizing, and controlling the data that we generate and that others suck in from our digital crumb trails. We also need new understandings about how personal data might be used. None of this is easy, yet it must be done. Fortunately, it's still early.

As any parent knows, possession is nine-tenths of the three-year-old, and possessive pronouns are as human as opposable thumbs. This is why we'll never be able to avoid expressions of ownership, even when our possessive pronouns apply to things that are not ours, or not even ownable in the literal sense. For example, when we drive a rental car, we still speak of "*my* tires," and "*my* engine." The commercial pilot's senses extend outward through *his* wings and *his* tail, even though the plane belongs to *his* employer. But cars and planes can still be treated as simple property. Data is not so simple, and never will be.

Whether or not data can be "owned" is a conversational tar pit, so let's not go there. Instead, let's look at the gathering, controlling, and managing of data by tools for those purposes. What matters here are means and ends. The means are tools in service of personal agency. The ends are desired effects. That is, what we *intend*. Those effects can't happen unless the data we require, most often called "personal," is available to us, with a *right of action*. (For more on what we mean by that, visit chapter 15.)

"Give me a place to stand, and I will move the world," Archimedes said. Such is leverage. We need that, too. Whether or not we own the places where we stand, and whether or not "my data" is oxymoronic, we still need the freedom and power to do more with personal data than we can now, when too much of it is in the hands of others who don't care, can't make good use of it, or are likely to misuse it.

To illustrate what I mean, here are a couple of stories.

Vectors

On June 1, 2007, I was walking up Massachusetts Avenue from Harvard Square, when I noticed a blue flash on the periphery of vision in my left eye. It showed up whenever I moved my eyes rapidly, or took a bouncing step. This didn't disturb me until I looked at the sky and saw that my left eye had become a snow globe. There were more floaters than I had ever seen before, some in focus (that is, against the retina) and some blurry (farther from the retina). I assumed this development related to the continuing blue flashes and immediately worried that my retina might be detaching.

So I went to the Harvard urgent care facility, where the doctor on duty promptly sent me by taxi to Massachusetts Eye and Ear, where, after much waiting around, the ophthalmologist told me I was witnessing something called posterior vitreous detachment, or PVD. It happens to most of us as we get older. And, while it carries a risk of retinal detachment, that wasn't happening in my case. He told me I shouldn't be worried or alarmed, when the same thing would happen to my right eye. (Which, a few months later, it did.)

When I got home after all this, I looked at the accumulated paperwork: from Harvard University Health Services (HUHS), from the taxi driver, and from Mass. Eye and Ear. All three had spelled my surname wrong, and in three different ways. There were other errors scattered around, including my birth date, my employer, and so on. To my knowledge, nothing in the medical information was wrong, but, not being a doctor, I couldn't be sure.

My experience through the next three years as an HUHS patient was a good one. The care was excellent and, in one case, saved my life. But there were also lots of glitches that had everything to do with poor communication of data (especially between hospitals, radiology labs, and various specialty centers).

That story has a happy ending because I lived, and I'm still doing fine. My mother wasn't so lucky. She died following a stroke that probably would not have happened if two of the medical departments attending her had communicated fully about the medication she required after a surgical error during a routine gallstone-removal procedure. The surgical error was a risk she accepted when she signed the release for the procedure. But the pharmaceutical error was a different matter. Had she been taking the proper anticoagulants, she might not have had the stroke.

Ours is not a litigious family, and at ninety, Mom had lived a long and very full life. But bad data is what killed her, and it's unlikely that big data could have saved her.

What both these cases call for is a combination of holy grails for medical system reformers. EMR (electronic medical records), EHR (electronic health records), and PHR (personal health records) are all intended to reduce errors and guesswork by making medical data easy to share between and among individuals and various health-care providers. All help make the patient what Joe Andrieu calls the *point of integration* for his or her own data, as well as the *point of origination* for what gets done with it: "When we put the user at the center, and make them the point of integration, the entire system becomes simpler, more robust, more scalable, and more useful."[3]

In respect to the story about my eye problem, Joe asked,

> But what if those systems were replaced with a VRM approach? What if instead of individual, isolated IT departments and infrastructure, Doc, the user was the integrating agent in the system? That would not only assure that Doc had control over the propagation of his medical history, it would assure all of the service providers in the loop that, in fact, they had access to all of Doc's medical history. All of his medications. All of his allergies. All of his past surgeries or treatments … All of these things could affect the judgment of the medical professionals charged with his care. And yet, trying to integrate all of those systems from the top down is not only a nightmare, it is a nightmare that apparently continues to fail despite massive federal efforts to re-invent medical care.[4]

EMR, EHR, and PHR are VRM solutions, meaning they match up with the lists of VRM purposes and tools I shared earlier. While my own leverage is on projects that will show results in less time, I want to honor the good continuing work of Adrian Gropper, Brian Behlendorf, Jon Lebkowski, and others in the VRM community working on health-care solutions. Many others like them have been on the VRM-in-health-care case since long before I showed up, and many more will still be working on it after I'm dead. I can't think of a bigger, tougher, or more important challenge, especially in the United States, where health care is an unholy mess.

-Driven versus -Centric

Joe's post, just cited, was highly clarifying for everybody working on VRM tools. But we still had a problem with "user-centric," because the point of view seemed to be anchored outside the user. Exactly who was being user-centric? Was it the user, or some second or third party?

Then, on April 21, 2008, VRM developer Adriana Lukas put up a post titled, "Two tales of user-centricities." She wrote,

> Last year at the IIW in Mountain View, I got talking to Bob Frankston about the difference I started to see between the *user-centric* and *user-driven*. Bob, in his inimitable fashion, used the tuna salad we were having for lunch during the conversation to coin an analogy. A ready-made tuna salad is user-centric—it has been decided what goes into it, in what proportions and what order. It has been designed around me and for me but I cannot add anything to it.
>
> Giving me ingredients, utensils and a recipe suggestion and letting me get on with it, leads to user-driven design—it can still be meant to become a tuna salad but I get to put it together, determine the proportions, skip or add ingredients. The process is driven by me ...
>
> Of course, there are times for user-centric and there are times for user-driven. Not everyone wants to make everything themselves and neither is it the best or most effective way to design all systems or tools. But there are cases when only user-driven will do. And VRM is one of them.[5]

The difference is one of perspective: "-centric" is anchored outside the individual, while "-driven" is anchored inside the individual. The difference is also one of *intent*. Am I doing the intending, or is somebody else intending for me? (I still bristle every time some company puts words in my mouth, saying "my" on my behalf. For example, MySpace was never anybody's space but the site owner's.)

One year later, as we continued to weigh the differences between user-centric and user-driven, Joe put up a series of blog posts on *user driven services*. (He leaves out the hyphen.) In it, he provides fresh guidance to both the customer and vendor sides of the marketplace:

> User Driven Services put users in charge. Users start each interaction, manage the flow of the experience, and control what and how data is captured, used and propagated. Users are the cause and the controller, working with service providers to co-create collaborations that create value for all parties.
>
> From self-serve gas stations and soda fountains to ATMs and self-checkout grocery stores, companies have been putting users in charge of different aspects of their services for years. With GetSatisfaction—which allows users to self-organize for cooperative customer support—and Facebook—which provides social context for user-generated content—users are not just self-servicing, they provide the core content behind the user experience. Now, through user-centric Identity and API access to most popular online services (Flickr, Twitter, Facebook, etc.), users can direct which parts of their experience are serviced by which providers, allowing unprecedented realtime flexibility in service creation.[6]

Joe then rolled out ten blog posts explaining the virtues of user-driven services. They include "Impulse from the User," "Data Portability," "Service Endpoint Portability," User Generativity," and "Self-managed Identity," among others. But the verb impelling them all was *drive*. His encompassing message: customers are not just going to be passengers anymore. They are going to be *drivers*—of themselves and of others helping on the their side of the demand-supply relationship.

Yet, there was still some ambiguity.

In June 2011, in a discussion thread on the VRM list titled, "VRM tool characteristics" (a thread that helped draft the list in chapter 17), Joe noted that ambiguity and wrote, "I expect that the idea that [the]customer is the recipient of value is so inherent to the entire conversation, that we just don't think about it. Like a fish who doesn't know about the water ... but if you think about it, corporate software does NOT have this mandate. Corporate software is there to create value for the corporation. VRM is there to create value for the individual ... There is something vital in the idea of tools that allow the individual to create value for themselves."[7]

Possessive Pronoun Mash-up

Following the exchanges above, Iain Henderson posted, "The Personal Data Ecosystem" at the Kantara Initiative's site.[8] In it, he sorted data into four categories, in four overlapping circles:

1. **My data** (me)—Stuff only I know or should have

2. **Your data** (service providers, governments, retailers)—Stuff they use to remember me, or have gathered about me

3. **Their data** (marketing data providers, credit bureaus, search services)—Stuff they've found out about me, somehow

4. **Everybody's data** (public domain)—Stuff everybody can find out

Iain expects that "over time some 80% of customer management processes will be driven from 'My Data'," and gives two reasons: "(a) because we are already seeing the beginning of the change in the current rush for 'user generated content' ... and (b) because the economics will stack up."[9] Those are the economics both of intent (customers expressing demand directly) and of cost-benefit. "Organizations care less about the sources of data than its usefulness."

It is no coincidence that the U.K. government in 2011 launched the "Midata" initiative.[10] Iain and his colleagues, along with many others in the U.K., had long been pressing the government to take a policy stand recognizing citizens as responsible parties for data collected from (and about) them. In the last national election, all three major political parties favored that position (compared to none in the United States). The winning coalition government followed up with Midata, a voluntary program the government is pursuing with industry to give individuals the ability to download their personal data in a portable electronic format.[11] The aim, says the government, is that individuals "will be able to use this data to gain insights into their own behaviour, make more informed choices about products and services, and manage their lives more efficiently."[12]

In April 2011, the U.K. Cabinet Office Behavioural Insights Team (of the Department for Business, Innovation and Skills) published, "Better Choices, Better Deals: Consumers Powering Growth." It says the office's effort "does not set out a new legislative programme. Nor will it see a range of new regulations laid in Parliament. Rather, it seeks to put in place a wide range of new programmes that have been developed in partnership with businesses, consumer groups and regulators."[13]

I met with three members of the U.K. team in August 2011, and sensed that what they're doing is studiously light-handed. From the same document:

> We will see two profound changes:
>
> - A shift away from a world in which certain businesses tightly control the information they hold about consumers, towards one in which individuals, acting alone or in groups, can use their data or feedback for their own or mutual benefit.
> - A shift away from seeing regulation as what Government-sponsored bodies do after consumers have suffered in some way, towards one in which individuals and groups feel more able to send the right signals to business, and hence secure the products and services they want.
>
> In short, we want to see confident, empowered consumers able to make the right choices for themselves—to get the best deals, demand better products or services, and be able to resolve problems when things go wrong.[14]

Midata is citizen-centric rather than citizen-driven at this stage, but it's looking for more of the latter than the former. More importantly, it states that expectation.

A couple years back, over beer at a pub somewhere in London, Iain explained to me why the U.K. was at the VRM forefront. "A stool needs three legs," he said. "The three in this case are business, the customer, and government. Having the government support both business and the customer is a big advantage."

U.K. members of the VRM community, including Iain, William Heath, and Alan Mitchell, have been on the case from the start. In November 2011, Alan told me "becoming VRM-ready" has been central to their argument to business. For the rest of the argument, he gave this list:

- Improved data accuracy and quality

- Reduced guesswork and waste

- New insights into customer needs and behaviors

- The chance to innovate new services

And it appears to be working. As of that same month, Callcredit (which keeps files on every adult in the U.K.), Scottish Power, and the Royal Bank of Scotland have all publicly lined up behind Midata.[15]

Personal Data Stores/Lockers/Vaults/Clouds

As of this writing, Mydex (the company Iain, Alan, and William cofounded), Azigo, Personal.com, Privowny, Qiy, and Singly are all working on PDSes (Personal Data Stores), also known variously as personal data lockers, vaults, and clouds. All are *points of integration* for one's personal data. All are described in different ways, which will change by the time you read this. Behind some of these are noncommercial and open source development projects, including the Locker Project, KRL, Pegasus, Project Danube, Tele-Hash, and WebFinger. Many open standards are also involved, including RSS, Atom, Activity Streams, JSon, evented APIs, and others.

Here is how Jeremie Miller put the challenge in a speech to the Web 2.0 Summit in November 2011:

> You need to have a home for your data. I'm trying aggressively to define this home, in … the best software, the best technology, the best legal terms. This home is *yours*—that *you* own, that *you* control. And this home is for *your* data.
>
> This ability for *you* to have it and share it out, is going to transform our industry, over the next ten years. There is going to be this tectonic shift, as everything sort of re-shapes and re-centers itself around people, around individuals, and around the mountains of data that they have … Everybody talks about "big data." This isn't big data. This is going to be the era of *small data*, of *my* data.[16]

Let that era begin.

SO, THEN

However this plays out, the end result is that the "small data" that's yours will be more important than the "big data" behind marketing's guesswork. The two in the long run will dance together. But for now the small data side needs to get its act together. And it will.

22

APIs

Baking an organization's core competence into API is an
economic imperative.

—Craig Burton[1]

THE ARGUMENT

Customer intentions need contexts, and ways to interact with
vendors in real time. Thus, to operate in the urban environs of
the World Live Web, every company needs to manifest what it
does in ways that can be engaged and put to use. That's what
APIs will do.

In the early 1980s, when computers on desktops began to replace the "dumb
terminals" of corporate computing systems, "local area networks"—better
known as LANs—were required. Competition was fierce between different
LAN data protocols (Ethernet vs. Token Ring), wiring topologies (bus vs.
ring vs. star), cabling (thick and thin twisted pair, coaxial, twin-axial, and
other types), and so on. Every issue of *Data Communications* and *Communications Week* was thick with ads and coverage of the competition between
companies such as Corvus, Sytek, Wang, IBM, 3Com, and Digital, all of
which sold vertical "solutions" to a problem that all of them compounded
through incompatibility with other companies' "solutions" at every level.

Then, almost overnight, Novell obviated the problem with NetWare,
a "network operating system," or NOS, which provided what companies

wanted from a LAN: a platform for *services*, starting with two that companies cared about most. Those were *file* and *print*: ways to store files and print things out on a network. NetWare didn't care what kind of protocol, wiring topology, or cabling a company used. It embraced all of them.

NetWare was a big hit, and by the late '80s the LAN conversation changed from one about "pipes and protocols" to one about services.

This conversational shift—from the vexing complexities of competing gear and technologies to the straightforward benefits of a network that functioned so well that everybody could take it for granted—continued with the later adoption of the Internet and the services we take for granted today: hypertext (the Web), email, instant messaging, syndication of postings, and so on.

Novell's jujitsu-like move on the LAN business was no accident. It was a deliberate strategy led by Craig Burton. (I met Craig in 1986, when Novell bought one of the clients of Hodskins Simone & Searls, the advertising agency where I was a partner. He has been a great friend and mentor ever since.)

I bring in the story of Craig and Novell because in 2011 Craig began telling me about a similar shift now taking place—one he expects to serve as groundwork for the intention economy. That shift begins, almost literally, with turning companies inside out.

High Risings

In the Hyperlinks Subvert Hierarchies chapter of *The Cluetrain Manifesto*, David Weinberger writes,

> Somewhere along the line, we confused going to work with building a fort.
>
> Strip away the financial jibber-jabber and the management corpospeak, and here's our fundamental image of business:
>
> - It's in an imposing office building that towers over the landscape.
>
> - Inside is everything we need.
>
> - And that's good because the outside is dangerous. We are under siege by our competitors, and even by our partners and customers. Thank God for the thick, high walls!
>
> - The king rules. If we have a wise king, we prosper.

- The king has a court. The dukes, viscounts, and other luminaries each receive their authority from the king. (The king even countenances an official fool. Within limits.)

- We each have our role, our place. If we each do the job assigned to us by the king's minions, our fort will beat all those other stinking forts.

- And then we will have succeeded—or, thinking it's the same thing, we will say we have "won." We get to dance a stupid jig while chanting "Number one! Number one!"

- This fort is, at its heart, a place apart. We report there every morning and spend the next eight, ten, or twelve hours inaccessible to the "real" world. The portcullis drops not only to keep out our enemies, but to separate us from distractions such as our families. As the drawbridge goes up behind us, we become businesspeople, different enough from our normal selves that when we first bring our children to the office, they've been known to hide under our desk, crying.

He adds, "the true opposite of a fort isn't an unwalled city. It's a conversation."[2]

Yet in the years since *Cluetrain* came out, conversation was something marketing talked about more than something whole companies actually did. This is about to change, thanks to APIs.

"Fort business won't go away," Craig tells me. "The corporate high-rises will still be there. On the Web, however, they will be turned inside out, so that a company's core competencies will be exposed to the world—in ways that can be engaged directly. The means for engagement are APIs. Companies with exposed APIs are the new skyline of the Web."[3]

API stands for application programming interface. Think of APIs as user interfaces for code. Most APIs on the Web today produce live feeds of data on request by other sites and services. Take, for example, the Google, Bing, and Yahoo maps that appear on a Web site or a smartphone app. When you search for a restaurant on Yelp and it shows you a Google map, Yelp has obtained that map through a request to the Google API, which responded with the required map. This is why Google, Bing and Yahoo are already big on the Web's skyline.

APIs such as these, however, are not yet fully evolved in the direction that Craig sees as the Live Web end-state. They are teats on the cows of dominant Web services, providing milk for the calves of dependent ones. (See chapter 3 for more on the calf-cow model.) Turn those cows upside down and make a skyline of their teats, and the two metaphors make a fun kind of sense together. But even upside-down, this API convention is still hierarchical, still calf-cow. That's a problem, because hierarchies are trees that don't grow to the sky.

The Network City

Commenting on the city model, Kynetx founder and CTO Phil Windley writes:

> I think there's more than a mere metaphor between the city/corporation insights and the ways we build software today. I'd argue that social systems, including cities, are models for the techniques and technologies we ought to be using. Networked systems scale better and are more flexible than hierarchical systems. They can absorb complexity better without suffering from the debilitating effects of tight coupling that hierarchical systems create. But I'm ready to go farther …
>
> While API-based systems are more flexible than the moribund systems that enterprise IT shops create, they don't go far enough. They are still request-response based. Request-response based systems are hierarchical and create unnecessary coupling. Cities and other social systems do not operate solely using a request-response model. The dual of request-response is *events*. Event-driven systems exhibit more of the network architecture that makes cities flexible and robust.[4]

So Phil and his team at Kynetx created the first spec for *evented APIs*. Evented APIs are not request-response, which is half-duplex (only one way at a time, taking turns), but conversational, and full-duplex (both ways at once, like a phone call). That way they can interactively listen, carry out orders, and obey rules that *you* write, or that you have written for you—say, by your fourth party.

Phil has made this easy with a language called KRL (kynetx rules language), and a *rules engine* for executing the rules. Both are open source. Together, they help create the Live Web (also the title of Phil's new book).

As Phil puts it, "KRL allows you to treat every API, and every app on your computer or phone, as social products and services that work with you and for you in the urban environment of the Live Web." For the first time, "social" is something *you* do, outside of any one company's silo. No one company, including Phil's, owns or controls your social context in any way. Whatever you want can be social with whatever else you want.

"This is like what has been called the Internet of Things," Phil says, "only more personal—in fact intensely personal. Your personal event network forms your own personal cloud where apps under your control interact with your personal data, services you use, and products you own, to accomplish the things that are important to you, freeing you from the tedious and mundane interactions that are still business-as-usual on the Static Web."[5]

When I asked Phil to draw his own personal cloud, he e-mailed it to me (see figure 22-1).

On the outside of the figure:

- **Things,** including bathroom scale, thermostat, fridge, sprinkler system, car, GPS, TiVo, and exercise gear[6]

- **Company APIs,** including a calendar, a travel service, company CRM system, and credit card company

On the inside are *apps* that can interact with all the APIs on the outside.

FIGURE 22-1

Phil's personal cloud

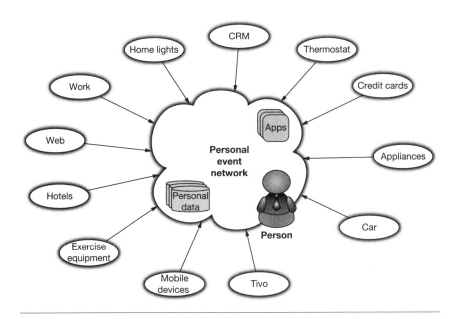

There are no limits to the variety of what goes inside or outside. You're the boss. Put whatever you want inside and interact with whatever you want on the outside. If neither is ready for you yet, don't worry. It will be. The upsides to participation far exceed the downside risks of exposure or whatever else companies making APIs or apps might worry about.

In Any Event

KRL lets you mash up contexts from any variety of relationships you already have. It also lets you create new ones. Let's look at what it can do, starting with the simple and working up to the complex.

A trivial but fun example is what I'm looking at right now on Twitter (see figure 22-2).

See those little numbers next to the handles of @jeffsonstein, @matclayton, and @stevegarfield? Twitter didn't put those there. Nor did PeerIndex, which supplied the numbers (which it calls a "relative measure of your online authority"). *I* put them there, using a free browser plug-in from Kynetx called HoverMe. That plug-in calls out to the PeerIndex API, obtains the little numbers, and puts them next to each tweeter's @-handle.

For even a casual programmer, writing plug-ins like HoverMe using KRL is easy. So are writing other programs to do just about anything, mostly by taking advantage of exposed competencies, not just of businesses and organizations, but of each individual.

That's why we'll have our own live and evented APIs as well. Markets will be conversations, not just for us, but for every device, app, and service we use. We will have our own ways of exposing our own core competencies, and we will be in full control of them.

FIGURE 22-2

KRL relationships

jeffsonstein `47` Jeff Sonstein
[ROFL] RT @matclayton `24` : To the police surveillance van outside our flat, renaming your wifi would make you stealthier pic.twitter.com/1GZbuLqO
54 seconds ago

stevegarfield `63` Steve Garfield
Just posted a photo @ Arnold Arboretum instagr.am/p/QOcF2/
1 minute ago

Now for our next hack: adding local Best Buy results to Amazon searches on the Web. Here's how the logic works:

1. *If* the item I've found at Amazon is also available at Best Buy,

2. *And* the item is in stock at the nearest Best Buy,

3. *Then* I see the price for the item at my nearest Best Buy, along with other helpful information, such as how far away that Best Buy is.

I have that hack, done with KRL, in my Chrome browser, right now. Here's a key thing: *neither Amazon nor Best Buy is involved*. I'm the one doing the shopping, and I'm the one with the rules that make Best Buy results appear in my Amazon search. The hack was done in KRL in just a few minutes, and it has been handy for me ever since.

Now for the complex scenario, involving a salesman we'll call Bob, who works for a company we'll call BigCo. Bob lives in Denver and is going on an overnight business trip to see a client in San Francisco.

Bob's personal cloud (like Phil's) has these apps on the inside:

- TripEase (which doesn't exist yet, but something like it will)

- Calendar

- Expensify

- OpenTable

- TomTom

- Quickbooks

- Singly

The APIs on the outside are the exposed competencies of:

- Marriott

- United Airlines

- Avis

- Visa

- Salesforce

We start as Bob confirms an onsite visit with his San Francisco client. When Bob schedules the meeting in his calendar, an appointment event is sent to his personal cloud. Evented applications and services Bob uses are listening for these events and respond by taking action on Bob's behalf. In this case, Salesforce fills out appointment details in his calendar, such as Bob's client's office location and directions for parking nearby.

Meanwhile, rules in Bob's TripEase app react to the same event, recognize the appointment is in San Francisco and that Bob will need travel arranged. TripEase knows Bob's travel preferences (e.g., a single room at a Marriott hotel, a compact car from Avis, an aisle seat on United, and a request to United for an upgrade to business class if a seat is available) and marks available choices from each on his calendar. TripEase also knows that Bob has memberships in loyalty programs with each of those companies and also with other companies, in case Bob's first-choice preferences aren't available. Bob sees the choices, makes them, and TripEase puts those in the Calendar.

In the background, TripEase also raises a new business trip event, causing Expensify to bring up an expense journal, so an accounting of expenses can be made at the end of the trip. So, when Bob gets to the airport and buys a sandwich with his Visa card, Expensify automatically adds that purchase to this trip's expense journal. And, because Expensify and TripEase are cooperating, Expensify has more context for purchases and can make better categorization decisions without Bob's involvement.

After landing in San Francisco, Bob turns on his smartphone, and its location function raises an event indicating Bob is now at SFO. Avis hears and responds to Bob's location event by preparing Bob's preferred car and paperwork. To help with that, TripEase also lets Avis know that Bob will decline Avis's insurance offer and return the car with a full tank of gas. If Avis does not already have this information, TripEase fills Avis in on the facts, and auto-signs Avis's agreement, so Bob doesn't have to bother with that. TripEase also puts Bob's appointment destination in the TomTom app on Bob's smartphone. After meeting with his client, Bob drives to the Marriott and parks there. When he arrives at the reception desk, he is greeted by name and given his preferred room (on the north side of a high floor) and a key to his room and the exercise facility. He also receives a notification from Open Table that two of his favorite restaurants have reservations available. He decides on one and proceeds to his room. Open Table also sends an e-mail and a text to his client with reservation information.

All these connections are made in the background, on Bob's behalf, by apps and services that he or his fourth party have already programmed, using KRL.

After checking out of the hotel (automatically, of course), driving his car back to Avis at SFO, flying back to Denver, and driving back to his house, TomTom tells TripEase that Bob has completed the trip and raises an end-of-trip event. Expensify sees the event and moves Bob's journaled expenses—air fare, hotel, rental car, gas purchases, dinner, personal driving mileage (to and from the airport), and parking fees—from his trip journal to his expense report. After reviewing and approving the report, Bob tells Expensify to send it to BigCo's Salesforce system, which is in the cloud Salesforce keeps for BigCo.

Expensify has also sent copies of expenses to Bob's own personal cloud, which comprises these:

1. His personal data store (PDS), which is where he keeps his personal data, fed from many sources, including all the apps and services mentioned. While Bob could keep his PDS on a self-hosted server, his preference is to use Singly, a fourth-party he pays to keep his data and relationships sorted out, secure, and up to date. Singly also has a rules engine he can use, but he isn't limited to that one alone.

2. His personal API. This can live anywhere, but would most likely live with his PDS.

3. His rules, written in KRL.

4. His memorandum book.

5. His journal and ledger, kept by QuickBooks.

His memorandum book is the modern version of what for centuries was the first step in double-entry bookkeeping: the place where everything that happens is first written down. This helps Bob (and his tax preparer) remember what happened when, as well as what it cost.[7] From there, it goes to his journal and then to his ledger, which can generate the usual reports. Meanwhile, he has an accountable and auditable trail of records.

To be fair to everybody else in this future game, KRL won't be the only way to do what I just described. It's just the one I know best today, because Phil and his colleagues at Kynetx have been highly involved in the VRM tool development community. So have some of the other companies I've mentioned.

The Troika

Craig Burton knows ubiquity. I watched him make it happen with Novell in the 1980s, and I've watched him teach how it works, over and over again.

He points out that by late 2011, there were a few thousand APIs in existence: a town, not a city. Still, there is a hockey-stick shape to the growth curve. This will continue upward until it flattens at ubiquity, which will be the sum of everything that can have an evented API, including every individual with a mobile device. Says Craig,

> There are three core things that make the Intention Economy start to work, and grow toward ubiquity. Call it a troika. They are:
>
> 1. Cloud-based code (code platforms like Kynetx that are API- and cloud-centric).
>
> 2. Cheap telephony-data (affordable mobile-telephony data pricing like Ting.com provides).
>
> 3. Personal data technology (cloud-based stores that are controlled by the individual. Singly is promising such a thing, Cloudmine.me has one up in beta).[8]

That's for both companies and customers. For companies specifically, he adds, "Get with it. Figure out your API strategy. Understand the API Economy Troika and how it relates to what you are doing." And, be a *ubiquitineur*, which he defines as, "An entrepreneur whose business and innovation practices are ubiquity-based as opposed to scarcity-based."[9]

In other words, build in the Live Web and not just the static one.

SO, THEN

Means for building the Live Web exist in the world today. They will provide evented interactions between everything and everybody, and demand for them will grow as the benefits to customers, vendors, and other involved parties become obvious.

And, even though neither humans nor companies have yet proven they can live as long and as well as cities (see chapter 10), they can use API-based tools to get onboard the superlinear train of city-like growth.

23

EmanciPaytion

Only free men can negotiate; prisoners cannot enter into contracts. Your freedom and mine cannot be separated.

—Nelson Mandela[1]

The most important single central fact about a free market is that no exchange takes place unless both parties benefit.

—Milton Friedman[2]

THE ARGUMENT

The market will have many more dances when customers can take the lead.

Somewhere in the vast oeuvre of John Updike, I stumbled across this line: "We live in the age of full convenience." It stuck my mind because it seemed perfect, yet had never been perfectly true—and never will be. In life, we often want more than we can get, and the delta between the two contains opportunity.

For example, sometimes when I give a talk here in the United States, I ask the audience a question: "How many people here listen to public radio?" Nearly all hands go up. Then I ask, "How many of you pay for it?" Around 10 percent of the hands stay up. (That's a typical listener/customer ratio for public radio.[3]) Then I ask, "How many of you would pay if doing that was *real easy*?" Many more hands go up, usually about double the last number.

Then, "How many of you would give if you didn't have to wait through the stations' fund-raising breaks?" More hands go up.

These hand raisings signal MLOTT (pronounced "m-lot"): money left on the table.

Clearly, there is more willingness to pay for public radio than there are means for doing so. This is surely the case for many other things as well. For example, I would love to be able to rent camera lenses that I can pick up when I arrive at an airport and then drop off when I pass back through. I've often wished for a business that provides a courier service to arriving business travelers, supplying projectors for laptops or forgotten laptop power adapters. When traveling, I also often find myself wanting to rent a specific car (say, one that seats seven, comes with a bike rack, and has satellite radio)—rather than the "or similar" that rental agencies happen to have on the lot at the time.

But, even though I'm usually willing to pay more for exactly what I want, that's not how The System has been working in the age of adhesionism, and I have almost no direct input to that system other than to reinforce it by renting only what it offers me.

The problem in a general way is that means of engagement are constrained by systems on the sellers' side that are rigged to ignore signals from buyers other than those that point to the standard list of offerings. Limited offerings are easy to rationalize, but the fact remains that there are many more signals that demand can send than it is able to now, or that supply is ready to hear. This fact suggests opportunity on both sides.

Public Advantage

Public radio has been begging for money since before the term *public radio* existed. Pacifica stations, starting in 1949 with flagship KPFA in Berkeley, California, called themselves "listener sponsored"—a term they still use. Noncommercial radio became "public" with the creation of National Public Radio (now just NPR) in 1970. More recently, the industry has been calling its category "Public Media," to include not only public radio and TV, but podcasts, streaming over the Net, on-demand "content," and many other kinds of stuff as well.

When ProjectVRM began, I thought public media (radio especially) might provide an ideal test bed for new VRM developments, especially around payment systems. Stations always need money, yet their systems for receiving it have always been limited by norms and practices that fall far short of what might be possible if listeners had more ways to give. Basically, stations make appeals for contributions on the air and on their Web sites and podcasts—then every few months, they hold fund-raising breaks when they turn off or interrupt programs to cajole listeners into making donations. This is what gets about 10 percent of listeners to help out. I figured we could easily raise that number just by improving means for giving on the listeners' side.

One attraction was that public radio didn't have many of the complications endemic to commercial retailing: no SKUs, no shipping, no pricing, no inventory management, no special hours. It had its own ways of taking in money, but there was nothing about them that precluded getting money in other new ways.

ProjectVRM also had connections through the Berkman Center. PRX (Public Radio Exchange), a public radio developer and producer like NPR, was located in Cambridge, Massachusetts, and led by Jake Shapiro, who had also held a number of Berkman positions over the years. Our first ProjectVRM meeting at Berkman was on funding for public radio, which quickly made us a number of friends. Two of those, Keith Hopper of Public Interactive (now part of NPR) and Robin Lubbock of WBUR, were both very supportive. Keith became especially involved, as we'll see shortly.

On the minus side, public radio had (and still has) a bad case of channel conflict. On the whole, listeners care more about programs than stations, and many of those programs are available directly by podcast, as well as over many different stations. Yet public radio is built for two-tier distribution. NPR and PRX sell programs to stations, which in turn sell them to the audience, which pays on a voluntary basis. If you like one program in particular, paying directly isn't usually an option.[4] You have to pay a station. This can cause problems. For example, take this blog post by Dave Winer on February 12, 2007:

WNYC spam

9 times out of 10, I don't give money to public radio stations, because once you do, you never hear the end of it.

A few weeks ago, in response to a request for support from On The Media podcast, I gave $100 to WNYC. I don't even live in NY. Now I'm getting a steady stream of spam from them with all kinds of special offers. This really sucks.

Of course I have asked to be removed from the spam list, and how tacky is it to ask for a pledge less than a month after getting a gift of $100.[5]

To its credit, WNYC has listened to people like Dave and has done its best to adjust its fund-raising systems. (Bill Swersey, director, Digital Media, for WNYC at the time, participated in early meetings and conversations with ProjectVRM.) But WNYC, along with the rest of public radio, is still on the cow side of the commercial Web's calf-cow system. In fact, so is every organization that takes voluntary payments for goods that cost nothing for individuals to obtain.

Music is similar in the sense that you can get it for nothing, while some people are willing to pay something. A few well-known artists have taken advantage of this fact by selectively giving away some of their work. (Radiohead and Nine Inch Nails, for example.) Still, while the music industry's business model is different than public radio's, both have plenty of MLOTT.

Looking at public radio and the music business, I thought, "Hey, how about making it easy for anybody to pay (or at least offer) whatever they want for anything? For example, how about making it possible both to signal interest in paying, and to escrow the payment itself, or a pledge to pay?" ProjectVRM's answer was EmanciPay.

EmanciPay

EmanciPay is a choosing system, rather than a payment system. Here are the kinds of things you might want to choose:

1. How much to pay

2. Where the seller can pick the payment up

3. Whether this is a pledge or a payment

4. What data to pass along with the payment

5. Terms of use for personal data

Our first target market for EmanciPay was (and still is) public radio. Let's look at two use cases I'll call *impulsive* and *considered*.

In the *impulsive* case, you hear an especially good *On The Media* show and decide you want to throw a couple of bucks at the program. You don't care that it comes from WNYC. You just like Brooke Gladstone and Bob Garfield, and feel like giving them something for a job well done. On your listening app, you bring up an interface that lets you select an amount, and you send it—but not straight to them. You have a payment service (say, a bank) that escrows the payment, waiting for WNYC to pick it up. You don't have to become a member of WNYC, or you can express a willingness to do that, through choices four and five in the EmanciPay system. Either way, you're in control. You're not inside the systems of the radio app or of WNYC. You're in your own system, which signals your intentions to the station.

In the *considered* case, you log all your listening and decide how much to pay (or pledge) to whom, based on what you've logged. Toward that end, Keith Hopper came up with *ListenLog*, which ProjectVRM built into a program that is now implemented in the Public Radio Player, an iPhone app from PRX. ListenLog tells what stations and programs I've been listening to, and for how long. In economic terms, it tells me what I value.

I can go a number of ways with ListenLog and the data it gathers:

- Decide how much to pay per minute or hour of listening, either up front or after totaling up findings.

- Decide what to pay to stations, programs, or other parties.

- Connect payment directly to listening.

- Share with others.

As I'm writing this, ListenLog is a prototype, a proof of concept. You should be able to take the code (it's open source) and add, modify, or substitute what you like. For example, you might like to build in choices about payment rates for different kinds of uses. You might want to make it automatic, but with controls that are *yours*, rather than anybody else's. Or you might tweak it to follow activities other than listening to media.

Now let's go back to music. At this moment in time—at my house and possibly in yours as well—much of the world's music listening takes place inside Apple's iTunes, which logs a play count. In my own case, Weird Al Yankovic's "Couch Potato" takes the lead with 104 plays, all by our son and his friends, back when they were about ten years old. Next is "Lay Lady Lay" by Bob Dylan, with sixty-eight plays. (I'm amazed that I've played it that much, but it's possible I have.) Apple doesn't provide a way for me to send more money to either of those guys (based on play count, or any other metric). Nor does it provide a way for me to send money to other artists I especially like or consider deserving of additional compensation. (One example is Mike Cross, a favorite of mine from my two decades as a North Carolinian).

I don't want to wait for Apple to work something out with Sound-Exchange and other performance rights collection agencies, or with the artists themselves.[6] I'd rather just keep track, put the money out there by some means, and tell the artists and agencies to come get it when they're ready.

Toward that goal, I joined a group of people, several of whom were active with ProjectVRM, working with the Society for Worldwide Inter-bank Financial Telecommunication (better known as SWIFT), on new EmanciPay business model prototypes for banks and other financial institutions. Whether or not those prototypes pan out, we (in the largest sense) will standardize methods for making payment choices, escrowing money, recording pledges, notifying intended recipients that money awaits, and making the whole system secure. But for now, we just want to get the ball rolling.

ProjectVRM's purpose with EmanciPay from the start has been to scaffold voluntary and genuine—rather than coerced—relationships between buyers and sellers in the marketplace. We want to give deeper meaning, for instance, to "membership" in nonprofits. (Under the current system, "membership" mostly means putting one's name on a pitch list for future contributions.) We want to make the market truly free by giving any customer means for taking the lead, as well as for following. That lead includes signaling sums of value and extending hands with good intentions toward genuine relationships.

EmanciTerm

Three things happen in a marketplace: *transaction, conversation,* and *relationship*.[7] In our industrialized world, *transaction* is the biggest thing (see figure 23-1).

FIGURE 23-1

Mass marketplace events

Relationship

Conversation

Transaction

In the emerging world, where natural markets still thrive and serve as examples, the ratios are reversed (see figure 23-2).[8]

FIGURE 23-2

Networked marketplace events

Relationship

Conversation

Transaction

In the mass marketplace, relationship wasn't just subordinated to transaction. It is demeaned. We actually think, for example, that a mass-market vendor can (and should) control all the means by which relationships with customers should proceed. Still, as human beings, all of us also know we are capable of relating in our own ways and on our own terms, with anybody or anything. We also know our motivations are not all reducible to price. Many things are priceless, even in the marketplace. For example, relationships.

The commercial online world is very young. Born in 1995, it is still in high school. (Or, in the words of Frank Stasio, host of WUNC's "The State of Things," "It's not old enough to download its own porn."[9]) In the brick-and-mortar world, we have highly developed understandings of identity, privacy, friendship, and correct ways of interacting with strangers and familiar folk. There is enormous room for personal and cultural differences within these, and for improvisation.

We have nothing like that yet in the networked marketplace. "Friending" and "following" on Facebook and Twitter are barely at the stone-tool stage of what will become of civilized social interaction online. Both those activities also only work on those companies' ranches. So, even if we become adept at using Facebook and Twitter, neither makes us adept as free agents in the vast marketplace outside Facebook and Twitter's corporate reaches.

To work in the wild frontier of the networked commons, we are going to need instruments for *relating* as independent agents, and not just for *transacting* and *conversing*.

That's the idea behind *EmanciTerm*. You offer your terms (including the legal ones listed in chapter 20). The seller makes its offer. It agrees or doesn't, and you work out the differences, if you can.

This kind of thing is not complicated in the everyday world. First, we have very clear agreements already, both tacit and explicit, about what is private and what's not, and about how and why we trust certain other people and institutions with private information about us. How we relate to our medical doctor, our financial adviser, our teacher, our student, our yoga instructor, our old friend, or the cop on the corner—all differ. And yet none of those require clicking "accept" to a pile of terms before we proceed.

We are years away from bringing this same level of casual ease to the online world. But those years will be decades if we don't provide ways for individuals to make clear their *intentions* in the marketplace—especially for how we wish to be respected by entities we don't yet know (or already know but don't yet trust or barely understand).

Ascribenation

Over lunch several years ago, Bill Buzenberg, executive director of the Center for Public Integrity (CPI), told me how hard it is for CPI to get credit for the good work it does. It would do deep digging on one subject or another, produce a comprehensive report, and then watch as news organizations told the story while minimally crediting CPI as a source or not mentioning it at all.

Thinking about what Bill wanted here, I came up with the term *ascribenation*, which I chose in part because it wasn't used by anybody yet and had no domain names using it at that time. In an April 2009 blog post, I defined ascribenation as "the ability to ascribe credit to sources—and to pay them as well."[10]

In July 2009, the Associated Press, noting the same problem, issued a press release with this lead paragraph:

> NEW YORK—The Associated Press Board of Directors today
> directed The Associated Press to create a news registry that will tag
> and track all AP content online to assure compliance with terms of
> use. The system will register key identifying information about each
> piece of content that AP distributes as well as the terms of use of that
> content, and employ a built-in beacon to notify AP about how the
> content is used.[11]

That turned into a proposed standard called Rnews.[12] Another nascent standard called hNews[13] also showed up. Both support ascribenation, though they don't call it that (at least not yet). For VRM purposes, however, being able to say who you might want to single out for payment through EmanciPay is an interesting challenge as well.

Micro-accounting

When we talk about EmanciPay and ascribenation, the conversation almost always comes around to micropayments, and what's wrong with them. So, to be clear, what we're talking about here isn't micropayments, but micro-*accounting*.

Accounting of small change has been around for a long time on the vendors' side. Your phone company has being doing it forever. (Making nickel-and-dime into a verb.) It has also been happening with music on radio for most of a century and on Internet music streams since the turn of the millennium.

For example, the Copyright Arbitration Royalty Panel (CARP), and later the Copyright Royalty Board (CRB), both came up with "rates and terms that would have been negotiated in the marketplace between a willing buyer and a willing seller."[14] This language first appeared in the 1995 Digital Performance Royalty Act (DPRA), and was updated in 1998 by the Digital Millennium Copyright Act (DMCA).[15] The rates they came up with have values such as $.0001 per "performance" (a song or recording), per listener, and have changed too many times over the years to bother citing.

Here's the deal: *EmanciPay creates the "willing buyer" that the DPRA thought the Net would not allow.* It also can help the music industry do something it has failed to do from the beginning: stigmatize nonpayment for worthwhile media goods in a nonhostile and noncoercive way.

Micro-accounting, such as we have with ListenLog, can add up to many different ways for creators to be compensated for their work, by the market. That is, *by customers.* An individual listener, for example, can say, in effect, "I want to pay $.01 for every song I hear on the radio," and "I'll send Sound-Exchange a lump sum of all the pennies for all the songs I hear over the course of a year (or any other time period), along with an accounting of what artists and songs I've listened to"—and make dispersal of those pennies SoundExchange's problem—or opportunity. (One it should like to have).

We can do the same thing for reading newspapers, blogs, and other journals. Heck, even for tweets, if Twitter is willing to risk a nonadvertising business model.

While all this might look complicated and labor-intensive for customers, it doesn't have to be, once automated processes are set up, and much more activity becomes accountable.

Accountability is key. Everybody, including customers, should be able to record and audit whatever they do in the marketplace, as well as in the rest of their lives.

On the customers' side, this is already happening through countless apps that track weight, exercise, spending, and other variables. Kevin Kelly, Gary Wolf, and friends have been on this case for years with their Quantified Self work. Adriana Lukas (a stalwart in the VRM community) and friends have been doing related work under the "self-hacking" label.

On the vendors' side, a number of us (myself included) have been working with SWIFT (the Society for Worldwide Interbank Financial Telecommunication) on creating new business models for financial institutions based on EmanciPay, EmanciTerm, trust frameworks, and other VRM ideas. The first of those is a piece of infrastructure called the Digital Asset Grid, or DAG, described as a "certified pointer system pointing at the location of digital assets and the associated usage rights," by SWIFT Innovation Leader Peter Vander Auwera.[16]

The vectors on both the demand and the supply side point toward a relationship that obsoletes old-fashioned marketing cruft (see chapter 8) and "confusopolies" (see chapter 14).

The difference between cruft and relationship is between what Umair Haque calls "thin value" and "thick value." In *The New Capitalist Manifesto* he defines "thin value" as *"artificial,* often gained through harm, or at expense to people, communities, or society."[17] By contrast, "thick value" is "sustainable" and "meaningful."[18] You can't get that by shooting messages at the feet of customers and saying "dance." You get that by learning how to follow as well as to lead.

SO, THEN

The pioneers of the emerging marketplace for customer-driven intention are prototypes such as EmanciPay, EmanciTerm, ListenLog, and trust frameworks. The settlers will be companies and development projects new and old. The civilization they develop will be built on real relationships, with thick value, rather than the thin value from which they need to escape.

24

VRM + CRM

The real and effectual discipline which is exercised over a workman is that of his customers. It is the fear of losing their employment which restrains his frauds and corrects his negligence.

—Adam Smith[1]

Let me not to the marriage of true minds admit impediments.

—William Shakespeare[2]

THE ARGUMENT

We need to manage our relationships. Not each other.

In a narrow sense, VRM is the customer-side counterpart of CRM (customer relationship management). Just as CRM is how one company relates to many customers, VRM is how one customer relates to many vendors.

In the past, CRM systems were containers within which all relating between customers and vendors took place. With VRM, however, both sides can hold up their own ends of the relationship burden, so relating can take place *between* the two rather than *within* the vendor's system alone.

As I reviewed earlier (in chapter 20), agreements between parties form laws unto themselves. A relationship, however, is its own entity. Such is the case with a marriage, a treaty, a partnership, a corporation. (My own marriage is symbolized literally: "the couple decides" is inscribed inside our wedding rings.) CRM was developed in a time when customers had little to bring to a relationship other than complete submission to whatever system the vendor provided. While a relationship of sorts existed, it was within the vendor's space. The customer was a manorial subject.

Now the customer is in a position to be self-reliant and fully engaging. What can he or she bring now to the market's table, and how will it engage with CRM systems, both as they stand today and as they evolve through interaction with customers' VRM tools and systems?

In chapter 5, we visited Iain Henderson's three-column list (table 5-1) of what happens in a relationship between a customer and a vendor over time. It showed how guesswork and waste flanked thin and dysfunctional interactions that were relationships in name only. Iain's approach to eliminating guesswork and waste is something he calls the customer-supplier engagement framework, or CSEF. It is based on many years of assessing CRM effectiveness using the CMAT model. (CMAT stands for customer management assessment tool and is defined—by many companies, all with the same wording—as "a range of tools and methodologies that provide a detailed, objective, benchmarked assessment of an organisation's capability to effectively manage its customers."[3])

Explains Iain,

> The CRM side is fully kitted up with the tools of their trade … data warehouses, web sites, CRM systems, and an army of people paid to do the work. The other (the buying side), has nothing more than some self-assembled, amateur tools … and their brains. They don't get paid to do it, and they typically don't have a lot of time set aside for the process … That imbalance between the 'haves' and the 'have nots,' as in any walk of life, leads the 'haves' to take advantage, and the 'have nots' to rebel against this in whatever way they can. Or (more often) they just don't engage as they might in a more balanced and equitable relationship.[4]

Getting that balance, Iain believes, requires moving some current CRM functions over to VRM—and to the relationship space where both sides interact. All of the following, for example, could go over to VRM or to the relationship space:

- Address and other contact details

- Location descriptors

- Lifestyle and stage

- Behaviors

- Preferences

- Existing relationships with various companies

- Intentions

Now look at the list of all the things Rapleaf got wrong about me, back in chapter 7. If I were in control of all the things Iain lists, plus other interesting variables (for example, the sum of all my miles with all the airlines I use—and what I like and don't like about each of those airlines), and if I shared that information in a trustable way, Rapleaf wouldn't need to do so much guesswork. Nor would Rapleaf's corporate customers.

Hope

Many people in the CRM world have come out to embrace VRM. *CRM Magazine* devoted its cover and much of its May 2010 issue to VRM, with a cover that read, in giant type, "I am not an eyeball." Its lead essay begins, "The victory, of course, belongs to the customer—who has always 'owned' her relationship with you, no matter what the letters of CRM might imply."[5] A story inside by Lauren McKay is titled, "It's Not Your Relationship to Manage," with a subtitle that adds, "Just as you finally come to grips with CRM, the customers themselves have turned the tables—and now they're managing you."

That sounds threatening, and in some ways, it has to be. CRM relationships today are defined and controlled by a single party, and cannot be extended to the customer side without vendors giving up some of that control, for the good of both parties.

UI

VRM tools will not be used only in connection with CRM systems, but the reciprocities of VRM + CRM require discussion of UI: user interfaces. Especially for individuals on the VRM side.

UI is everything, of course. It's what makes something not only useful and usable, but actually *used*. There isn't a graveyard big enough for all the great ideas and great products that failed to invite use, simply because they lacked a good UI.

The closest we have so far is a simple symbol: the r-button. It's actually a pair of buttons, one for you (VRM) and one for the other party (CRM). They look like two little magnets, facing each other: ⊂⊃. They can be a solid color or gray, indicating active or passive states, or the presence or absence of possible actions if you click on one. The first ones we worked with in the VRM development community were red, because that was the color of the marker I used when I first drew a pair of r-buttons on a whiteboard. I wasn't meaning to create a symbol or a UI element at the time, but the way it happened suggests there might be more to it than just serving as a place holder.

I was standing there talking to developers at PRX when I drew a racetrack-shaped oval on a whiteboard, dragged my finger down the middle to divide it in two, and said, "So this is the customer on the left, and the vendor on the right." One of the PRX guys said, "That's a good UI symbol," and it took off from there. We use the left (user-side) r-button for ListenLog on PRX's Public Radio Player. We used both in an EmanciPay prototype developed as an open source project with students at MIT and King's College London. And it's been a handy way to symbolize customer and vendor, supply and demand, and other reciprocities. But that doesn't mean we should stick with it.

It does mean we have a long way to go before VRM tools have UIs that demand use. This I believe will be the most important challenge for VRM development, once tools become sufficiently mature and usable.

Many VRM tools will be purely infrastructural and won't need an attractive UI. But for uses that involve conscious expressions of intent, good UIs are essential.

SO, THEN

The main benefit of VRM + CRM will be genuine relationships, rather than ones in name only. But we won't have those relationships if the tools don't get used. For that, UIs will matter. Without the ability to express intent with ease, the Intention Economy will get off to a slow start.

PART IV

The Liberated Vendor

Empowered customers make companies competitive.

—Christopher S. Rollyson

Companies need to dance with, not on, their customers.

—Adele Menichella

25

The Dance

There is never a good sale for Neiman Marcus that's not a good buy for the customer.

—Stanley Marcus[1]

The consumer is not a moron. She is your wife.

—David Ogilvy[2]

THE ARGUMENT

The Intention Economy is a dance in which vendors and customers both lead and follow each other.

In 2007, we got an apartment near Cambridge, Massachusetts, so I could be near the Berkman Center and Boston-area colleagues working on ProjectVRM. But choosing where to rent was not an easy decision. First, we wanted to find the right school for our son, who was then entering fifth grade. Second, my wife wanted to shop at a Trader Joe's. We found both nearby.

At first, I didn't get why she liked Trader Joe's so much. The quality of the food mattered, of course, as did the low prices, the uncomplicated selection of gourmet-friendly goods, and the low-pressure atmosphere in the store.[3] A few items there (such as cheeses, condiments, and crackers) were among her favorites from any store. And she liked the sense that there weren't any duds, which meant anything in the store was at least worth trying out. Still, I wondered why Trader Joe's did so well. As a less discriminating shopper, TJ's didn't seem *that* special to me, although I liked the place.

The first clues came with an August 2010 article in *Fortune* titled, "Inside the secret world of Trader Joe's." It explained,

> The privately held company's sales last year were roughly $8 billion, the same size as Whole Foods' (WFMI, Fortune 500) and bigger than those of Bed Bath & Beyond, No. 314 on the Fortune 500 list. Unlike those massive shopping emporiums, Trader Joe's has a deliberately scaled-down strategy: It is opening just five more locations this year. The company selects relatively small stores with a carefully curated selection of items. (Typical grocery stores can carry 50,000 stock-keeping units, or SKUs; Trader Joe's sells about 4,000 SKUs, and about 80% of the stock bears the Trader Joe's brand.) The result: Its stores sell an estimated $1,750 in merchandise per square foot, more than double Whole Foods'. The company has no debt and funds all growth from its own coffers.[4]

But then *Fortune* went off on a chewy tangent: the company's "secrecy":

> You'd think Trader Joe's would be eager to trumpet its success, but management is obsessively secretive. There are no signs with the company's name or logo at headquarters in Monrovia, about 25 miles east of downtown Los Angeles ... Trader Joe's and its CEO, Dan Bane, declined repeated requests to speak to Fortune, and the company has never participated in a major story about its business operations.

However, I got lucky where *Fortune* didn't, over a long lunch with Doug Rauch, a senior fellow with Harvard's Advanced Leadership Initiative. Doug worked for thirty-one years at Trader Joe's, the last fourteen as president of the company. Now retired, he spoke freely, starting out by explaining that Trader Joe's isn't secretive, rather just disinterested in speaking to anybody other than its customers. Turns out publicity is just one of many games the company does not play.

Here are my notes, which I wrote down after getting home from lunch with Doug:

1. The word "consumer" isn't used at TJ's. "It's a statistical category," Doug says. "We say 'customer,' 'person,' or 'individual.'"

2. TJ's raison d'être is to serve as "a purchasing agent for the customer." It sees itself as completely old-fashioned that way.

3. "We don't do gimmicks." Not just loyalty cards, ads, and promotions, but anything that manipulates the customer and insults his or her intelligence. "Those things are a huge part of retailing today, and have huge hidden costs." TJ's also doesn't cut its posted prices, ever.

4. TJ's has no interest in industry fashion—at all. It avoids industry meetings, associations, conferences, and similar gatherings, because too many of those things are about the latest retail fashions, most of which are about pushing things at customers. That's not TJ's style because that's not its substance. It doesn't push.

5. TJ's truly believes that markets are conversations—with customers. A key job for top company executives, Doug explained, is walking the floors at stores and "shopping along with customers."

6. Distribution is about creating the shortest and most efficient possible conduits between first sources and customers in stores.

7. "We have stores. They have storefronts." Doug said the aisles of typical grocery stores tend to be "slots" filled by other companies. The store itself might be responsible for a fraction of the SKUs the customer sees.

8. "We're not a one-stop shop, because our customers don't shop in one store, and we both know that." Not being a one-stop shop also makes TJ's fit better in the local marketplace.

9. It cuts costs with its suppliers in partnership, and not by muscling them. This is especially true with packaging costs. Nearly all TJ products carry the company's own labels, even if they come from name-brand sources. "We own what we buy." More importantly, it carries no promotional burdens: no two-for-ones, no promotional tie-ins, nothing built only for special displays. These uncomplications are pleasing to suppliers. So are the savings, all of which are passed along to customers rather than stuffed into margins.

10. "We believe in honesty and directness between human beings," Doug said. "We do this by engaging with the whole person, rather than just with the part that 'consumes.'" Whole means authentic. This is especially the case where TJ's management walks the stores. TJ's wants to know the bad and the good, all the time, directly from

customers. "We'll even open packages with customers to taste and talk about the goods." As a result, "There's nothing sold at Trader Joe's that customers haven't improved."

11. Its only promotional vehicle—the opt-in *Fearless Flyer*—is meant to be "a narrative about different things we're selling, or what we're up to." For example, the current *Fearless Flyer* has a two-page report on cheese: its history, ingredients, what goes into making it.[5] Of French Brie, it says, "We actually sell more Brie than any other retailer in the country, and we continually taste and re-taste to make sure the various Bries we offer are the best quality and always represent terrific value ... It also enables us to offer this high-quality cheese at the fantastic price of $7.99 a pound." Confession: until this minute I had never read a *Fearless Flyer*. But I love TJ's Brie and have bought it many times.

12. It likes to hire foodies, and develop them into experts—on wine, on candy, on nutrition, whatever—and it often recruits those foodies from the customer base and from within the company.

13. Being privately owned isn't selfish, because publicly owned companies are also in the business of pleasing Wall Street. Besides, most stock holdings are short term anyway. "If we were public, Trader Joe's wouldn't be your store."

Thus, Trader Joe's provides a controlled study in how markets as conversations can succeed, at "scale," without gimmicks. By interacting with customers and constantly inviting customer input, Trader Joe's models the attitude required not only for VRM-friendliness but for surviving in a world where customers are going to be ready to provide input, whether retailers like it or not.

I was introduced to Doug by José Alvarez, Senior Lecturer of Business Administration at Harvard Business School. José's most recent position outside the academy was as president and CEO of Stop & Shop/Giant-Landover. Before that he was at Shaw's. While he had lots to do with the kind of innovations we reviewed back in chapter 6, what he teaches about retail is anchored in deep history—especially in what we've forgotten. That forgotten history is encapsulated in a one-liner he dropped on me during lunch one day: *The original purpose of the merchant was to serve as an agent for the customer.*

If you made or bought textiles in the Venice of 1250 A.D., for example (that's roughly when the merchant Marco Polo headed for the Orient on company business), you needed materials—wool, flax, cotton—from elsewhere, since Venice itself was a collection of islands comprised entirely of stone structures on pilings pounded into a swamp. Your merchant got what you needed. There existed, in a very real way, what Craig Burton calls the "demand chain." After my conversation with Doug I understood for the first time what "Trader Joe's" literally meant. I also understood what "agency" meant in the first place (see chapter 11).

Customers, Not Consumers

The word *consumer* first appeared in the early fifteenth century, when it meant "one who squanders or wastes."[6] By 1776, when Adam Smith published *The Wealth of Nations* (in which *consumer* appears forty-eight times), the word had gained an economic meaning, as the counterpart of *producer*.[7] By the middle of the twentieth century, however, consumers had become members of mass markets: living embodiments of appetite, or what REX (Relationship Economy Expedition) founder Jerry Michalski calls "gullets with wallets and eyeballs."[8]

Consumers have power only in groups, most of which are categories seen by retailers rather than unions representing common interests of individuals. This is why Consumers Union was formed in 1936, and why it remains a powerful institution today. It is also why governments maintain consumer price indexes (CPIs) and consumer protection bureaus and agencies. (When I look up "customer protection agency" on Google, it assumes I mean "consumer" and instead gives me results for that.[9])

Here's the difference: while consumers are herd animals (meaning they *look* that way from above), customers are human in the most profound way—they require respect for who and what each of them are, which is different from everybody else.

No human characteristic is more distinctive than difference. Even genetically identical twins, who begin life as a single fertilized cell, can become as unique as any other two human beings who have ever lived.[10]

As individual human beings, the respect we want goes beyond mere courtesy. We want understanding by others that what we bring to conversations, relationships, and transactions are more than words, commitments, and money. We also bring what only we know, believe, think, and can say.

None of that can be fully represented, much less duplicated, by anybody or anything else, including "big data" constructions. We have full agency only as ourselves. The agency of those representing us works best when it carries forward the personal essences that are ours alone. Chief among those, for the purposes of business, is our intentions.

Just getting our attention, as consumers, won't cut it anymore—no matter how "personalized" a seller makes our "experience" as a target of their guesswork.

Beyond the Echo Chamber

Within the world's value chains, the term *vendor* customarily applies to upstream sources of goods and services, while *customer* refers to downstream buyers of those services. The retailer Safeway is a customer of General Mills, and a vendor to customers who walk into Safeway stores. General Mills would never call Safeway a "consumer," which testifies both to the collective nature of consumers and the individual natures of customers. To their credit, retailers like Safeway also don't tend to call their customers "consumers" either—at least not to their faces—because workers at Safeway stores interact with customers face-to-face every day.

Trader Joe's is not alone in not calling customers "consumers." Target, for example, calls customers "guests" Thus, on the corporate Web page titled "Target's unique guests," the word "consumer" does not appear. The page also says clueful things like "Target attracts guests just as unique as its stores," and "Target guests are thoughtful about how they spend and where they shop. They know that any retailer can match price, but what about value? Target guests strive to make the most of their time and money by recognizing the difference between price and the more enduring concept of value."[11]

This consciousness about customers helps distinguish Target from other big-box discount retailers. Yet the word "guest" also carries the scent of euphemism. Several years ago I was talking about VRM with a high-level executive at Target. After telling me about the many ways Target works distance itself from other big-box retailers (commitment to diversity, high percentage of women in executive ranks, commitment to product quality, calling customers "guests" and so on), he summed up his case with this line: "We do everything we can to own the customer." I replied, "What's another word for owning a human being?" He said, "Oh my gosh: it's *slavery*. Why do we talk like that?" The answer is that business in general talks like that, and mostly to itself.

For example, consider trade shows.

Take the National Retail Federation's 2012 Big Show, which ran in New York in January.[12] The first item on the agenda was "Critical Developments in Retail Marketing: Understanding Consumers, Building Brands." The session was sponsored by IBM, and the speaker was Jon Iwata, IBM's senior vice president of Marketing and Communications. From the agenda's Web page: "A new IBM study reveals that 71% of retail Chief Marketing Officers feel underprepared to manage the explosion of data. CMOs are excited by the vast knowledge available to them about customers and by the means to reach and serve them in new ways, but they are challenged by how to use that information to understand what's happening right now, act on information in real time, and even successfully predict outcomes."[13]

Let's put this in context. IBM is one of the biggest vendors of IT (information technology) gear and services to retailers. The company was doing big data long before the term "IT" showed up, and its competence around big data is surely a helpful thing for many retailers. But nothing big data offers today, in any business, is a substitute for intentionally delivered intelligence from real customers who are engaged, one-to-one, with retailers in the marketplace—in their own ways, and on their own terms. Fort Business (see chapter 22) can't do this by talking only to itself, or by looking only to its own vendors for guidance.

Still, retailers are realists, and there are signs, even at trade shows, that customer leadership is inevitable in any case. Here is the description copy for a Big Show 2012 breakout session titled "Winning Today's Digitally-Enhanced Shopper":

> Today's path to purchase has become dynamic and fluid with multiple touch points, interactions, and engagement—many of which occur outside of the physical store. While brand influence continues to play a significant role in the path, the shopper's voice is becoming stronger and the shopper is in control. Mobile, digital, and social change drivers are transforming shopping trips—before, during, and after. Rules have changed. The shopper has gone digital and retailers must find innovative new ways to engage with today's digitally enhanced shopper. The keys to engagement, influence, and loyalty require understanding the shopper's mind-set and engaging in the right conversations.[14]

"Mind-set" doesn't cover what customers will bring to the table that retailers are setting. Among other things, we want to know what goes into the products and services we buy, and not just what's happening at the near ends of supply chains. The main reason we want to know that stuff is that we care about more than paying the least we can. Baiting with bargains is a game that's less fun for everybody to play when all the true costs are exposed.

Without Gimmicks

Thomas Harper's *Online Etymology Dictionary* offers this for the origin of *gimmick*: "1926 (in Maine & Grant's 'Wise-Crack Dictionary,' which defines it as 'a device used for making a fair game crooked'), Amer.Eng., perhaps an alteration of gimcrack, or an anagram of magic."[15] Among other definitions, *Merriam-Webster* says gimmick means "a trick or device used to attract business or attention <a marketing gimmick>."[16]

There are many marketing gimmicks, but all serve to both attract shopper attention and mask intrinsic worth—at costs to both the seller and the shopper. For example, the "75¢ off any two Old El Paso products" offered to me by the scanning gizmo at Stop & Shop (see chapter 6) has nothing to do with the worth of those products as food, or the value of Old El Paso as a brand.[17] In fact, the discount demeans the brand. Both stores and brands are surely aware of this, and perhaps even build that cost into their pricing calculations. But the masking is still there, and that's one reason why Trader Joe's (and a handful of other major grocery sellers—notably Whole Foods) offer a single non-discount price. But they remain the exception. Gimmickry still rules.

In *Our Dumb World*, which may be the funniest book ever written, *The Onion* calls the United States "Land of Opportunism"—a place where lotteries "allow thousands to lose instantly" and "the #5 combo" is listed under "traditional cuisine."[18]

In her book *Cheap: The High Cost of Discount Culture*, Ellen Ruppel Shell digs deeply into the tragic truths that make *The Onion*'s funny one-liners about the United States ring so true. About the aftermath of the recent financial meltdown, she writes,

> Our fixation on all things cheap led us astray. We have blundered before and risen chastened but stronger. From this latest fiasco we have learned the hard lesson that we cannot grow a country and a future on a steady diet of "great deals."

Americans love a bargain, and that is not about to change. But sometimes what looks like a bargain is really just a bad loan.[19]

Discounting is also a drug, which best explains why a business so doomed as Groupon's original coupon game not only got traction, but a $5 billion to $6 billion takeover offer from Google that the founders *turned down*.[20] When I first saw that news I thought it *was* an *Onion* story. In fact, Groupon's putative valuation at this writing has soared as high as $30 billion. According to Andrew Ross Sorkin, editor at large of the *New York Times DealBook*, that high-hype mark was achieved by Lloyd Blankfein, CEO of Goldman Sachs, who "flew to Chicago personally to pitch his firm to underwrite what was supposed to be the hottest initial public offering of the year." The pitch succeeded. Later (on October 17, 2011), Sorkin wrote, "The valuation will be lucky to be more than $10 million."[21]

I'm no analyst, but I can say with confidence that Groupon is a value-subtract for nearly every enterprise that buys its jive. Its worth to the economy is less than zero because it is pure gimmick, as were Green Stamps and as are nearly all the half-billion promotional sites that come up in a Google search for "coupons."

An old saying goes, "Cocaine makes you feel like a man. Problem is, the man wants more cocaine." Coupons are cocaine for business.

To get off the discounting drug, it helps to know that businesses can survive—and thrive—without Groupons, or coupons, or any gimmick at all. As I reported in chapter 8, one reason Kmart tanked while Walmart rocked (at least according to Lee Scott, Walmart's former CEO) was that Kmart hooked its customers on coupons while Walmart didn't.

The lesson: when your company and your customers both get hooked on discounts, you don't have a clear sense of what your products and services are actually worth or how you can increase their intrinsic value.

Some customers, of course, will remain hooked on coupons for the duration. But most customers don't need coupons, and neither do the companies that distribute them. They also don't need most of the overhead-fattening practices listed in the chapter 8: advertising and buyback allowances, contests, co-op, dealer premiums, display allowances, diverting, forward-buying, variable trade spending, trade deals, slotting fees, spiffs, and the rest of them. Not if what they offer is attractive and valuable to begin with.

The Bigger Delusion

Live long enough, and you get to see a series of market crashes. The one closest to home for me is still the dot-com crash, which I experienced both as a techie in Silicon Valley and as a journalist covering it, live. Here's an excerpt from "Lessons in Mid-Crash," which I wrote for *Linux Journal* in August 2001:

> It's now obvious that the crashing will continue, right up to the point when every public- and venture-funded technology company that was never a real business ceases attempting to become one. In most cases, that will happen when they finish burning their investors' money—after crashing their investors' cars while smoking one another's exhaust.
>
> When the "internet economy" was still a high-speed traffic jam somewhere back in 1999, I was at a party in San Francisco. Most of the folks there were young, hip "entrepreneurs." Lots of all-black outfits, spiky haircuts, goatees and face jewelry. I fell into conversation with one of these guys ... (who) was on his second or third startup and eagerly evangelizing his new company's "mission" with a stream of buzzwords.
>
> "What does your company do, exactly?" I asked.
>
> "We're an arms merchant to the portals industry," he replied.
>
> When I pressed him for more details (How are portals an industry? What kind of arms are you selling?), I got more buzzwords back. Finally, I asked a rude question. "How are sales?"
>
> "They're great. We just closed our second round of financing."
>
> Thus I was delivered an epiphany: *every company has two markets—one for its goods and services, and one for itself—*and the latter had overcome the former. We actually thought selling companies to investors was a real business model.[22]

The situation was even worse than that, because the dot-com crash was just one symptom of a larger economic disorder called *financialization*, which brought on the housing market crash of the late '00s. In *American Theocracy: The Peril and Politics of Radical Religion, Oil, and Borrowed Money in the 21st Century*, Kevin Phillips calls financialization "a process whereby financial services, broadly construed, take over the dominant economic, cultural, and political role in a national economy."[23] In his next book, *Bad Money: Reckless Finance, Failed Politics, and the Global Crisis of American Capitalism*, he writes, "… in less than half a century, finance has ascended from its image as a mistrusted casino (a memory from 1929) to secular altar, from emotional cockpit to Efficient Market, and from a battle-field of scamps to a playing field of such Efficient Market exemplars as spec-ulators, arbitrageurs, credit-derivatives designers, and corporate raiders."[24]

Financialization can also cause psychosis within companies: a detach-ment of the corporate mind from reality, which is the business itself, rather than its worth to Wall Street.

Let's face it: few entrepreneurs go into business saying, "I just can't wait to maximize shareholder value." They go into business because they see opportunity in some obsession or other, and want to make that obsession appeal to customers. Here's how Peter Drucker put the difference in an interview with *Fortune* in 1998:

> There's one thing securities analysts will never understand, and that's business, because they believe that money is real. Securities analysts believe that companies make money. Companies make shoes. No securities analyst can really understand that. Yes, your stock price is exceedingly important because it controls the cost of your most expensive resource—capital … and there is no profit unless you earn the cost of capital.[25]

Unless your business makes money from money, you make shoes. One hundred percent of the people who wear shoes are called customers, not stockholders. If you make stockholders happy without doing the same first for customers, your company is dancing on the edge of a cliff. Because once customers have a better choice, they'll leave.

Perfect examples: Nordstrom and Zappos.

In 1999, at the height of the dot-com boom, Nordstom pioneered selling shoes online. With help from Benchmark Capital, a big-name Silicon Valley venture capital firm, Nordstrom put up a slick new shoe store, featuring the latest and greatest in e-commerce Web site design. Here's what Stefanie Olsen of CNET News.com reported at the time:

> The Nordstromshoes.com site, which offers approximately 20 million pairs of shoes, seeks to draw customers online with a new national sweepstakes … The Make Room for Shoes promotion will give away free shoes for life, among other prizes.

Nordstromshoes.com customers can return their purchases to any of Nordstrom's brick-and-mortar stores. Store clerks can order items through the Web site for customers who are unable to find what they are looking for in Nordstrom's stores.

The retailer also plans to spend $17 million this holiday season promoting its new online shoe store.

Nordstrom estimates that the online shoe business will grow from $121 million this year to some $902 million in 2003, but competition will be intense. Banana Republic, Macy's, and Nike, among others, all sell shoes online.[26]

But the competition didn't come from any of those usual suspects. It came from ShoeSite.com, which had launched a few months earlier. Around the time Nordstromshoes.com came online, ShoeSite.com became Zappos. The rest is history, including Nordstromshoes.com (that address now redirects to shop.nordstrom.com/c/shoes). Zappos (slogan: "Powered by Service") out-Nordstromed Nordstrom. While Nordstrom succeeded in the brick-and-mortar by offering high levels of customer service made possible by deep product and size inventories, Zappos beat them at all of that in the online world. In 2009, Zappos sold to Amazon.com for $1.2 billion in stock. It still operates independently.

Zappos won by loving customers and letting them lead. From the beginning, it saw relationships as an investment rather than an expense. It also saw conversation as an advantage, rather than a waste of time. In other words, the more the better.

According to Jane Judd, senior manager of customer loyalty at Zappos, "The key is for personal, emotional connection and to engage the consumer."[27] This means, for example, no time limit on the phone. The current record time for a customer call to Zappos is eight hours and twenty-eight minutes, a sum Zappos regards with pride.[28]

Zappos also wins by being *really* different, rather than incrementally so. In *Different: Escaping the Competitive Herd*, Youngme Moon (Donald K. David Professor at Harvard Business School) writes, "In category after category, it has become apparent that competitive differentiation is a myth. Or to put it more precisely, in category after category, companies have gotten so collectively locked into a particular cadence of competition that they appear to have lost sight of their mandate—which is to create meaningful grooves of separation from one another. Consequently, the harder they compete, the less differentiated they become."[29]

It's easy to miss a great line—a sub-subhead—almost hidden in the stylistic arrangement of text on *Different*'s title page. It reads, "Standing out in a world where conformity reigns but exceptions rule." To fully dig what that means, consider Apple, which she calls "yet another reminder, against a sea of competitive homogeneity, of how utterly charismatic difference can be."[30] Listen to Steve Jobs do the voice-over for a one-minute TV ad titled, "The Crazy Ones," which launched Apple's "Think Different" campaign after Steve returned to the company. Here's the copy:

> Here's to the crazy ones, the misfits, the rebels, the troublemakers, the round pegs in the square holes, the ones who see things differently. They're not fond of rules. You can quote them, disagree with them, glorify or vilify them; but the only thing you can't do is ignore them, because they change things. They push the human race forward. And while some may see them as the crazy ones, we see genius, because the ones who are crazy enough to think that they can change the world, are the ones who do.[31]

Richard Dreyfus voiced the ad that aired on TV. But after Steve Jobs died, the version with Steve's own voice showed up on YouTube. It's eerie, because it makes clear how truly different Steve was—and how determined he was to make his company and its products different as well.

Learning New Moves

What "different" companies do is return to the free and open place that markets were to begin with. Here's what David Weinberger and I wrote about that place in the "Markets are Conversations" chapter of *The Cluetrain Manifesto*:

> The first markets were filled with people, not abstractions or statistical aggregates; they were the places where supply met demand with a firm handshake. Buyers and sellers looked each other in the eye, met, and connected. The first markets were places for exchange, where people came to buy what others had to sell—and to talk.
>
> The first markets were filled with talk. Some of it was about goods and products. Some of it was news, opinion, and gossip. Little of it mattered to everyone; all of it engaged someone. There were often conversations about the work of hands: "Feel this knife. See how it fits your palm." "The cotton in this shirt, where did it

come from?" ... Some of these conversations ended in a sale, but don't let that fool you. The sale was merely the exclamation mark at the end of the sentence.

Market leaders were men and women whose hands were worn by the work they did. Their work was their life, and their brands were the names they were known by: Miller, Weaver, Hunter, Skinner, Farmer, Brewer, Fisher, Shoemaker, Smith.

For thousands of years, we knew exactly what markets were: conversations between people who sought out others who shared the same interests. Buyers had as much to say as sellers. They spoke directly to each other without the filter of media, the artifice of positioning statements, the arrogance of advertising, or the shading of public relations.

These were the kinds of conversations people have been having since they started to talk. Social. Based on intersecting interests. Open to many resolutions. Essentially unpredictable. Spoken from the center of the self. "Markets were conversations" doesn't mean "markets were noisy." It means markets were places where people met to see and talk about each other's work.

Conversation is a profound act of humanity. So once were markets.[32]

Yet talking isn't all that good companies do. They also dance.

Right now, most retail market categories are dance floors where every customer hears dozens, hundreds, or thousands of companies, each with a megaphone, calling out dance moves. What those companies need to do instead is put down the megaphone, and—in the manner of Trader Joe's and Zappos—shop along with customers. Dance. Sure, lead sometimes, but follow, too.

Not easy. Throughout the industrial age, business on the whole has always taken the lead—or thought it had to. But for customers to take charge—which they will, at least half the time—they have to take the lead, too.

It helps that vendors and customers both bring qualities to the dance floor that the other does not, and that both need each other for the economy to work and for civilization to thrive. They don't always need to love each other or even to know each other. But they do need to respect, understand, and learn from each other. They can't do that to full effect if one side tries constantly to dominate the other.

One thing companies are free to do is please and delight customers with products and services that are truly worthwhile. The chances of doing that only go up if customers are both heard and engaged as equals, and not as slaves or suckling calves.

The Personal Edge

My friend Antonio Rodriguez is a serial entrepreneur who once reported to me an interesting exchange he had with a venture capitalist. When the VC asked him, "What's your lock-in?" Antonio answered, "Our lock-in is love. We want our customers to love our company."

You don't have to like all your customers. But you do have to love them. And love goes two ways, not just one. So does intent. If your business rationalizes trapping customers or baiting them with gimmicks, you don't have a dance—just a lot of jerking around. But if you truly relate with your customers, you'll discover moves together that just weren't possible when you ran the whole show by yourself.

SO, THEN

Think of the dances that followed jazz, big band music and rock and roll into the world. All of them were invented by the dancers themselves, and none of them were predictable before the music started.

The networked marketplace today is a lot like where we were when radio got started in the 1920s. But history will move a lot faster now, because everybody and everything is far more networked. Life in the city is bound to get a lot more interesting. There's no way around it. The choice is to dance or die.

You're not in business alone. Your customers are with you, even if you don't know it. Start dancing with them and you'll both be set free.

26

Commons Cause

Cities are the greatest creations of humanity.
—Daniel Libeskind[1]

THE ARGUMENT

The Internet is a commons with the characteristics of a world-wide city. Adapting to life there is essential. Companies will not only get along better, but will seize more opportunities and (if they're lucky) live a lot longer.

Think of the Internet as a World Wide City, and you can see why it has scaled so well. It supports and embraces abundance and difference. Its value grows with each person, each device, each kind of work that connects to it.

The World Wide City is also a World Wide Commons. This is the vast new marketplace where connected companies live now. We need to keep it vast to take advantage of the opportunities it provides to connect and to produce because of those connections.

The networked marketplace is not reducible to the companies and governments that provide its wired and wireless infrastructure. The Net is a second world within and alongside the physical one that we've inhabited from the start, and yet the Net is still very young. We need to understand it, even as we continue to build it and build on it. Regardless of how our understanding grows, we should be clear that the Net is bigger and more essential than anything or anybody that would limit it.

Companies should be intentional about saving and growing the Net. Limiting the Net can only limit what can be done on it, and that would be bad for business.

Genius As a Resource

Ed McCabe, one of the best copywriters in the history of advertising (and a hero of mine when I was in that business), said, "I have no use for rules. They only rule out the possibility of brilliant exceptions."[2]

Humanity is built for exceptions. The more than 3 billion DNA base pairs in the human genome are platforms for incalculable variety among individuals. The great schoolteacher John Taylor Gatto put it this way:

> I've come to believe that genius is an exceedingly common human quality, probably natural to most of us. I didn't want to accept that notion—far from it—my own training in two elite universities taught me that intelligence and talent distributed themselves economically over a bell curve ... The trouble was that the unlikeliest kids kept demonstrating to me at random moments so many of the hallmarks of human excellence—insight, wisdom, justice, resourcefulness, courage, originality—that I became confused ... Was it possible I had been hired not to enlarge children's power, but to diminish it? ... slowly I began to realize that the bells and the confinement, the crazy sequences, the age-segregation, the lack of privacy, the constant surveillance ... were designed exactly as if someone had set out to prevent children from learning how to think and act, to coax them into addiction and dependent behavior ...
>
> I dropped the idea that I was an expert, whose job it was to fill the little heads with my expertise, and began to explore how I could remove those obstacles that prevented the inherent genius of children from gathering itself.[3]

Like the kids in Gatto's classes, customers have been categorized, confined, segregated, surveilled, and denied their privacy by an industrial age value system that seeks to normalize at all costs. The highest of those costs is ignoring an essential fact of human life: that we are all different, that every human being is more than a "resource" and an "asset." We are all sovereign sources of intelligence and advantage. Some of what we say and do is typical of others, but much more of it is not. This fact is more than a Good Thing. It is essential to the growth of civilization and to addressing its inevitable problems.

Human difference is one of the biggest reasons why cities thrive in ways that companies, especially as they become large, do not. The nature of cities is to welcome and embrace abundant differences: different companies, different arts, different cuisines, different schools, different forms of transportation, different faiths, different habitats, different public spaces, different forms of recreation—all occupied and sustained by different people, each with their own character, each with their own intentions.

Genius is also the ultimate hedge. If, as companies, we are forced to deal with a mass of difference, it should help to know that those differences are the first sources of innovation as well as disruption. With the help of our many different selves, we can make many more, and better, bets on what will work.

Taking and Giving

In economics, we like to speak of rational actors, rational choices, rational behavior. Yet not all commerce is impelled by rational intentions and actions. There are emotional ones as well. Both the rational and the emotional have moral dimensions.

Most formal moralities are modeled on bookkeeping. Consider the scales of justice and our belief that we should pay for our crimes. "Debt," "owe," and "repay" are a few among the many financial words in our moral lexicon. Christians, for example, believe that Christ died to pay for humanity's sins.

But there is also a morality of generosity: of giving without expectation of exchange. Such, for example, is the love we give to our spouses and our kids. What we give is without price and without keeping records of it.

In *The Gift*, Lewis Hyde sorts these into *logos* and *eros*. He describes *logos* as "reason and logic in general" and says "a market economy is an emanation of *logos*." He describes *eros* as "the principle of attraction, union, involvement which binds together."[4] He explains,

> Not surprisingly, people live differently who treat a portion of their wealth as a gift. To begin with, unlike the sale of a commodity, the giving of a gift tends to establish a relationship between the parties involved. Furthermore, when gifts circulate within a group, their commerce leaves a series of interconnected relationships in its wake, and a kind of decentralized cohesiveness emerges.[5]

When we look at the successes we've discussed, for all their differences (and the virtues of difference itself), they share this combination of logos and eros, of rational exchange and emotional wealth creation that arises from giving outside the accounting system. It goes deeper than policy. It's a reason for being. Trader Joe's isn't on Earth just to serve the German company that owns it. Nor do Apple and Zappos exist to serve stockholders. They are here for customers. Trader Joe's does it with simple human contact. Apple does it by hiring obsessives, calling them "geniuses," and providing customers with lots of hand-holding. Zappos does it by taking conversation-as-marketing to an extreme.

In each case, there is giving as well as taking. And the giving isn't all in exchange. Some of it is pure *eros*.

Intent

To live is to move. That's why we use the language of travel to talk about life. (For more on that, see chapter 9.) Much of our movement is unconscious, but the movement that matters isn't. It is intentional. Our will looks for ways, all the time.

As customers, we don't intend just to consume. We intend to use, to enjoy, to invest, to share, to care, to talk. We also intend for the companies we keep to stay in business. (Companies might like to kill each other, but customers prefer choices between companies that aren't being killed.)

Thus, *intent* is the operative noun and *intend* the operative verb that together bring a marketplace to life. Whether our intentions are *logos, eros,* or some mix of the two, they move money in one direction, goods in the other, intelligence in both directions, and growth in the economy we all share.

For most of the industrial age, companies have been obsessed with getting the attention of prospects and customers. That obsession was born in a time when reaching and connecting with more than a handful of people was difficult and expensive. Reaching large markets required advertising in mass media and other forms of attention getting. This is no longer the case.

SO, THEN

We can all connect now, more easily than ever. We can make our intentions known personally and in ways that can cause and sustain genuine relationships. And, where no relationship is required, we can connect, do business, and move on, with less cost and hassle than ever.

The Attention Economy will persist, because the rationales for it won't go away and were never wrong. The Intention Economy will grow because that's where the money is. And the love, too.

We're in this thing together, and it's bigger than any of us. If we keep it that way, it'll be good for everybody.

27

What to Do

The demand chain and the supply chain need to pull each other, side by side. There need to be dialogs of process, up and down the whole system: seller to buyer, buyer to seller—and even buyer to buyer, and seller to seller.

—Craig Burton[1]

THE ARGUMENT

It's always good to buy a hot commodity in the past. Today, VRM is a future hot commodity, and the Intention Economy is still on the horizon. So now is a good time to start watching developments and investing in them.

There are vendors and customers all up and down the supply chain. But it is the ones at the end of that chain—retailers—that interact personally with customers. Retailing is therefore also the category directly involved with customers' VRM tools. That's why I've focused on retailing in this part of the book.

Of course, there are many other kinds of businesses, both out in the world and back up the supply chain. What follows is guidance for a small collection of large verticals and some general advice for all companies anticipating VRM and the Intention Economy, in order to meet them in the great middle we call the marketplace.

Then, last but far from least, we visit Customer Commons, a new dot-organization that will have lots of work to do once customers become truly free agents in the free and open marketplace.

Verticals

There is no end to vertical business categories. What I hope is that the following five categories cover enough territory to hint toward ways that VRM and the Intention Economy will affect the rest of them.

Banking and Finance

EmanciPay, described in chapter 23, is just one of the new business offerings that might open up for banks and similar services. No doubt there will be others. The main question for banks in the Intention Economy is how they can better play the game they invented centuries ago: paying for savings and charging for loans. Better signaling from actual and potential customers should reduce risk and improve the ability to make offerings and monitor performance. Banks can also work as fourth-party agents for customers.

The transcendent fact for banking in the Intention Economy is that every good customer is both a saver and a borrower—even if all they borrow is the money they spend on credit card purchases, while paying off bills completely once a month. In recent years, large banks have been trying to scrape off small customers, who have been taking their business elsewhere (usually to credit unions).[2] Those small customers, however, are sources of intelligence about what's happening "on the ground" in the marketplace. Losing them is more costly to large banks than spreadsheet numbers alone might suggest.

The business of banking and finance has always been in money itself. The big money made by making bets on what companies and other securities are worth is now the tail wagging the banking dog. Even leaving aside the securitization failures that brought on the Great Recession, the fact remains that the worth of all securities is inherently derivative. They are a step, or two, or three, removed from the first sources of value, which comes from what people and companies buy, create, save, and do.

The networking of everything on the Live Web makes the first sources of value far more manifest. As more value creation gets hooked together, mostly following the intentions of individuals, more of it will also be accountable. In the past, banks and financial institutions have been good at accounting. It should pay them to see the possibilities that arise when far more accounting of actual work is done in the world.

Supply Chain

The road from first sources to final customers is not a conveyor belt. It is a series of tight relationships and value additions that are always two-way rather than just one. So, instead of seeing the supply chain as a conveyor belt, think about pull between supply and demand as *funicular* in the manner of trolleys connected to either end of a cable looped over a pulley at the top, so one goes up as the other goes down. And think of this happening at every stage.

According to Michael Stolarczyk, author of *Logical Logistics: A Common-Sense Primer for Your Supply Chain*, supply chains not only convey goods in the mechanical sense, but involve constant learning for everyone involved. "Collaborating creates value and executive empathy makes mutual innovation possible." he says. "Understanding what your partners are going through is rarely enough. You have to be interested and attuned as well. This requires feeling: making emotional as well as mechanical connections."[3]

That empathy begins on the customer side of the "Chinese wall" I talked about in chapter 2. All of us are customers, no matter what we do in business. That means we all live at the far ends of supply chains. Having empathy for the customer—for ourselves—is one requirement. But so is having empathy as customers for suppliers working for common cause at every stage back up the demand chain.

This isn't possible in either direction without far more transparency than we have today, even with the Internet connecting every business operation. For most of the industrial age (which is still going on), hiding the mechanics and operations of everything a company did was generally considered a Good Thing, and in most cases a requirement for management. Now companies need to turn inside out, as Craig Burton said (in chapter 22), and have their exteriors bristling with APIs that expose core competencies. For supply chain logistics to become what Michael Stolarczyk calls "locative," you need an ever-updating assortment of smart handheld mobile devices, GIS (geographical information systems), maps from Google, and other APIs, AR (augmented reality) visualizations, cloud-based platforms for data and processing, and even social media apps that layer data on location. Whatever it takes.

Look back at what Bob the salesman does in the scenario we visited in chapter 22. Think of him as a smart agent moving through the supply-demand chain of life—or just of one business trip. Look at all the ways he, his apps, and the APIs of various services all interact, based on how he and his fourth party program them to interact. Now think of a product as an agent as well, moving from first source to final customer, and the funicular intelligence feedback loops that are established and improved along the way. The less fixed, closed, and siloed all of those are, the better the whole system and each part of it can learn, adapt, improve, and compete in an increasingly open marketplace.

Knowing the intentions of every contributor to that system, especially as they change through learning over time and from experience, is going to be a requirement for both survival and success.

Health Care

Everything in VRM is at the human level, literally. No business is more human than health care—or more screwed up, at least in the United States.

Not surprisingly, VRM development work has been going on in health care since long before ProjectVRM showed up to cheer it on. PHRs (personal health records) have been an ideal since the turn of the millennium, if not longer. Meant to serve as a single-purpose PDSs (personal data stores), their failure to catch on in a big way should be instructive to the many PDS development projects and businesses currently incubating in the VRM community.

Large Health 2.0 conferences have also been held for years, focusing on "patient-generated health care," "participatory medicine," and other VRM-ish virtues. The same conferences have also been encouraging development. Large companies such as Google and Microsoft have obliged with PHRs of their own (e.g., Google Health and Microsoft HealthVault), with minimal success. Google Health folded in 2011, and Microsoft's efforts have also hardly set the world on fire.

So the problem is not a lack of trying or even knowing what the problems are. It's that the health-care business could hardly be more siloed and fractured between incompatible and noncommunicating systems, with walls thickened by fear of exposure and lawsuits. Still, there are many good people working on solutions, starting with PHR and EHR (electronic health records), controlled by patients rather than by providers alone.

Adrian Gropper (an MD and longtime advocate and developer of health-care VRM solutions), says medical errors, many caused by bad or missing data, kill many thousands of people per year in the United States. He adds,

> The errors in closed, proprietary systems derive from lack of open
> source, absent peer review and everyone re-inventing the same

bugs. Aside from buying closed systems, hospitals also seem to differentiate themselves by the idiocies and idiosyncrasies of their information systems. Hospitals, groups and some doctors also resist cloud systems, which are inherently lower in cost and easier to maintain, even though the bugs in a cloud system are much more public and the errors more manageable.[4]

Adds Marty Heaner, another VRM advocate in health care,

> The major stumbling block is data flow. Today's medical systems are not designed to share data. If data is going to flow, then the EMRs (Electronic Medical Records) and integrated hospital management systems must evolve to add APIs and interfaces that allow them to link to Personally Controlled Health Records (PCHRs) to both read in and write out data. This is not going to happen quickly and without a fight.

I think the incentives need to come from customers—patients—working to maximize their own health, with their own devices and services. This will have a funicular[5] effect on health-care provisioning, because it will provide better knowledge and data direct from the individual. The empathy required is already there. Means for applying it are missing.

Toward that I'll give Adrian the last word: "The only way to apply VRM to health information exchange is to enable patients to control real time connections and queries by doctors. In my world, the patient is the driver and the doctor is the valet."[6]

Law

There are two VRM challenges in law. One is keeping the Net open and free. The other is establishing freedom of contract dealings between vendors and customers.

Keeping the Net open and free has always been a cause for the Berkman Center and one of the reasons I was drawn to it. Although I can't find any bylaws or mission statements saying so, the best explanation I ever heard for the Berkman Center's founding mission went like this: "To keep old laws from screwing up the Net and to help new laws save it." That should also remain a mission for any businessperson who cares about the Net and wishes it to remain the business-friendly environment it still is, in spite of many attempts to fence it in.

Toward *freedom of contract*, the main challenge for businesses at this stage is to keep legal departments on a leash while customers and their developer friends come up with new and better terms of engagement that work for both sides and create new business. On the Live Web, lopsided and customer-hostile contracts of adhesion (see chapters 4 and 20) are worse than obsolete. They maintain private marketplaces that are free only to the extent that customers can choose captors. They also prevent an immeasurable sum of economic activity by severely limiting what customers can bring to the market's table and enlarging that table in the process.

The Intention Economy will require both a free Internet and free customers. Whatever legal folks can do to make both happen (including staying out of the way) will be a Good Thing.

Government

In addition to being a serial entrepreneur, a great programmer, and a computer science PhD, Phil Windley is a retired U.S. Navy commander who also served as CIO for the state of Utah. So, when he talks about how government works and what it ought to do, I listen. That's what I did one day in early 2004, when I ran into Phil at the airport in Salt Lake City. This was when Howard Dean was briefly the front-runner in the Democratic primaries, and there was a lot of noise about how the Internet was going to make all the difference in that year's presidential election. (It didn't.)

Phil and I talked for a long time, standing in a concourse between flights. I don't remember anything I said (and I doubt Phil does either), but two pieces of Phil's wisdom stick with me still. One was, "Democracy is about elections and governance, and governance is what gets the job done." The other was, "Everyone wants the roads fixed."

Four years and a few months later, on Election Day 2008, I got up at 4 a.m. to watch Barack Obama (the real Howard Dean, it turned out) give his acceptance speech, live on a flat screen in the corner of a pub underneath Smithfield's, the meat-packing house on the north side of London. Joining me were folks from MySociety, whose largest and most dramatic success was a simple Web site called FixMyStreet.com—a service that cost little to build and provided results beyond measure, mostly by making connections between individual citizens and U.K. government entities in charge of fixing streets.

The success of FixMyStreet and similar grass-roots efforts are among the reasons why the U.K. government's Midata project (reviewed in chapter 21) is working to make sure that citizens are respected as the parties best positioned to control their own data.

Here in the United States, the Personal Democracy Forum (as both publication and event) has become a fixture at the center of the move to personalize democracy. So has the work of Britt Blaser, a former Air Force pilot, real estate developer, and the prime mover behind NewGov.us. Britt's corollary to Phil Windley's two principles is, "Government is the story; Politics is just the punch line. All politics is yokels." He also says, "What if they formed a party and everybody came?"[7]

He doesn't mean that as a joke. He means NewGov.us should be the party where every voter comes to manage his or her politicians "as easily as you manage your iTunes: rate, promote, collect and discard them and never attend a party meeting." His final goal for this is a "participatory surplus."[8]

There are many other grass-roots efforts to do GRM—government relationship management—but these two are the ones involved today in the VRM movement. Watch for them, or start one of your own.

Meanwhile, I take hope in Abraham Lincoln's call, in his Gettysburg Address, for "a new birth of freedom" leading to "government of the people, by the people, for the people." We have the same ends today. But we've also got better means.

The Checklist

So here are a few things to do, rules to obey, and developments to watch for:

- **Turn your company inside out,** if it isn't already. Expose your core competencies through live, evented APIs.

- **Follow and adopt tools** being developed by the VRM community.

- **Put a leash on legal.** Make lawyers write the least onerous agreements they can, for customers that are captive, with you, in the calf-cow commercial Web we still have today.

- **Support a free and open Internet.** Oppose everything in business and government that seeks to make the Net less than it was born to be: the best virtual environment ever created for business.

- **Try out personal data stores for yourself,** and help improve them.

- **Embrace freedom, open source, open standards, and open markets** everywhere you can. They're going to win anyway.

- **Look for ways to make** VRM + CRM work.

- **Think outside the Static Web box,** and look for all the ways you can bet on the Live Web as it emerges.

- **Stop collecting customers' data** without their permission, and make personal data available to customers as a matter of course.

Customer Commons

ProjectVRM was always just a project rather than a stand-alone organization. Its community will persist as long as it needs to, as will its wiki, blog, and gatherings. VRM itself, however, has much larger implications, and its tools will have effects that will, in the long run, work for all customers in the Intention Economy.

Customer Commons is an organization for those customers. At this writing (mid-November 2011), Customer Commons is still in the planning stages. But its "About" page at CustomerCommons.org already says these three things, written by entrepreneur Mary Hodder:

1. We are a community of customers.

2. We are funded only by customers.

3. We serve the interests and aspirations of customers.

@CustomerCommons on Twitter says the same thing.

One thing we know for sure is that Customer Commons will, like Creative Commons (on which it is modeled), be the place where simple terms of engagement will be compiled and made available for everybody to use. (For more on those, see chapters 4, and 20.)

Beyond that it's up to you, me, and every other customer who wants to make truly free markets happen.

SO, THEN

The Intention Economy will be driven by customers. Paving the roads will make the ride better for all of us.

Almost There

The journey is the reward.

—Steve Jobs[1]

$$\Delta x \; \Delta p \geq \frac{\hbar}{2}$$

—Werner Heisenberg[2]

Subjects and Objects

Physicist Werner Heisenberg's uncertainty principle says you can't know position and momentum with full accuracy at the same instant. That is, if something is moving, you can't say exactly where it is; and if you know exactly where it is, you can't say where it's going or how fast. He also says observation itself has influences.[3]

So, in a Heisenbergian sense, I know where VRM development has been, where it is now (when I write this), and the direction it is headed. What I can't know is where it will be when you read this. Heisenberg also said, "The uncertainty relation does not hold for the past."

Searls's corollary for the future is that you can know neither position nor momentum, but that shouldn't stop you from trying to influence both. Or, *don't be the pinball. Be the machine.* So, I beg your patience with motions that don't go according to plan, and your respect for the good intentions of work that will continue in any case, improved by experience and other helpful influences, perhaps including yours.

Our plan in the VRM movement has always been ambitious: to liberate customers, facilitate better relationships between customers and vendors, and invigorate markets as a result. This requires changing a great deal of what business is doing. The flywheels of business as usual are immense, but so are the engines of change. Steady innovation and disruption, about which Clayton Christensen has studied and written a great deal, will accelerate in the networked world.[4] It will also follow Larry Downes's law of disruption: *Technology changes exponentially, but social, economic, and legal systems change incrementally.*[5]

Thanks to the Internet and rapid cycles of technology creation, use, and improvement, we have little choice but to change what we are doing anyway, and to change it again. We'll calibrate those changes better if customers help us with it. At least that much should be clear by now.

How the Intention Economy comes about (or if it comes at all) is anybody's guess, but it's also the calling of a few who will become many. Life is a casino with no house, so go ahead and influence your own bets. Every species is a mistake that works.

The VRM development community is busy making mistakes that result in new species today, and will continue to make them, as fast as they can. So should those of us on the vendor side. There's nothing but frontier between us. Might as well get started settling it, cultivating the farmland, and building whole new towns and cities.

Parting Thoughts

One day last spring, I went into the Barnes & Noble store near here. Aside from the Coop in Harvard Square, it's the biggest bookstore around. For a shopping list, I took along a printout of the books in my Amazon shopping cart. The nice woman behind the service counter thanked me for giving the store a shot, at least for this one visit. Then she carefully went down the list of twelve books, finding only one of them in stock. It was Eli Pariser's *The Filter Bubble*, which had come out a few days earlier (and which we discussed back in chapter 2). She pointed to one of the tables where new books are featured. I thanked her and turned to go get the book. But she didn't want to let me go yet.

"I'm afraid most of what we have here just moves through," she said.

"Like magazines?" I replied.

"Yes, like magazines. Sorry about that."

I write a column every month for *Linux Journal*, a magazine that was sold on the rack at Barnes & Noble before becoming all-digital (i.e., no print version) in September 2011. My lead-time up until then was three months, which is typical of monthlies. That means, for example, that the column I wrote for December was due in the first week of September. Now the lead time is two months, because it's still a magazine. Show me a good print medium, and I'll show you a latency issue. Even with blogging, which until tweeting was the most current way one could possibly write, one could sense the space between the *now* of writing and the *then* of publishing.

So, as I said at the beginning of part III, the biggest challenge in writing this book has been making it both current and durable. If that proves to be the case, it will be because its simple thesis—that a free customer is more valuable than a captive one—endures.

I believe that thesis will be proven, sooner or later, in the marketplace. It's a good idea, and always has been.

QUESTIONS

In technology, the best endings are open. So it goes for work on VRM and the Intention Economy.

I promised to wrap up with some questions, so here we are. The following are mine. I invite you to add your own:

- Can advertising people ever finally cross the Chinese wall between their work and who they are as real people and customers?

- What will be the VRM user interface, or interfaces? What symbols will we use, and what will they mean?

- Will *adhesionism* be with us for the duration? To prevent that, how should we work to change law as well as practice?

- Will CRM embrace VRM, or fight it? Or, if the answer is both, who and what will do the embracing and the fighting?

- Will exposing MLOTT be enough of a motivator for those currently ignoring it?

- Can we understand the Net as a rising tide of open capacity that lifts all economic boats, or will incumbent business and government powers succeed in limiting its scope to what they alone allow?

- Will fourth parties (or user agents) emerge as a large, new business category?

- Can retailing move past gimmickry and into genuine communication and relationship with customers?

- What should we be researching now, and in the future, about VRM?

Those are just a few of mine. If this book does its job, you should have many more of your own. So, bookmark this chapter and write your questions in the blank space below. Or go to IntentionEconomy.com and post your questions, answers, and other comments there. And, of course, post them in your own places and spaces, whatever they happen to be. Use the hashtag #intentioneconomy.

We have a lot to start talking about.

NOTES

Prologue

1. Doc Searls, "The Intention Economy," *Linux Journal*, March 8, 2006, http://www.linuxjournal.com/node/1000035.

2. The project was named by Mike Vizard on *The Gillmor Gang* show, in October 2006, in response to my characterization of the project as the customer-side counterpart of CRM. When Mike suggested calling our new category VRM, it struck a chord, and the label stuck.

3. Doc Searls, "The Intention Economy: What happens when customers get real power," Berkman Center for Internet & Society, speech, March 24, 2009, http://cyber.law.harvard.edu/events/luncheon/2009/03/searls.

4. Geoffrey Moore, *Crossing the Chasm*, rev. ed. (New York: Harper Paperbacks, 2002).

5. Nassim Nicholas Taleb, *The Black Swan: The Impact of the Highly Improbable* (New York: Random House, 2007), 141.

Introduction

1. In this book we use the term "vendor" to mean any kind of seller, including both retailers and their suppliers.

2. PriceWaterhouseCoopers MoneyTree report shows about $2.008 billion invested by U.S. venture capitalists on software in Q3 of 2011 and another $682 million in media and entertainment. Some percentage of that goes toward companies either supported by advertising or with advertising as a business model, but it's hard to tell. Source page: https://www.pwcmoneytree.com/MTPublic/ns/nav.jsp?page=industry.

Chapter 1

1. See http://thinkexist.com/quotation/the_only_way_to_deal_with_an_unfree_world_is_to/346776.html.

2. Roy Amara, who for many years ran the Institute for the Future, said, "We tend to overestimate the effect of a technology in the short run and underestimate the effect in the long run," and said it so often that it become known as "Amara's Law." But he was not the first to make the point. In *Libraries of the Future*, J. C. R. Licklider writes, "A modern maxim says: People tend to overestimate what can be done in one year and to underestimate what can be done in five or ten years" (Cambridge, MA: MIT Press, 1965). Without this maxim, we wouldn't have Silicon Valley.

3. Zeo is a real company. It's at MyZeo.com. All the companies mentioned in this chapter exist today. Most are also active in the VRM development community.

4. See http://kantarainitiative.org/confluence/display/infosharing/.

5. Joe Andrieu, "Introducing User Driven Services," http://blog.joeandrieu.com/2009/04/26/introducing-user-driven-services/.

6. Community Interest Corporations, or CICs, are social enterprises that commit their profits and assets toward a public good. The first were created in the U.K. under the

Companies (Audit, Investigations and Community Enterprise) Act of 2004, http://www
.legislation.gov.uk/ukpga/2004/27/contentsCompanies.

7. See http://cyber.law.harvard.edu/projectvrm/Ascribenation.

Chapter 2

1. Ralph Keys, *The Quote Verifier: Who Said What, Where, and When* (New York:
St. Martin's Press, 2006), 1-2. While this line is customarily attributed to John Wanamaker,
he was neither the first nor the only source. In *The Quote Verifier: Who Said What,
Where, and When* (New York: St. Martin's Press, 2006), Ralph Keys writes,

"In the United States this business truism is most often attributed to department
store magnate John Wanamaker (1838–1922), in England to Lord Leverhulme (William
H. Lever, founder of Lever Brothers, 1851–1925). The maxim has also been ascribed
to chewing gum magnate William Wrigley, adman George Washington Hill, and adman
David Ogilvy. In *Confessions of an Advertising Man* (1963), Ogilvy himself gave the nod
to his fellow Englishman Lord Leverhulme (Lever Brothers was an Ogilvy client), adding
that John Wanamaker later made the same observation. Since Wanamaker founded his
first department store in 1861, when Lever was ten, this seems unlikely. *Fortune* magazine
thought Wanamaker expressed the famous adage in 1885, but it gave no context. While
researching *John Wanamaker, King of Merchants* (1993), biographer William Allen
Zulker found the adage typed on a sheet of paper in Wanamaker's archives, but without a
name or source. Wanamaker usually wrote his own material longhand. *Verdict*: A maxim
of obscure origins, put in famous mouths.

2. Gandalf, http://www.gandalf.it/m/johnson2.htm.

3. Private e-mail.

4. "Worldwide Ad Market Approaches $500 Billion," *eMarketer Digital Intelligence*,
June 13, 2011, http://www.emarketer.com/Article.aspx?R=1008438.

5. Stephanie Reese, "Quick Stat: Advertisers Will Spend $500 Billion in 2011,"
eMarketer, September 6, 2011.

6. "Fact Sheet: U.S. Advertising Spend and Effectiveness" *nielsenwire*, June 10,
2011, http://blog.nielsen.com/nielsenwire/media_entertainment/fact-sheet-u-s-advertising-
spend-and-effectiveness/.

7. "Quadrennial events to help ad market grow in 2012 despite economic trou-
bles," *ZenithOptimedia*, December 5, 2011, http://mediame.com/tags/zenith_optimedia/
quadrennial_events_help_ad_market_grow_2012_despite_economic_troubles.

8. "Share of ad spending by medium," *MarketingCharts.com* (combining data from
Nielsen and Adcross), http://www.marketingcharts.com/television/share-of-ad-spending-
by-medium-may-2008-5828/.

9. "Television advertisement," *Wikipedia*, http://en.wikipedia.org/wiki/Television_
advertisement.

10. Renee Hopkins Callahan, "Hulu Is A Big Hit," *Forbes*, January 22, 2009,
http://www.forbes.com/2009/01/22/hulu-amazon-newscorp_leadership_clayton_in_
rc_0121claytonchristensen_inl.html.

11. "Great Expectations: How Advertising for Original_Scripted TV_Programming
Works Online, http://comscore.com/Press_Events/Presentations_Whitepapers/2010/
Great_Expectations_How_Advertising_for_Original_Scripted_TV_Programming_
Works_Online.

12. Ibid., 2.

13. Ibid., 7.

14. Ibid., 7–9.

15. Hugh MacLeod, *If You Talked to People*, 2008, http://gapingvoid
.com/2008/10/31/mass-marketing-and-the-heroic-lone-individual/.

16. Jonathan Taplin, Web page, USC Annenberg School of Communication, http://
www-bcf.usc.edu/~jtaplin/.

17. *Digital Hollywood*, September 23–25, 2002, http://www.digitalhollywood.com/LA2002Agenda.html.

18. Doc Searls, "The Real Battle," *Linux Journal*, October 5, 2002, http://www.linuxjournal.com/article/6360.

19. Darren Murph, "Research affirms that DVR owners do indeed blaze by commercials," *Engadget HD*, http://hd.engadget.com/2008/08/05/research-affirms-that-dvr-owners-do-indeed-blaze-by-commercials/.

20. John Senior and Rafael Asensio, "TV 2013: Is it All Over?" *Oliver Wyman Journal (OWJ25-8)*, http://www.oliverwyman.com/ow/pdf_files/OWJ25-8-Future_of_TV.pdf.

21. Terry Heaton, "Media's Real Doomsday Scenario," *The Pomo Blog*, September 20, 2010, http://www.thepomoblog.com/papers/pomo112.htm.

22. Bob Garfield, "Future May Be Brighter, but It's Apocalypse Now," *Advertising Age*, March 23, 2009, http://adage.com/article/news/garfield-chaos-scenario-arrived-media-marketing/135440/.

23. Julia Angwin, "The Web's New Gold Mine: Your Secrets," *Wall Street Journal*, July 30, 2010, http://online.wsj.com/article/SB10001424052748703940904575395073512989404.html.

24. Ibid.

25. Ibid.

26. Steve Stecklow, "On the Web, Children Face Intensive Tracking," *Wall Street Journal*, September 17, 2010, http://online.wsj.com/article/SB1000142405274870390430457549790352187146.html.

27. "How concerned are you about advertisers and companies tracking your behavior across the Web?" *Wall Street Journal*, http://online.wsj.com/community/groups/media-marketing-267/topics/how-concerned-you-about-advertisers?dj_vote=12190.

28. Emily Steel, "Some Data-Miners Ready to Reveal What They Know," *Wall Street Journal*, December 3, 2010, http://online.wsj.com/article/SB100014240527487043770045756508021367221966.html.

29. Scott Thurm and Yukari Iwatani, "Your apps are watching you," *Wall Street Journal*, December 17, 2010, http://blogs.wsj.com/digits/2010/12/19/how-one-apps-sees-location-without-asking/.

30. Ibid.

31. Emily Steel and Julia Angwin, "On the Web's Cutting Edge, Anonymity in Name Only," *Wall Street Journal*, August 4, 2010, http://online.wsj.com/article/SB10001424052748703294904575385532109190198.html.

32. Steve Stecklow and Paul Sonne, "Shunned Profiling Technology on the Verge of Comeback," *Wall Street Journal*, November 24, 2010, http://online.wsj.com/article/SB10001424052748704243904575630751094784516.html.

33. Julia Angwin and Steve Stecklow, "'Scrapers' Dig Deep for Data on Web," *Wall Street Journal*, October 12, 2010, http://online.wsj.com/article/SB10001424052748703358504575544381288117888.html.

34. Question of the day: "Would you use an Internet "do-not-track" tool if it were included in your Web browser?" *Wall Street Journal*, December 30, 2010, http://online.wsj.com/community/groups/question-day-229/topics/would-you-use-internet-do-not-track?dj_vote=13831.

35. "FTC Staff Issues Privacy Report, Offers Framework for Consumers, Businesses, and Policymakers," http://www.ftc.gov/opa/2010/12/privacyreport.shtm.

36. Lymari Morales, "U.S. Internet Users Ready to Limit Online Tracking for Ads," Gallup, January 13, 2011, http://www.gallup.com/poll/145337/Internet-Users-Ready-Limit-Online-Tracking-Ads.aspx.

37. Daniel Ruby, "Ad Layout Series: Above The Fold Ads Get 44% Higher CTR," Chikita Research, September 22, 2010, http://chitika.com/research/2010/ad-layout-series-above-the-fold-ads-get-44-higher-ctr/.

38. Davis Dyer, Frederick Dalzell, and Rowena Olegario, *Rising Tide: Lessons from 165 Years of Brand Building at Procter & Gamble* (Boston: Harvard Business School Publishing, 2004).

39. "The F&M Schaefer Brewing Company," BeerHistory.com, http://www.beer history.com/library/holdings/schaefer_anderson.shtml.

40. Hugh McLeod, "the hughtrain," *Gapingvoid*, June 27, 2004, http://gapingvoid .com/2004/06/27/the-hughtrain/.

41. See http://www.google.com/corporate/history.html.

42. See http://investor.google.com/financial/tables.html.

43. "$6.4 Billion in Q3 2010 Sets New Record for Internet Advertising Revenues," http://www.iab.net/about_the_iab/recent_press_releases/press_release_archive/press_ release/pr-111710.

44. Ronan Shields, "AdMob serves 16.7bn ads during March," *New Media Age*, April 28, 2010, http://www.nma.co.uk/news/admob-serves-167bn-ads-during-march/3012743. article.

45. "We've officially acquired AdMob!" *The Official Google Blog*, May 27, 2010, http://googleblog.blogspot.com/2010/05/weve-officially-acquired-admob.html.

46. "UK: Mobile advertising revenues will grow 840% by 2015," *MobileSquared*, September 9, 2010, 9:46 am, http://www.mobilesquared.co.uk/news/2648.

47. Eli Pariser, *The Filter Bubble: What the Internet is Hiding from You* (New York: Penguin Press, 2011), 109–110.

48. Nicholas G. Carr, *The Shallows: What the Internet is Doing to our Brains*. (New York: W. W. Norton & Company, 2010), 222.

49. Eli Pariser, *The Filter Bubble: What the Internet Is Hiding from You*. (New York: The Penguin Press, 2011.) 115.

50. Richard E. Kihlstrom and Michael H. Riordan, "Advertising as a Signal," *Journal of Political Economy* 92, no. 3 (1994): 427–450.

51. Tim Ambler and E. Ann Hollier, "The Waste in Advertising is the Part That Works," *Journal of Advertising Research*, December 2004, 375–390.

52. Don Marti, "Ad Targeting—Better is Worse?" http://zgp.org/~dmarti/business/ targeting-better-is-worse/.

53. "Our Company," *Reedge*, http://www.reedge.com/our-company.

54. "Some really smart folks decided to build something better," *RocketFuel*, http:// www.rocketfuelinc.com/about.

55. Eric Clemons, "Why Advertising Is Failing On The Internet," *TechCrunch*, May 22, 2009, http://techcrunch.com/2009/03/22/why-advertising-is-failing-on-the-internet/.

56. "The end of the free lunch—again," *The Economist*, March 19, 2009, http:// www.economist.com/node/13326158?story_id=13326158.

57. Eric Clemons, "Why Advertising Is Failing On The Internet" *TechCrunch*. March 22, 2009. http://techcrunch.com/2009/03/22/why-advertising-is-failing-on-the-internet/

58. Douglas Harper, *Online Etymology Dictionary*, http://www.etymonline.com/ index.php?allowed_in_frame=0&search=mania.

59. The word "advertimania" was new when I researched it online. So I posted it on my blog, *Doc Searls Weblog*, on September 28, 2011, both to introduce it to the world and to test time-to-index for Bing and Google. http://blogs.law.harvard.edu/ doc/2011/09/28/advertimania/.

60. Julia Angwin, "The Web's New Gold Mine: Your Secrets," http://online.wsj .com/article/SB10001424052748703940090457539507351298404.html.

61. Christopher Meyer and Stanley M. Davis, *Blur: Speed of Change in the Connected Economy* (New York: Capstone Publishing, 1999).

62. Personal conversation.

63. Personal e-mail.

64. A search for "privacy policy" (with quotes) consistently yields close to a billion results on Google. This is because any site with something to sell has, as a pro forma matter, a privacy policy.

Chapter 3

1. Frederick Douglas, http://www.biography.com/people/frederick-douglass-9278324?.
2. Craig Burton, personal conversation.
3. Tim Berners-Lee, *Weaving the Web: The Original Design and Ultimate Destiny of the World Wide Web by its Inventor* (New York: HarperOne, 1999), 227.
4. "Internet grows to nearly 202 million domain names in third quarter of 2010," Verisign press release, November 29, 2010, http://bit.ly/f8LVfU; VB.com counted 69,215,937 registered.com domains on the last day of 2008, and 78,776,555 and 84,000,293 on the last days of 2008 and 2009, http://www.vb.com/domain-time-line.htm.
5. On just one laptop, I have 687 login-password combinations in Firefox, and 79 in Chrome.
6. Mark Zuckerberg, "Facebook Across the Web," *The Facebook Blog*, December 4, 2008.
7. Jennifer Van Grove, "Each Month 250 Million People use Facebook Connect on the Web," *Mashable*, December 8, 2010.
8. Kim Cameron, "Introduction," http://www.identityblog.com/?p=838.
9. Phred Dvorak and Stuart Weinberg, "Rim, Carriers Fight Over Digital Wallet," *Wall Street Journal*, March 18, 2011, B1.

Chapter 4

1. Henry David Thoreau, "Slavery in Massachusetts," delivered at an anti-slavery celebration in Framingham, Massachusetts, on July 4, 1854, after the conviction in Boston of fugitive slave Anthony Burns, http://thoreau.eserver.org/slavery.html. Additional source: Henry David Thoreau, *Walden and other writings of Henry David Thoreau*, (New York: Random House, 1937), 669.
2. For Deepa's account, see http://www.flickr.com/people/itzfromme/.
3. Thomas Hawk, http://www.flickr.com/photos/; Thomas Hawk, "Deepa Praven's Protest After Flickr Deletes Her Paid Pro Account Without Warning or Explanation, http://thomashawk.com/2011/01/deepa-pravens-protest-after-flickr-deletes-his-paid-pro-account-without-warning-or-explanation.html.
4. See http://blogs.law.harvard.edu/doc/2011/01/12/what-if-flickr-fails.
5. "Adhesion Contract," *West's Encyclopedia of American Law*, 2nd ed (Farmington Hills, MI: The Gale Group, Inc., 2008). Accessed via *The Free Dictionary*, http://legal-dictionary.thefreedictionary.com/Adhesion+Contract.
6. Kessler passes back credit for coining the term, writing, "Thus, standardized contracts are frequently contracts of adhesion; they are *à prendre ou à laisser*." A footnote in that passage reads, "The word 'contract of adhesion' has been introduced into the legal vocabulary by Patterson, *The Delivery of a Life Insurance Policy* (1919) 33 HARV. L. REV. 198, 222."
7. Friedrich Kessler, "Contracts of Adhesion—Some Thoughts about Freedom of Contract," *Columbia Law Review* 43, no. 5 (July 1943): 631. Also Kessler, Friedrich, "Contracts of Adhesion-Some Thoughts About Freedom of Contract" (1943), faculty scholarship series, paper 2731, http://digitalcommons.law.yale.edu/fss_papers/2731.
8. Google Accounts, http://www.google.com/accounts/TOS.
9. Douglas Adams, *The Hitchhiker's Guide to the Galaxy* (New York: Ballantine Books, 1979).
10. Second Life, Privacy Policy, http://secondlife.com/corporate/privacy.php.
11. In 2007, Marc Bragg challenged the contractual provision in Linden Labs's Terms of Service that required him to travel to California to arbitrate a claim he had against the company. Linden Labs Terms of Service then had a mandatory arbitration provision. Under California law, however, a contract could be held to be unconscionable both procedurally and substantively. The court decided that mandatory arbitration was likely to cost well over $20,000, while also requiring Bragg to travel to

California. The court concluded that the arbitration clause is not designed to provide Second Life participants with an effective means of resolving disputes with Linden. Rather it was one-sided and tilted unfairly, in almost all cases, in Linden's favor. (*Bragg v. Linden Research, Inc.*, 487 F. Supp. 2d 593 E.D.Penn. 2007.) The case was eventually settled for an undisclosed amount, and the result did nothing to change the way companies write Terms of Service. Except, perhaps, to make them even more one-sided than before.

12. *West's Encyclopedia of American Law.* http://legal-dictionary.thefreedictionary.com/Adhesion+Contract.

13. Kessler, "Contracts of Adhesion," 630.

14. Ibid., 640.

15. Renee Lloyd, personal correspondence.

16. Kessler, "Contracts of Adhesion" 641.

17. West's Encyclopedia of American Law.

18. ProCD, Inc. v. Zeidenberg, 86 F3d 1447 (7th Cir.1996).

19. Ibid., 1449.

20. Flickr pro, Additional Terms of Service, http://www.flickr.com/atos/pro/.

21. Y! Media Kit, http://advertising.yahoo.com/media-kit/flickr.html.

22. Zack Shepherd, "5,000,000,000," *Flickr Blog*, September 19, 2010, http://blog.flickr.net/en/2010/09/19/5000000000/.

23. In a search for "privacy policy" on January 26, 2011, Google came up with 908 million results. The same search (http://www.google.com/search?q=%22privacy+policy%22) yielded 1,820 million results on November 2, 2011. Since privacy policies nearly always accompany adhesive contracts (usually called "terms of service," "service agreements," or similar noun phrases), and not all adhesive contracts require a privacy policy, we might assume that there are at least a billion Web sites that present adhesive contracts.

24. "Contracts: Click-Wrap Licenses," *Internet Law Treatise*, Electronic Frontier Foundation, http://ilt.eff.org/index.php/Contracts:_Click_Wrap_Licenses.

Chapter 5

1. Iain Henderson, "Sales Process … meet Buying Process; and why context trumps segmentation," *Information Answers*, August 7, 2009, http://informationanswers.com/?p=386.

2. Geoffrey James, "Strong Market Growth Predicted Through 2012," http://www.sellingpower.com/magazine/article.php?i=839&ia=2584. The report cites Gartner, which does not make its research available directly.

3. See https://www.trefis.com/company?hm=CRM.trefis&driver=0104#.

4. Doc Searls, "Will the real History of CRM please stand up?" *Doc Searls Weblog*, December 1, 2008.

5. Gartner, "Magic Quadrant for Sales Force Autoation," July 28, 2010, http://www.gartner.com/technology/media-products/reprints/oracle/article145/article145.html; Donal Daly, "Gartner's CRM Magic Quadrant & Sales Effectiveness," *Sales 20 Network*, August 26, 2010, http://sales20network.com/blog/?p=807.

6. Michael Maoz, "You failed at Customer Service, so now try Social Processes," *Gartner Blog*, October 27 2010, http://blogs.gartner.com/michael_maoz/2010/10/27/you-failed-at-customer-service-so-now-try-social-processes/.

7. Steve Lohr, "Customer Service? Ask a Volunteer," *New York Times*, April 25, 2009, http://www.nytimes.com/2009/04/26/business/26unbox.html.

8. Eric von Hippel, *Democratizing Innovation* (Cambridge, MA: MIT Press, 2006).

9. Paul Greenberg, *CRM at the Speed of Light*, 4th ed., *Social CRM 2.0 Strategies, Tools, and Techniques for Engaging Your Customer* (New York: McGraw-Hill Osborne Media, 2009), 4, 45.

Chapter 6

1. Stephen Wright, from one of his stand-up acts, http://www.youtube.com/watch?v=F5ErMolRE8M&.

2. I heard George Burns say this long ago and have quoted it often. Alas, today nearly all citations of the quote trace back to me and not to George. So, until we find a more solid source, you'll just have to take my word for it.

3. The original source here was the About page at shsolutions.com, which provided a history of S&H, the original Green Stamps company. The company has now changed its name to greenpoints.com, but its About page link goes nowhere.

4. I have been challenged on this assumption, but I've heard the same from many other customers. So, while perception may not be reality, it's close enough to make something of a case.

5. Color me cranky, but I hate it when some company I don't know uses the first-person singular pronoun on my behalf.

Chapter 7

1. Chris Dale, "Don't believe everything you read in the papers," *The e-Disclosure Information Project*, December 12, 2010, http://chrisdale.wordpress.com/2010/12/16/dont-believe-everything-you-read-in-the-papers/.

2. From a presentation by Tim Christin, then an executive with Acxiom, at the Kynetx Impact conference in November 2009.

3. "Our goal is to personalize your experiences," https://www.rapleaf.com/about.

4. "Personalization Info," Rapleaf, https://www.rapleaf.com/people/see_your_info.

5. Emily Steele, "A Web Pioneer Profiles Users By Name," *Wall Street Journal*, October 25, 2011; Emily Steele, "Thousands of Web Users Delete Profiles From RapLeaf," *Wall Street Journal*, http://online.wsj.com/article/SB10001424052702304248704575574653801361746.html; Julia Angwin, "Privacy Advocate Withdraws from RapLeaf Advisory Board," *Wall Street Journal*, http://blogs.wsj.com/digits/2010/10/24/privacy-advocate-withdraws-from-rapleaf-advisory-board/; Jennifer Valentino-DeVries, "How to Get Out of RapLeaf's System," *Wall Street Journal*, October 24, 2010, http://blogs.wsj.com/digits/2010/10/24/how-to-get-out-of-rapleafs-system/; Courtney Banks, "Rapleaf's Founder on Privacy and Business," *Wall Street Journal*, October 24, 2010, http://blogs.wsj.com/digits/2010/10/24/rapleafs-founder-on-privacy-business/; Caitlin, "The 12 Days of Personalization," Rapleaf Blog, December 22, 2010, http://blog.rapleaf.com/the-12-days-of-personalization-2/.

6. Caitlin, "Day 12: A Valuable Box Office," Rapleaf Blog, http://blog.rapleaf.com/day-12-the-12-days-of-personalization/.

7. Christopher Locke, *The Cluetrain Manifesto* (New York: Basic Books, 2000), 87, http://www.cluetrain.com/book/apocalypso.html.

8. McKinsey & Company, "Big Data: The next frontier for innovation, competition and productivity," http://www.mckinsey.com/mgi/publications/big_data/pdfs/MGI_big_data_full_report.pdf and http://www.mckinsey.com/mgi/publications/big_data/.

9. Ibid., 90.

10. See http://jeffjonas.typepad.com/jeff_jonas/2009/08/your-movements-speak-for-themselves-spacetime-travel-data-is-analytic-superfood.html.

11. See http://commerce.senate.gov/public/?a=Files.Serve&File_id=85b45cce-63b3-4241-99f1-0bc57c5c1cff.

12. See http://www.ftc.gov/os/2010/12/101201privacyreport.pdf.

13. See http://www.commerce.gov/sites/default/files/documents/2010/december/iptf-privacy-green-paper.pdf.

Chapter 8

1. "Horoscope: August 30, 2011," *The Onion*, 47, no. 35, http://www.theonion .com/articles/your-horoscopes-week-of-august-30-2011,21249/.

2. "TLC Videos: Extreme Couponing All-Stars: Panic at the Supermarket!" *TLC Videos*, http://tlc.discovery.com/videos/extreme-couponing/

3. Food Marketing Institute, "Supermarket Facts: Industry Overview 2010," http://www.fmi.org/facts_figs/?fuseaction=superfact.

Chapter 9

1. David Weinberger, *Small Pieces, Loosely Joined: a unified theory of the Web* (New York: Perseus Books, 2002), 24.

2. In the *Blade Runner FAQ*, Murray F. Chapman lists thirty product placements. Chapman's research, spanning several years in the early 1990s, is extensive: http://www .faqs.org/faqs/movies/bladerunner-faq/.

3. I might be wrong on one or more of those, and I might have missed some other locations. In any case, my point is the same: the Net works by reducing the apparent distance of everything on it to zero—and the cost as well.

4. See http://en.wikipedia.org/wiki/VisiCalc; Bob Frankston, "Understanding Ambient Connectivity," http://www.frankston.com/public/?name=AmbientConnectivity.

5. Google search for "the Internet is," http://www.google.com/search?hl=en&q= "the+Internet+is".

6. See http://web.mit.edu/Saltzer/www/publications/endtoend/endtoend.pdf.

7. David Isenberg, "The Rise of the Stupid Network," http://isen.com/stupid .html.

8. My favorite sources for more wisdom on this are George Lakoff and Mark Johnson. A good place to start is with *Philosophy in the Flesh: the Embodied Mind and Its Challenge to Western Thought* (New York: Basic, 1999). Other recommendations are in the bibliography.

9. In *Small Pieces*, David also writes, "I purposefully conflate the Internet with the Web throughout the book." His point here therefore applies to the Net, and not just to the Web.

10. David Weinberger, *Small Pieces*, 9.

11. Doc Searls, "Uncollapsing Open Source Distinctions: A Conversation with Craig Burton," *Linux Journal*, August 2000, http://www.linuxjournal.com/article/4158.

12. Google search for RSS, http://www.google.com/search?q=rss. A search in February 2011 yielded 6 billion results, and searches in months previous to that grew from 3 billion to 4 billion results.

13. Doc Searls, "Bet on nature," *Doc Searls Weblog*, http://doc-weblogs.com/ 2001/02/08.

14. Wikipedia entries such as this one (on the Internet protocol suite) change almost constantly. This link goes to the latest revision as of February 14, 2011, http:// en.wikipedia.org/w/index.php?title=Internet_Protocol_Suite&oldid=413851023.

15. Patent 4,063,220. Listed inventors are Robert M. Metcalfe, David R. Boggs, Charles P. Thacker, and Butler W. Lampson. The assignee is Xerox Corporation, which worked with Digital Equipment Corporation and Intel on the standard, and the successful strategy for ubiquitizing it.

Chapter 10

1. Walt Whitman, *Leaves of Grass*, The Project Gutenberg, 1998. (First published by Whitman in *Song of Myself*, 1855.)

2. William J. Mitchell, *City of Bits: Space, Place, and the Infobahn* (Boston: MIT Press, 1995), 24.

3. Geoffrey West, "The surprising math of cities and corporations," A speech at TED, July 2011, http://www.ted.com/talks/geoffrey_west_the_surprising_math_of_cities_and_corporations.html.

4. Ibid.

5. Ibid.

Chapter 11

1. Ralph Waldo Emerson, *Essays: First Series*, 1841.

2. "agency *noun*," *Oxford Dictionary of English*, Angus Stevenson, ed. (Oxford: Oxford University Press, 2010); Oxford Reference Online, Oxford University Press, Harvard University Library, http://www.oxfordreference.com/views/ENTRY.html?subview=Main&entry=t140.e0013280.

3. Disclosure: for a few months Acxiom was a consulting client of mine. Tim Christin, who hired me, thought Acxiom was in a good position to be a fourth party: an agency for individuals. But it's hard for a company to change its species, and that's what we were asking Acxiom to do. Eventually, Tim moved on and so did I. Still, to Tim and Acxiom's credit, the company did invest early in Kynetx, a developer of tools ideal for VRM. We visit those tools in chapter 22, and fourth parties in chapter 19.

4. Abraham H. Maslow, "A Theory of Human Motivation," *Psychological Review* 50 (1943): 370–395.

5. Ibid., 383.

6. Clay Shirky, *Here Comes Everybody: The Power of Organizing Without Organizations* (New York: Penguin Press, 2008), 23.

Chapter 12

1. Eric S. Raymond, *The Cluetrain Manifesto* (New York: Basic Books, 2000), 87.

2. Linus Torvalds and David Diamond, *Just for Fun: the Story of an Accidental Revolutionary* (New York: HarperBusiness, 2001).

3. Linus has said this, or something very much like it, to me—or in my presence— many times. One sample can be found in "Caring Less," a column I wrote for Linux Journal's February 2003 issue, http://www.linuxjournal.com/article/6427.

4. Netcraft, http://necraft.com.

5. Yochai Benkler, "Coase's Penguin, or Linux and The Nature of the Firm," *Yale Law Journal* 112 (2002); *The Wealth of Networks* (New Haven, CT: Yale University Press, 2006).

6. Some of Linux's top kernel hackers, called maintainers, worked at IBM at the time, and still do.

7. Doc Searls, "Is Linux Now a Slave to Corporate Masters?" *Linux Journal*, April 30, 2008.

8. Brian Profitt, "Morton Gets Googled," *Linux Today*, August 3, 2006, http://www.linuxtoday.com/developer/2006080303126NWCYKN.

9. Eric S. Raymond, "Goodbye, 'free software'; hello, 'open source,'" http://www.catb.org/~esr/open-source.html.

10. Credit where due: the term open source was first used in its current context by Bruce Perens, in the Debian Free Software Guidelines, which evolved into the Open Source Definition. The definition still anchors used the Open Source Initiative, which was cofounded by Perens and Eric Raymond and remains the canonical institution of the open source movement.

11. Personal correspondence.

12. Richard Stallman, "GNU Operating System," http://www.gnu.org/gnu/manifesto.html.

Chapter 13

1. Hal Abelson, Ken Ledeen, and Harry Lewis, *Blown to Bits: Your Life, Liberty and Happiness after the Digital Explosion* (Boston: Addison Wesley, 2008), 4–5.

2. Kevin Kelly, "Better than Free" *The Technium*, http://www.kk.org/thetechnium/archives/2008/01/better_than_fre.php.

3. Lawrence Lessig, *Code and Other Laws of Cyberspace* (New York: Basic Books, 1999), 4.

4. "A Cloudy Crystal Ball—Visions of the Future," 1992-07-16, Presentation, 24th Internet Engineering Task Force.

5. ITU History Portal, http://www.itu.int/en/history/.

6. DOCSIS, http://www.cablelabs.com/cablemodem; About CableLabs, http://www.cablelabs.com/about/mission/.

7. See http://techonomy.com/program-outline/.

8. Susan Crawford., "The New Digital Divide," *New York Times*, December 3, 2011, http://www.nytimes.com/2011/12/04/opinion/sunday/internet-access-and-the-new-divide.html.

9. Ivan G. Seidenberg, "Bringing High-Speed Internet to All," *New York Times*, Letters, December 7, 2011, http://www.nytimes.com/2011/12/08/opinion/bringing-high-speed-internet-to-all.html.

10. James Bailey, "Why Broadband Is a Basic Human Right: ITU Secretary Hamadoun Touré," Forbes, November 14, 2011, http://www.forbes.com/sites/techonomy/2011/11/14/why-broadband-is-a-basic-human-right-itu-secretary-hamadoun-tour/.

11. 1984 was when AT&T was broken up.

12. See http://www.itu.int/3g.

13. Scott Adams, "Making Money Scheme," *The Scott Adams Blog*, April 6, 2011, http://dilbert.com/blog/entry/money_making_scheme/.

14. Ryan Singel, "Wireless Oligopoly is the Smother of Invention," *Wired*, http://www.wired.com/epicenter/2010/06/wireless-oligopoly-is-smother-of-invention/#ixzz0vVTWU3nu.

15. In fact, "Markets are conversations," the alpha thesis of *The Cluetrain Manifesto*, was inspired by this writer's conversations with Reese Jones.

16. See http://www.frankston.com/public/?name=FSM.

Chapter 14

1. Jeff Jarvis, *What Would Google Do?* (New York: HarperBusiness, 2009), 270.

2. In telco parlance, OEMs are equipment makers such as Nokia, Motorola, and Samsung, while operators are phone companies such as AT&T, Verizon, and T-Mobile.

3. That was the idea, anyway. Within the practical realities of the telco business, only Google writes Android code, and in its licensing deals, Google isn't much different than Microsoft has been from the start with Windows. But let's remember that it was this kind of dealing that also made Windows a de facto dominant horizontal platform for two decades.

4. Google did buy Motorola in 2011, but the reason was clearly to acquire the patent portfolio and keep the company afloat, rather than to get into competition with other Android OEMs.

5. "Doc Searls on Steve Jobs," DaveNet, September 4, 1997, http://scripting.com/davenet/stories/DocSearlsonSteveJobs.html.

6. Yes, it has changed since then. But, contrary to the usual reports, there are not "caps" on data. Just flat charges for each additional gigabyte used.

7. Jarvis, *What Would Google Do?*, 79–80.

8. Jonathan Zittrain, *The Future of the Internet and How to Stop It* (New York: Yale University Press, 2009), 68, 70.

9. "Google's Android becomes the world's leading smart phone," *Canalys*, January 31, 2011, http://www.canalys.com/pr/2011/r2011013.html.

10. Brainy Quote, http://www.brainyquote.com/quotes/quotes/a/alberteins130982.html.

11. From John Gillmore's Web site: "This was quoted in *Time Magazine's* December 6, 1993 article 'First Nation in Cyberspace', by Philip Elmer-DeWitt. It's been reprinted hundreds or thousands of times since then, including the *NY Times* on January 15, 1996, *Scientific American* of October 2000, and *CACM* 39(7):13," http:toad.com/gnu.

12. Doc Searls, "Framing the Net," *Publius*, February 4, 2009, http://publius .cc/2008/05/16/doc-searls-framing-the-net.

13. CNBC, "The Stadium Curse: Naming Deals Gone Bust," CNBC.com, http:// www.cnbc.com/id/34960125/The_Stadium_Curse_Naming_Deals_Gone_Bust.

Chapter 15

1. Tom Peters, *Re-Imagine!* (New York: Dorling Kindersley Limited, 2003), 59.

2. Advanced Google Books search for "neither the state nor the market," http://www .google.com/search?tbo=p&tbm=bks&q=%22neither+the+state+nor+the+market%22& num=10.

3. Garrett Hardin, "The Tragedy of the Commons," *Science* 162 (1968): 1243–1248, http://www.sciencemag.org/content/162/3859/1243.full.

4. Ibid.

5. Hyde notes, "Garret Hardin has indicated that his original essay should have been titled 'The Tragedy of the Unmanaged Commons,' though better still might be 'The Tragedy of Unmanaged, Laissez-Faire, Common-Pool Resources with Easy Access for Noncommunicating, Self-Interested Individuals" See Lewis Hyde, *Common as Air* (New York: MacMillan, 2010), 44.

6. Hyde, *Common as Air*, 24–25.

7. *Estovers*, Hyde says, "comes from the French *estovoir*, 'to be necessary'; a common of estovers is actually a right of subsistence." Sourcing a line using *estovers* in the Magna Carta, he adds, "Rights in common assured a baseline of provision: they were the social security of the premodern world, the 'patrimony of the poor,' a stay against terror."

8. Hyde, *Common as Air*, 28.

9. Ibid., 31, 34–35.

10. Ibid., 37.

11. In *Commoners: Common Right, Enclosure and Social Change in England, 1700–1820* (Cambridge: Cambridge University Press, 1993), J. M. Neeson contends that a cultural memory of the commons persists in "a lasting connection between population and land" (306).

12. Ibid., 43–44.

13. Mike Linksvayer, "Lewis Hyde, author of Common as Air: Revolution, Art, and Ownership," *Creative Commons*, August 27, 2010, https://creativecommons.org/weblog/ entry/23204.

Chapter 16

1. Andy Wachowski and Lana Wachowski, *The Matrix Reloaded*, 2003.

2. William Shakespeare, *As You Like It*, Act 2, scene 1, 12–17.

3. Yes, these may have slowed down or halted in some places, at least temporarily. But our species has been making war and using up irreplaceable resources with impunity for the duration, and we are far from proving we can stop either practice.

4. Clay Shirky, *Cognitive Surplus: Creativity and Generosity in a Connected Age* (New York: Penguin Press, 2010), 1.

5. Ibid., 2.

6. Ibid., 12.

7. Ibid., 15.

8. Christopher Locke, "Internet Apocalypso." *The Cluetrain Manifesto* (New York: Perseus Books, 2000), 12.

9. Frederick Taylor, *Principles of Scientific Management* (Sioux Falls, South Dakota: NuVision Publications, LLC, 2007) 49. The original was a monograph self-published in 1911.

10. Peter Drucker, *Management: Tasks, Responsibilities, Practices* (New York: Harper Paperbacks, 1993, originally published in 1973), 325.

11. Friedrich Kessler, "Contracts of Adhesion—Some Thoughts about Freedom of Contract," *Columbia Law Review* 43, no. 5 (July 1943): 642.

12. Peter Drucker, *The Practice of Management* (New York: Harper & Row, 1954, 1982, 1986), viii.

13. Peter Drucker, quoted by Elizabeth Haas Edersheim, in *The Defininitive Drucker* (New York: McGraw Hill, 2007), 45.

14. William Hollingsworth Whyte, *The Organization Man* (New York: Simon and Schuster, 1956), 447–448.

15. Daniel Bell, *The Coming of Post-industrial Society: a Venture in Social Forecasting* (New York: Basic, 1973).

16. Alvin Toffler, *The Third Wave* (New York: Bantam Books, 1980), 12.

17. John Naisbitt, *Megatrends* (New York: Warner Books, 1982).

18. Ibid., 251.

19. Alvin Toffler, *Powershift: Knowledge, Wealth and Violence at the Edge of the 21st Century* (New York: Bantam Books, 1990), 212.

20. John Naisbitt and Patricia Aburdene, *Megatrends 2000: Ten New Directions for the 1990's* (New York: William Morrow, 1990), 298.

21. Ibid., 302.

22. Ibid., 308–309.

23. Regis McKenna, *Relationship Marketing: Successful Strategies for the Age of the Customer* (Menlo Park, CA: Addison Wesley, 1991), 43, 47, 119.

24. Don Peppers and Martha Rogers, *The One to One Future: Building Relationships One Customer at a Time* (New York: Doubleday, 1993), 4–5.

25. Ibid., 209.

26. Rick Levine, Christopher Locke, Doc Searls, and David Weinberger, *The Cluetrain Manifesto: The End of Business as Usual* (New York: Perseus Books, 2000), xii.

27. Daniel H. Pink, *Free Agent Nation: The Future of Working for Yourself* (New York: Business Plus, 2001), 18–19.

28. Don Tapscott and Anthony D. Williams, *Wikinomics* (New York: Penguin, 2006), 124–150.

29. Raymond Fisk, "A Customer Liberation Manifesto," *Service Science* 1, no. 3 (2009): 135, http://www.sersci.com/ServiceScience//upload/12512062260.pdf.

30. John Hagel III, John Seely Brown, and Lang Davison, *The Power of Pull: How Small Moves, Smartly Made, Can Set Big Things in Motion* (New York: Basic Books, 2010), 158.

31. David Siegel, *Pull: The Power of the Semantic Web to Transform Your Business* (New York: Portfolio, 2009), 22, 120.

32. Ibid., 152–153.

33. Rick Levine, Christopher Locke, Doc Searls, and David Weinberger, *The Cluetrain Manifesto: 10th Anniversary Edition* (New York: Basic Books, 2009), 18.

34. This is one of Veblen's most famous lines, yet it is hard to find the first source. Perhaps the reader can help with that.

Chapter 17

1. Alan Mitchell, "Is VRM a 'phenomenon'?" *Right Side Up*, May 19, 2008, http://rightsideup.blogs.com/my_weblog/2008/05/is-vrm-a-phenom.html.

2. Berkman Center for Internet & Society, http://cyber.law.harvard.edu/about.

3. Doc Searls, "Markets Are Relationships," *The Cluetrain Manifesto: 10th Anniversary Edition* (New York: Basic Books, 2009.), 17.

4. One could also substitute "individuals" here and broaden the meaning beyond commercial interactions alone.

5. Elliot Noss, personal conversation, August 2011.

Chapter 18

1. Eric Von Hippel, *Democratizing Innovation* (Cambridge, MA: MIT Press, 2005), 1.

2. Karim Lakhani and Jill A. Panetta, *The Principles of Distributed Innovation, Research Publication No. 2007-7* (Cambridge, MA: Berkman Center for Internet & Society, October 2007).

3. Brian Behlendorf, "Re: [projectvrm] VRM tools," October 13, 2011, https://cyber.law.harvard.edu/lists/arc/projectvrm/2011-10/msg00157.html.

4. Katherine Noyes, "Which Browser Has Your Back? That Would Be Firefox," *PCWorld*, October 12, 2011, http://www.pcworld.com/businesscenter/article/241661/which_browser_has_your_back_that_would_be_firefox.html.

5. Mozilla.org, *The State of Mozilla Annual Report 2010*, http://www.mozilla.org/en-US/foundation/annualreport/2010/opportunities/.

6. Doc Searls, "Enough with browsers. We need cars now," ProjectVRM, September 24, 2011, http://blogs.law.harvard.edu/vrm/2011/09/24/enough-with-browsers-we-need-cars-now/.

7. Ibid.

8. John Smart, *Human Performance Enhancement in 2032: A Scenario for Military Planners* (2004–2011), http://accelerating.org/articles/hpe2032army.html#pcdt.

9. Ibid.

10. Venessa Miemis, "Re: [projectvrm] Some VRM project mentions in the WSJ," ProjectVRM Mailing List, October 11, 2011, https://cyber.law.harvard.edu/lists/arc/projectvrm/2011-10/msg00072.html.

11. Everett M. Rogers, *Diffusion of Innovations* (New York: Free Press, 1995), 37.

12. Geoffrey Moore, *Chrossing the Chasm*, rev. ed. (New York: Harper Paperbacks, 2002).

13. Clayton M. Christensen and Michael E. Raynor, *The Innovator's Solution: Creating and Sustaining Successful Growth* (Boston: Harvard Business School, 2003), 45.

14. Ibid., 45–46.

Chapter 19

1. Juston Paskow, "It takes two to tango, but four to square dance …," @justinpaskow, March 6, 2011, https://twitter.com/#!/justonpaskow/status/44273131350790144. Also, "It Takes Two to Tango; Four to Square Dance," Agile 2009 Conference, http://agile2009.agilealliance.org/node/286/index.html. This is one of those cases where one thinks of a one-liner, looks on the Web in confidence that somebody else has already thought of it, and sure enough: there it is. In this case, I thought, "Hmm … It takes two to tango, but four to square dance." These are the top-two results. I gave Justin the quote credit in the text because his line exactly matched the one I had in mind. But I at least want to give the two other guys props as well, even if it's only in an endnote.

2. "Third Party Agent Program," http://usa.visa.com/merchants/risk_management/thirdparty_agents.html?ep=v_sym_third-party-agent.

Chapter 20

1. Personal conversation with Renee Lloyd, an attorney, former Berkman fellow, and contributor to ProjectVRM. June 2011.

2. Rudyard Kipling, *The Man Who Would Be King* (New York: Doubleday, 1899), 41.

3. Friedrich Kessler, "Contracts of Adhesion—Some Thoughts about Freedom of Contract," *Columbia Law Review* 43, no. 5 (July 1943): 640–641.

4. Yes, we'll never know. And that's also my point. At least with *freedom of contract*, we'll find out.

5. *Eldred v. Ashcroft* began as *Eldred v. Reno* in 1999 and ended in 2003 with defeat for the plaintiff in the Supreme Court. The case challenged the constitutionality of the 1998 Sonny Bono Copyright Term Extension Act (CTEA), which extended by twenty years the already-extended terms of the Copyright Act of 1976 (one in a long series that each extended the original fourteen years suggested by the Constitution). The 1998 terms ranged from seventy to one hundred twenty years from creation or from the death of the author (or surviving author)—in other words, essentially forever. Or, comporting with the late Sonny Bono's expressed wishes, "forever less a day."

6. Thomas L. Friedman, *The World is Flat: A Brief History of the Twenty-First Century*, 1st ed. (New York: Farrar, Straus and Giroux, 2005), 81.

7. "Owner Data Agreement," Personal.com, http://www.personal.com/personal/owner-data-agreement.

8. Information Sharing Workgroup, http://kantarainitiative.org/confluence/display/infosharing/Home.

Chapter 21

1. World Economic Forum, "Personal Data: The Emergence of a New Asset Class" (Geneva: World Economic Forum, 2011), http://www.weforum.org/issues/rethinking-personal-data.

2. John Hagel III and Mark Singer, *Net Worth: Shaping Markets When Customers Make the Rules* (Boston: Harvard Business School Press, 1999), 3.

3. Joe Andrieu, "VRM: The user as point of integration," JoeAndrieu.com, June 14, 2007, http://blog.joeandrieu.com/2007/06/14/vrm-the-user-as-point-of-integration/.

4. Ibid.

5. Adriana Lukas, "Two tales of user-centricities," *Media Influencer*, April 21, 2008, http://www.mediainfluencer.net/2008/04/two-tales-of-user-centricities/.

6. Joe Andrieu, "Introducing User Driven Services," JoeAndrieu.com, http://blog.joeandrieu.com/2009/04/26/introducing-user-driven-services/.

7. Joe Andrieu, "Re: [projectvrm] VRM tool characteristics." June 15, 2011, https://cyber.law.harvard.edu/lists/arc/projectvrm/2011-06/msg00151.html.

8. Iain Henderson, "The Personal Data Ecosystem," *Kantara Initiative*, June 2009, http://kantarainitiative.org/wordpress/2009/06/iain-henderson-the-personal-data-eco-system/.

9. Ibid.

10. At first, it was called "Mydata," but that was duplicative of something else, so they changed it.

11. Department for Business, Innovation and Skills, "Midata—access and control your personal data," 2011, http://www.bis.gov.uk/policies/consumer-issues/personal-data.

12. Department for Business, Innovation and Skills, "The midata vision of consumer empowerment," November 3, 2011, http://www.bis.gov.uk/news/topstories/2011/Nov/midata.

13. U.K. Cabinet Office Behavioural Insights Team, "Better Choices, Better Deals: Consumers Powering Growth," Department for Business, Innovation and Skills, 2011, http://www.bis.gov.uk/assets/biscore/consumer-issues/docs/b/11-749-better-choices-better-deals-consumers-powering-growth.pdf.

14. Cabinet Office Behavioral Insights Team, *Better Choices: Better Deals—Consumers Powering Growth*, (London: Department for Business Innovation & Skills, April 2011).

15. Rory Clellan-Jones, "Midata: Will the public share government's enthusiasm?" BBC News Technology, November 3, 2011, http://www.bbc.co.uk/news/technology-15580059.

16. Jeremie Miller, "High Order Bit," Web 2.0 Summit, October 18, 2011, http://www.youtube.com/watch?v=pTNO5npNq28&.

Chapter 22

1. Craig Burton, "The API Computing Magic Troika and the API Economy," *Craig Burton: Logs, Links, Life and Lexicon: and Code*, October 26, 2011, http://www.craig-burton.com/?p=3381.

2. David Weinberger, "The Hyperlinked Organization," *The Cluetrain Manifesto: 10th Anniversary Edition* (New York: Basic Books, 2011), 187–188.

3. Personal conversation, October, 2011.

4. Phil Windley, "On hierarchies and networks," *Technometria*, September 16, 2011, http://www.windley.com/archives/2011/09/on_hierarchies_and_networks.shtml.

5. Phil Windley, via email, November 6, 2011.

6. The hot new entry here is a simple and smart replacement for just about any household thermostat, by Nest, a company started by Tony Fadell, the former vice president of engineering at Apple. He began there by leading development of the iPod and its descendants.

7. With so much more being made accountable in the evented world, and with more and more data being kept and managed by individuals and their fourth-party agents (such as Singly, in this case), it makes sense to return to double-entry bookkeeping, which served civilization well from the time of Marco Polo until the single-entry simplicities of Quicken and QuickBooks caused most of us to drop it. Simply put, what double-entry bookkeeping does is provide ways to connect what happens in the real world with the numbers produced by the final stage of bookkeeping and accounting: the ledger and the reports it produces.

8. Craig Burton, "The API Computing Magic Troika and the API Economy," *Craig Burton: Log, Links, Life and Lexicon*, October 26, 2011, http://www.craigburton.com/?p=3381.

9. Ibid.

Chapter 23

1. Jamie Murphy and Peter Hawthorne, "South Africa Mandela Declines Offer of Freedom," *Time Magazine*. February 25, 1985, http://www.time.com/time/magazine/article/0,9171,961237,00.html.

2. Milton Friedman, "Commanding Heights," interview on PBS, conducted October 1, 2000, http://www.pbs.org/wgbh/commandingheights/shared/minitext/int_miltonfriedman.html.

3. "Audience/Contributor," *Hearing Voices*, February 4, 2011, http://hearingvoices.com/news/2011/02/audiencecontributer; data sources: CPB's ISIS database, RRC, Arbitron, PBS Research, Nielsen. See "170 Million Americans for Public Broadcasting: The Numbers," http://www.170millionamericans.org/numbers.

4. There are a few exceptions. "This American Life," from Chicago station WBEZ, makes direct appeals on its podcasts.

5. Dave Winer, "WNYC Spam." *Scripting News*, February 12, 2007.

6. "Clearing rights" is pro forma in Hollywood and the recording industry, but it is so beset with regulatory complications (and therefore high legal costs) that nobody outside those industries bothers. As a result, for example, there are no podcasts of popular music. Streams, yes; podcasts, no. That's because there are blanket royalty payment agreements covering all artists for streaming, while there are none for podcasters. Thus, podcasters have to clear rights, separately, for every artist they play.

7. I obtained this insight separately from two very different people: Eric Raymond and Sayo Ajiboye. Eric is a libertarian atheist, and Sayo is a doctor of divinity.

8. "Emerging world" is the label used by *The Economist*. I like it better than alternatives, so I use it here.

9. Frank Stasio, *Home → The State of Things → SOT Audio Archive → WWW2010*, http://wunc.org/tsot/archive/sot0429c10.mp3.

10. Doc Searls, "Saving the Globe From its World of Hurt," *Doc Searls Weblog*, April 9, 2009, http://blogs.law.harvard.edu/doc/2009/04/09/saving-the-globe-from-its-world-of-hurt/.

11. "Associated Press to build news registry to protect content," *Associated Press*, July 23, 2009, http://www.ap.org/pages/about/pressreleases/pr_072309a.html.

12. Rnews Feed Aggregator, Sourceforge.net, http://rnews.sourceforge.net/.

13. hNews 0.1, Microformats wiki, http://microformats.org/wiki/hnews.

14. "Digital Performance Right In Sound Recording" list, Copyright Arbitration Royalty Panels, United States Copyright Office, http://www.copyright.gov/carp/index.html#performance; Copyright Royalty Board, http://www.loc.gov/crb/.

15. "Digital Performance Right in Sound Recordings Act of 1995," United States Copyright Office, http://www.copyright.gov/legislation/pl104-39.html; Digital Millennium Copyright Act, Public Law 105–304, October 28, 1998, http://www.copyright.gov/legislation/pl105-304.pdf.

16. Peter Vander Auwera, "Digital Asset Grid: Let's meet at the SWIFT Dance Hall," *swiftcommunity.net Blogs*, October 8, 2011, https://www.swiftcommunity.net/blogs/28/blogdetail/22333.

17. Umair Haque, *The New Capitalist Manifesto: Building a Disruptively Better Business* (Boston: Harvard Business Review Press, 2011), 19.

18. Umair Haque, "The Value Every Business Needs to Create Now," *HBR Blog Network*, September 31, 2009.

Chapter 24

1. Adam Smith, *An Inquiry into the Nature and Causes of the Wealth of Nations*, part 2, (London: W. Strahan and T. Cadell, 1776), 86, http://geolib.com/smith.adam/won1-10.html.

2. William Shakespeare, sonnet 116 (1609).

3. CMAT serves as a CRM industry standard, and this quote appears in the literature of many companies in the CRM business. Here is one: http://www.cmframeworks.com/cmat.htm.

4. Iain Henderson, "The Customer—Supplier Engagement Framework," *Information Answers*, January 25, 2010, http://informationanswers.com/?p=449.

5. Editors, "V Is for Victory—But the Victory Isn't Yours," *CRM Magazine*, May 2010.

Chapter 25

1. Joyce Searls: "When I was a young trainee at the Broadway Department Stores in Los Angeles, I had the privilege of being Stanley Marcus's escort on a visit to our stores. He told me his father's advice to him: 'Remember, there is never a good sale for Neiman Marcus that's not a good buy for the customer.' He said he believed and lived it every day."

2. David Ogilvy, *Confessions of an Advertising Man* (London: Southbank Publishing, 1983), 21.

3. In a way, it seemed like Garrison Keillor's "Ralph's Pretty Good Grocery," in his fictional town of Lake Wobegon. The slogan was, "If you can't find it at Ralph's, you can probably get along without it."

4. Beth Kowitt, "Inside the secret world of Trader Joe's," *Fortune*, August 23, 2010.

5. Trader Joe's, "Cheese, glorious cheese," *Fearless Flyer*, October 2011, http://www.traderjoes.com/fearless-flyer/article.asp?article_id=272.

6. Douglas Harper, *Online Etymology Dictionary*, http://www.etymonline.com/index.php?allowed_in_frame=0&search=consumer.

7. Adam Smith, *An Inquiry into the Nature and Causes of the Wealth of Nations* (London: Methuen & Co., Ltd., 1776). Also online at the Library of Economics and Liberty, George Mason University, http://www.econlib.org/library/Smith/smWN.html.

8. Doc Searls, "Markets are Relationships," *The Cluetrain Manifesto 10th Anniversary Edition* (New York: Basic Books, 2009), 19.

9. The search URL: http://www.google.com/search?&q=customer+protection+agency.

10. Bella English, "Led by the child who simply knew," *Boston Globe*, December 11, 2011.

11. "Target's unique guests," *Target.com*, http://pressroom.target.com/pr/news/target-guests.aspx.

12. "Retail's Big Show 2012," *National Retail Federation*, http://events.nrf.com/annual2012.

13. "Critical Developments in Retail Marketing: Understanding Consumers, Building Brands," *National Retail Federation*, January 16, 2011, http://events.nrf.com/annual2012/Public/SessionDetails.aspx?SessionID=1641.

14. "Winning Today's Digitally-Enhanced Shopper," *National Retail Federation*, January 16, 2011, http://events.nrf.com/annual2012/Public/SessionDetails.aspx?SessionID=1680.

15. Thomas Harper, "Gimmick," *Online Etymology Dictionary*, http://www.etymonline.com/index.php?term=gimmick&allowed_in_frame=0.

16. "Gimmick," *Merriam-Webster*, http://www.merriam-webster.com/dictionary/gimmick.

17. Regis McKenna and Geoffrey Moore (who worked for McKenna early in his career) have both said a "whole" product is far more than its essential qualities. A whole product includes everything that gives the customer a reason to buy. The hard part here is to separate pure gimmicks from substantive variables such as quality control, product history, and reputation, and the variety of ways a product fits with or is surrounded by other products that enhance its value. Obviously, Old El Paso products are made whole by their packaging, the cuisines and recipes in which they are used, and so on. What makes the discount in this case a gimmick is that it has nothing to do with why I want to buy an Old El Paso product, other than the enticement of the discount, which in fact might cheapen my own regard for the product.

18. The Onion, *Our Dumb World: Atlas of the Planet Earth* (New York: Little, Brown, 2007), 9–10.

19. Ibid., 230

20. Evelyn M. Rusli and Clair Cain Miller, "Google is Said to Be Poised to Buy Groupon," *New York Times DealBook*, November 30, 2010, http://dealbook.nytimes.com/2010/11/30/google-is-said-to-be-close-to-buying-groupon/.

21. Andrew Ross Sorkin, "The Missed Red Flags on Groupon," *New York Times DealBook*, October 17, 2011, http://dealbook.nytimes.com/2011/10/17/the-missed-red-flags-on-groupon/.

22. Doc Searls, "Lessons in Mid-Crash," *Linux Journal*, September 1, 2001, http://www.linuxjournal.com/article/4837.

23. It helps to remember that Phillips began his career as senior strategist for Richard Nixon's successful campaign for president in 1968, and his long series of books started with The Emerging Republican Majority in 1969. Among other distinctions, he coined the term Sun belt, and correctly projected its coherence as an economic base and a conservative Republican stronghold, long before both facts became obvious. Kevin Phillips, *American Theocracy: The Peril and Politics of Radical Religion, Oil, and Borrowed Money in the 21st Century* (New York: Penguin, 2007), 268.

24. Kevin Phillips, *Bad Money: Reckless Finance, Failed Politic, and the Global Crisis of American Capitalism* (New York: Viking, 2008), 70.

25. Brent Shendler, Peter Drucker, and Lixandra Urresta, "Peter Drucker Takes The Long View The original management guru shares his vision of the future with FORTUNE's Brent Schlender," *Fortune*, September 28, 1998 http://money.cnn.com/magazines/fortune/fortune_archive/1998/09/28/248706.

26. Stefanie Olsen, "Nordstrom makes strides with online shoe store," CNET News .com, November 2, 1999, http://news.cnet.com/2100-1017-232353.html.

27. Rachel Lamb, "Cultivating relationships increases customer loyalty, transactions: Zappos exec," *Luxury Daily*, July 1, 2011, http://stage.luxurydaily.com/customer-satisfaction-dependent-on-sales-professionals-zappos-exec/.

28. Dave Everett, "Cultivating relationships increases customer loyalty, transactions: Zappos exec," DaveEverett.net, http://daveeverett.net/cultivating-relationships-increases-customer-loyalty-transactions-zappos-exec/660/.

29. Youngme Moon, *Difference: Escaping the Competitive Herd* (New York: Crown Business, 2010), 11.

30. Ibid., 188.

31. Copy by Chiat/Day writers Rob Siltanen and Ken Segall, and art director Craig Tanimoto. Voice-over by Steve Jobs, "The Crazy Ones," 1997. On YouTube, http://www.youtube.com/watch?v=8rwsuXHA7RA.

32. Doc Searls and David Weinberger, "Markets are Conversations," *The Cluetrain Manifesto* (New York: Perseus Books, 2000), 76–77.

Chapter 26

1. Quote is widely credited to Libeskind, http://www.brainyquote.com/quotes/authors/d/daniel_libeskind.html.

2. From "The Real McCabe," an ad for itself that ran in the *Wall Street Journal* as one in a series that ran in the late 1970s and early 1980s. I remember it well because I was a copywriter at my new advertising agency at the time, and modeled my work on McCabe's. I was lucky to find an undated graphic copy of the original here: http://www.aef.com/images/creative_leaders/McCabe.gif.

3. John Taylor Gatto, *Dumbing Us Down: The Hidden Curriculum of Compulsory Schooling* (Gabriola Island, BC, Canada: New Society Publishers, 2002, 1992), xxxii.

4. Lewis Hyde, *The Gift: Creativity and the Artist in the Modern World* (New York: VintageBooks, 2007, 1979), xx.

5. Ibid.

Chapter 27

1. Craig Burton, by email, October 2011.

2. Suzanne Kapner, "Credit Unions Poach Clients," *Wall Street Journal*, November 7, 2011, http://online.wsj.com/article/SB100014240529702037335045770219723580858522.html.

3. Michael Stolarczyk, private correspondence, September, 2011.

4. Adrian Gropper, private correspondence, November, 2011.

5. Ibid.

6. Ibid.

7. Britt Blaser, private correspondence, September 2011.

8. Ibid.

Epilogue

1. Walter Isaacson, *Steve Jobs* (New York: Simon & Schuster, 2011), 143.

2. The formula for Werner Heisenber's uncertainty principle.

3. What Heisenberg said was also in German and more complicated than what I just said he said. But, toward the direction of his inquiry, my claim is the same: we can't measure the future, but we can work to make it better.

4. Christensen's five books (so far)—all with "Innovative" or "Innovator" in the title, are essential reading for any corporate manager who wishes either to cope with or prosper in the Intention Economy.

5. Larry Downes, *Laws of Disruption: Harnessing the new forces that govern life and business in the digital age* (New York: Basic Books, 2009), 17.

BIBLIOGRAPHY

Abelson, Harold, Ken Ledeen, and Harry R. Lewis. *Blown to Bits: Your Life, Liberty, and Happiness after the Digital Explosion*. Upper Saddle River, NJ: Addison-Wesley, 2008.

Amelio, Gil. *On the Firing Line: My 500 Days at Apple*. New York: HarperBusiness, 1998.

Anderson, Chris. *Free: the Future of a Radical Price*. New York: Hyperion, 2009.

Anderson, Chris. *The Long Tail*. New York: Hyperion, 2006.

Ariely, Dan. *Predictably Irrational, Revised and Expanded Edition: The Hidden Forces That Shape Our Decisions*. New York, Harper Perenial, 2010. Originally published in 2008 by Harper Collins.

Ariely, Dan. *The Upside of Irrationality: The Unexpected Benefits of Defying Logic at Work and at Home*. New York: Harper, 2010.

Bakshi, Rajni. *Bazaars, Conversations, and Freedom: for a Market Culture beyond Greed and Fear*. New Delhi: Penguin, 2009.

Bell, Daniel. *The Coming of Post-industrial Society; a Venture in Social Forecasting*. New York: Basic, 1973.

Benkler, Yochai. "Coase's Penguin, or Linux and The Nature of the Firm." *Yale Law Journal* 112 (2002).

Benkler, Yochai. *The Penguin and the Leviathan: How Cooperation Triumphs over Self-Interest*. New York: Crown Business, 2011.

Bhargava, Rohit. *Personality Not Included: Why Companies Lose Their Authenticity—and How Great Brands Get It Back*. New York: McGraw-Hill, 2008.

Blissett, Guy, Trevor Davis, Bill Gilmour, Patrick Medley, and Mark Yeomans. *The Future of the Consumer Products Industry*. IBM Institute for Business Value, 2010.

Blackmore, Susan, and Richard Dawkins. *The Meme Machine*. Oxford, UK: Oxford University Press, 2000.

Blackshaw, Pete. *Satisfied Customers Tell Three Friends, Angry Customers Tell 3,000: Running a Business in Today's Consumer Driven World*. New York: Doubleday, 2008.

Boldrin, Michele, and David K. Levine. *Against Intellectual Monopoly*. New York: Cambridge University Press, 2008.

Bollier, David. *Viral Spiral: How the Commoners Built a Digital Republic of Their Own*. New York: The New Press, 2008.

Boyle, James. *The Public Domain: Enclosing the Commons of the Mind*. New Haven, CT: Yale University Press, 2008.

Brand, Stewart. *How Buildings Learn: What Happens after They're Built*. New York: Penguin, 1995.

Bunt, Lucas N. H., Phillip Jones, and Jack D. Bedient. *The Historical Roots of Elementary Mathematics*. Englewood Cliffs, NJ: Prentice Hall, 1976.

Nicholas Carr. *The Big Switch*. New York: W.W. Norton & Co., 2008.

Caples, John, and Fred E. Hahn. *Tested Advertising Methods*. Upper Saddle River, NJ: Prentice Hall, 1997.

Christensen, Clayton M. *The Innovator's Dilemma: When New Technologies Cause Great Firms to Fail*. Boston: Harvard Business School Press, 1997.

Christensen, Clayton M., and Michael E. Raynor. *The Innovator's Solution: Creating and Sustaining Successful Growth*. Boston: Harvard Business School Press, 2003.

Christensen, Clayton M., Scott D. Anthony, and Erik A. Roth. *Seeing What's Next: Using the Theories of Innovation to Predict Industry Change*. Boston: Harvard Business School Press, 2004.

Christensen, Clayton M., and Michael Horn. *Disrupting Class: How Disruptive Innovation Will Change the Way the World Learns*. New York: McGraw-Hill Professional, 2008.

Christensen, Clayton M., Jerome H. Grossman, and Jason Hwang. *The Innovator's Prescription: A Disruptive Solution for Health Care*. New York: McGraw-Hill Professional, 2011.

Clawson, Calvin C. *The Mathematical Traveler: Exploring the Grand History of Numbers*. Cambridge, MA: Perseus Books, 1994.

Clippinger, John Henry. *A Crowd of One: the Future of Individual Identity*. New York: PublicAffairs, 2007.

Coburn, Pip. *The Change Function: Why Some Technologies Take off and Others Crash and Burn*. New York: Portfolio, 2006.

Covey, Steven R. *The 7 Habits of Highly Effective People*. New York: Free Press, 1989.

Covey, Steven R. *The 8th Habit: From Effectiveness to Greatness*. New York: Free Press, 2004.

Cruikshank, Jeffrey L., and Arthur W. Schultz. *The Man Who Sold America: the Amazing (but True!) Story of Albert D. Lasker and the Creation of the Advertising Century*. Boston: Harvard Business Press, 2010.

De Roover, Raymond. *The Rise and Decline of the Medici Bank—1397–1494*, 2nd ed. New York: Beard Books, 1999.

Downes, Larry. *The Laws of Disruption: Harnessing the New Forces That Govern Life and Business in the Digital Age*. New York: Basic, 2009.

Drucker, Peter F. *The Practice of Management*. New York: Harper & Row, 1954, 1982, 1986.

Drucker, Peter F. *Management Challenges for the 21st Century*. New York: HarperBusiness, 1999.

Drucker, Peter F. *Post-capitalist Society*. New York: HarperBusiness, 1993.

Drucker, Peter F. *Peter Drucker, Management: Tasks, Responsibilities, Practices*. New York: Harper Paperbacks, 1993, 1973.

Drucker, Peter F. *The Essential Drucker: Selections from the Management Works of Peter F. Drucker*. New York: HarperBusiness, 2001.

Edersheim, Elizabeth Haas, and Peter F. Drucker. *The Definitive Drucker*. New York: McGraw-Hill, 2007.

Eisenstein, Elizabeth L. *The Printing Press as an Agent of Change: Communications and Cultural Transformations in Early Modern Europe*. Cambridge, UK: Cambridge University Press, 1979.

Eisler, Riane Tennenhaus. *The Chalice and the Blade: Our History, Our Future*. San Francisco: HarperSanFrancisco, 1988.

Eves, Howard Whitley. *An Introduction to the History of Mathematics*, 6th ed. Belmont, CA: Brooks Cole, 1990.

Gatto, John Taylor. *Dumbing Us Down: The Hidden Curriculum of Compulsory Schooling*. Gabriola Island, BC, Canada: New Society Publishers, 2002, 1992.

Gansky, Lisa. *The Mesh: Why the Future of Business Is Sharing*. New York: Portfolio Penguin, 2010.

Garfield, Bob. *The Chaos Scenario: [amid the Ruins of Mass Media, the Choice for Business Is Stark: Listen or Perish]*. Nashville, TN: Stielstra Publishing, 2009.

Geijsbeek, John B. *Ancient Double-entry Bookkeeping: Lucas Pacioli's Treatise (A.D. 1494—the earliest known writer on bookkeeping)*. Denver: self-published, 1914.

Goldsmith, Jack L., and Tim Wu. *Who Controls the Internet?: Illusions of a Borderless World.* New York: Oxford University Press, 2008.

Greenberg, Paul. *CRM at the Speed of Light*, 4th ed.: *Social CRM 2.0 Strategies, Tools, and Techniques for Engaging Your Customer.* New York: McGraw-Hill Osborne Media, 2009.

Gupta, Sunil, and Carl Mela. "What Is a Free Customer Worth?" *Harvard Business Review*, November 2008.

Hagel, John, and John Seely Brown. *The Only Sustainable Edge: Why Business Strategy Depends on Productive Friction and Dynamic Specialization.* Boston: Harvard Business School Press, 2005.

Hagel, John, and Marc Singer. *Net Worth: Shaping Markets When Customers Make the Rules.* Boston: Harvard Business School Press, 1999.

Hagel, John, John Seely Brown, and Lang Davison. *The Power of Pull: How Small Moves, Smartly Made, Can Set Big Things in Motion.* New York: Basic, 2010.

Hammond, John Winthrop, and Arthur Pound. *Men and Volts; the Story of General Electric.* Philadelphia: J.B. Lippincott, 1941.

Haque, Umair. *The New Capitalist Manifesto: Building a Disruptively Better Business.* Boston: Harvard Business Review Press, 2011.

Hart, Stuart L. *Capitalism at the Crossroads: Next Generation Business Strategies for a Post-crisis World.* Upper Saddle River, NJ: Wharton School Publishing, 2010.

Hedges, Chris. *Empire of Illusion: the End of Literacy and the Triumph of Spectacle.* New York: Nation, 2009.

Henderson, Cal. *Building Scalable Web Sites.* Sebastapol, CA: O'Reilly Media, 2006.

Hyde, Lewis. *Common as Air: Revolution, Art, and Ownership.* New York: Farrar, Straus and Giroux, 2010.

Hyde, Lewis. *The Gift: Creativity and the Artist in the Modern World.* New York: Vintage, 2008.

Isaacson, Walter. *Steve Jobs.* New York: Simon & Schuster, 2011.

Jarvis, Jeff. *Public Parts.* New York: Simon & Schuster, 2011.

Jarvis, Jeff. *What Would Google Do?* New York: Collins Business, 2009.

Jewel Companies, Inc. *The Jewel Concepts.* Chicago: self-published, 1982.

Johnson, Steven. *Where Good Ideas Come From: the Natural History of Innovation.* New York: Riverhead, 2010.

Kasanoff, Bruce. *Making It Personal: How to Profit from Personalization without Invading Privacy.* Cambridge, MA: Perseus, 2001.

Emir Kamenica, Sendhil Mullainathan, and Richard Thaler, "Helping consumers know themselves." Working paper, Social Science Research Network. January 17, 2011.

Kelly, Kevin. *What Technology Wants.* New York: Viking, 2010.

Kipling, Rudyard. *The Man Who Would be King.* New York, Doubleday, 1899.

Kling, Arnold S., and Nick Schulz. *From Poverty to Prosperity: Intangible Assets, Hidden Liabilities and the Lasting Triumph over Scarcity.* New York: Encounter, 2009.

Lakhani, Karim, and Jill A. Panetta. *The Principles of Distributed Innovation.* Research Publication No. 2007-7. Cambridge, MA: Berkman Center for Internet and Society, October 2007.

Lakoff, George, and Mark Johnson. *Metaphors We Live by.* Chicago: University of Chicago Press, 1980.

Lakoff, George, and Mark Johnson. *Philosophy in the Flesh: the Embodied Mind and Its Challenge to Western Thought.* New York: Basic, 1999.

Lakoff, George, and Rafael E. Nunez. *Where Mathematics Comes From: How the Embodied Mind Brings Mathematics into Being.* New York: Basic, 2000.

Lanier, Jaron. *You Are Not a Gadget: a Manifesto.* New York: Alfred A. Knopf, 2010.

Lessig, Lawrence. *Code and Other Laws of Cyberspace.* New York: Basic, 1999.

Lessig, Lawrence. *The Future of Ideas: the Fate of the Commons in a Connected World.* New York: Random House, 2001.

Levine, Rick, Christopher Locke, Doc Searls, and David Weinberger. *The Cluetrain Manifesto*. New York: Perseus Books, 2000.

Levine, Rick, Christopher Locke, Doc Searls, and David Weinberger. *The Cluetrain Manifesto: 10th Anniversary Edition*. New York: Basic Books, 2009.

Levinson, Marc, *The Great A&P And The Struggle For Small Business In America*. New York: Hill and Wang, 2011.

Lewis, David, and Darren Bridger. *The Soul of the New Consumer: Authenticity—What We Buy and Why in the New Economy*. London: Nicholas Brealey Publishing, 2000.

Locke, Christopher. *Gonzo Marketing: Winning through Worst Practices*. Cambridge, MA: Perseus, 2001.

MacLeod, Hugh. *Ignore Everybody: and 39 Other Keys to Creativity*. New York: Portfolio, 2009.

Malone, Thomas W. *The Future of Work: How the New Order of Business Will Shape Your Organization, Your Management Style, and Your Life*. Boston: Harvard Business School, 2004.

McAfee, Andrew. *Enterprise 2.0: New Collaborative Tools for Your Organization's Toughest Challenges*. Boston: Harvard Business School Press, 2009.

McKenna, Regis. *Real Time: Preparing for the Age of the Never Satisfied Customer*. Boston: Harvard Business Press Books, 1997.

McKenna, Regis. *Relationship Marketing: Successful Strategies for the Age of the Customer*. Menlo Park, California: Addison-Wesley, 1991.

McKenna, Regis. *Total Access: Giving Customers What They Want in an Anytime, Anywhere World*. Boston: Harvard Business Press Books, 2002.

Mitchell, William J. *City of Bits: space, place and the infobahn*. Boston: The MIT Press, 1995.

Moon, Youngme. *Different: Escaping the Competitive Herd*. New York: Crown Business, 2010.

Moore, Geoffrey. *Crossing the Chasm*, revised ed. New York: Harper Paperbacks, 2002.

Naisbitt, John. *Megatrends: Ten New Directions Transforming Our Lives*. New York: Warner, 1982.

Naughton, John. *A Brief History of the Future: from Radio Days to Internet Years in a Lifetime*. Woodstock, NY: Overlook, 2000.

Normann, Richard, and Rafael Ramierez. *Designing Interactive Strategy: from Value Chain to Value Constellation*. Chichester, England: Wiley, 1994.

O'Connor, J. J., and E. F. Robertson. "Luca Pacioli," in *Biographies*. School of Mathematical and Computational Sciences, University of St. Andrews, Scotland, 1999. http://www-groups.dcs.st-and.ac.uk/~history/Biographies/Pacioli.html.

Ogilvy, David. *Confessions of an Adverstising Man*. London, UK: Southbank Publishing, 1983.

Ogilvy, David. *Ogilvy on Advertising*. New York: Crown, 1983.

Oram, Andrew. *Peer-to-Peer: Harnessing the Benefits of a Disruptive Technology*. Beijing: O'Reilly, 2001.

Ostrom, Elinor. *Governing the Commons: the Evolution of Institutions for Collective Action*. CambridgeUK: Cambridge University Press, 2008.

Quinn, Feargal. *Crowning the Customer: How to Become Customer Driven*. Atlantic City, NJ: Raphael Marketing, 1992.

Patel, Sameer. *Putting Relationship Back in Customer Relationship Management*. Presentation, Enterprise 2.0 Conference 2011, Boston, June 29, 2011. http://www.e2conf.com/boston/2011/presentations/free/59-sameer-patel.pdf.

Phillips, Kevin. *Bad Money: Reckless Finance, Failed Politics, and the Global Crisis of American Capitalism*. New York: Viking, 2007.

Phillips, Kevin. *American Theocracy: The Peril and Politics of Radical Religion, Oil, and Borrowed Money in the 21st Century*. New York: Penguin, 2006.

Pink, Daniel H. *Drive: the Surprising Truth about What Motivates Us*. New York: Riverhead, 2009.

Pink, Daniel H. *Free Agent Nation: the Future of Working for Yourself*. New York: Warner, 2002.

Reagle, Joseph Michael. *Good Faith Collaboration: the Culture of Wikipedia*. Cambridge, MA: MIT Press, 2010.

Ries, Al, and Jack Trout. *Positioning: the Battle for Your Mind*. New York: Warner, 1986.

Rosenberg, Scott. *Say Everything: How Blogging Began, What It's Becoming, and Why It Matters*. New York: Three Rivers, 2009.

Rushkoff, Douglas. *Coercion: Why We Listen to What "They" Say*. New York: Riverhead Books, 1999.

Samuels, Edward. *The Illustrated Story of Copyright*. New York: St. Martin's Griffin, 2002.

Schewick, Barbara Van. *Internet Architecture and Innovation*. Cambridge, MA: MIT Press, 2010.

Schmandt-Besserat, Denise. *Before Writing Volume I: From Counting to Cunieform*. Austin, TX: University of Texas Press, 1992.

Schmandt-Besserat, Denise. *How Writing Came About*. Austin, TX: University of Texas Press, 1996.

Schmandt-Besserat, Denise. *The History of Counting*. New York: Morrow Junior Books, 1999.

Sheldrake, Phillip. *The Business of Influence*. West Sussex, UK: John Wiley & Sons, Ltd., 2011.

Shell, Ellen Ruppel. *Cheap: The High Cost of Discount Culture*. New York: Penguin Press, 2009.

Shirky, Clay. *Cognitive Surplus: Creativity and Generosity in a Connected Age*. New York: Penguin, 2010.

Siegel, David. *Pull: the Power of the Semantic Web to Transform Your Business*. New York: Portfolio, 2009.

Smith, Adam. *An Inquiry into the Nature and Causes of the Wealth of Nations*. (London: Methuen & Co., Ltd., 1776.) Also online at the Library of Economics and Liberty, George Mason University. http://www.econlib.org/library/Smith/smWN.html.

Stross, Randall E. *Planet Google: One Company's Audacious Plan to Organize Everything We Know*. New York: Free Press, 2008.

Stephenson, Neal. *In the Beginning … Was the Command Line*. New York: Avon Books, 1999.

Stolarczyk, Michael. *Logical Logistics —A Common Sense Primer for your Supply Chain*, Createspace, 2011.

Strunk, William, Jr., and E. B. White, *The Elements of Style*, 4th ed. New York: Longman, 1999.

Sunstein, Cass R. *Infotopia: How Many Minds Produce Knowledge*. New York: Oxford University Press, 2006.

Thaler, Richard H., and Cass R. Sunstein,. *Nudge: Improving Decisions About Health, Wealth, and Happiness*. New Haven, Connecticut: Yale University Press, 2008.

Tapscott, Don, and Anthony D. Williams. *Wikinomics: How Mass Collaboration Changes Everything*. New York: Portfolio, 2006.

Taptiklis, Theodore. *Unmanaging: Opening up the Organization to Its Own Unspoken Knowledge*. Houndmills, Basingstoke, Hampshire, UK: Palgrave Macmillan, 2008.

Taylor, Jim, and Wacker, Watts, with Means, Howard. *The 500 Year Delta What Happens After What Comes Next*. New York: Harper Business, 1997.

The Onion, *Our Dumb World: Atlas of the Planet Earth*. New York: Little, Brown, 2007.

Van Cleve, Charles M. *Principles of Double-Entry Bookkeeping*. New York: James Kempster Printing Company, 1913.

Vandermerwe, Sandra. *Customer Capitalism: the New Business Model of Increasing Returns in New Market Spaces*. Naperville, IL: Nicholas Brealey Publishing, 1999.

von Hippel, Eric. *Democratizing Innovation*. Cambridge, MA: MIT Press, 2005.

Weinberger, David. *Everything Is Miscellaneous: the Power of the New Digital Disorder*. New York: Times, 2007.

Weinberger, David. *Small Pieces Loosely Joined: a Unified Theory of the Web*. Cambridge, MA: Perseus, 2002.

Weinberger, David. *Too Big to Know: Rethinking Knowledge Now That the Facts Aren't the Facts, Experts Are Everywhere, and the Smartest Person in the Room Is the Room*. New York: Basic Books, 2011.

Whitman, Walt, *Song of Myself*. Stilwell, KS: Digireads.com Publishing, 2006.

Whyte, William Hollingsworth. *The Organization Man*. New York: Simon and Schuster, 1956.

Williams, Sam. *Free as in Freedom: Richard Stallman's Crusade for Free Software*. Beijing: O'Reilly, 2002.

Wolff, Michael. *Burn Rate: How I Survived the Gold Rush Years of the Internet*. New York: Simon & Schuster, 1998.

Wu, Tim. *The Master Switch: the Rise and Fall of Information Empires*. New York: Alfred A. Knopf, 2010.

Zak, Paul J. *Moral Markets: the Critical Role of Values in the Economy*. Princeton, NJ: Princeton University Press, 2008.

Zittrain, Jonathan L. *The Future of the Internet: and How to Stop It*. London: Penguin, 2009.

Zuboff, Shoshana, and James Maxmin. *The Support Economy: Why Corporations Are Failing Individuals and the Next Episode of Capitalism*. New York: Viking, 2002.

INDEX

Abelson, Hal, 123
Aburdene, Patricia, 158
Acxiom, 79–80
Adams, Douglas, 55
Adams, Scott, 126
adhesion contracts
    adhesionism, 154–155
    defined, 8, 54
    enforceability of, 57–58
    genesis of, 54–55
    legality of, 56
    path towards the end of adhesion,
      156–162
    personal freedom and, 154–155
AdMob, 33
advertimania, 40–42
advertising, online
    growth in, 3–4, 32–33
    missing anonymity in, 36–38
    public reaction to advertisers' data
      collection, 30
    scope of tracking done by Internet
      businesses, 28–30
    tolerance for online TV advertising,
      22–25
"Advertising as a Signal" (Kihlstrom
  and Riordan), 35
advertising bubble
    advertimania, 40–42
    annual sum spent on advertising, 22
    branding and, 31–32
    Chinese wall, 21–22, 24, 247
    data filtration, 34
    delusions about advertising, 39–42
    demographic breakdown of
      viewers, 24t
    future of advertising, 26–27
    geo-targeted mobile advertising,
      83–84
    goal of knowing user intent, 38–39
    industry's tolerance for waste, 30–31

online advertising (*see* advertising,
    online)
platform choices, 25–26
quantitative versus emotional
    factions, 22
as a shock to the marketplace, 14, 15
signaling through advertising,
    34–36
AdWords, 32–33
agency
    defined, 111–112
    meaning of customer agency in the
      marketplace, 112–113
    original purpose of the merchant,
      226–227
    self-actualization and, 113–114
Alvarez, José, 226
Amara's Law, 7
Amazon.com, 101
ambient connectivity, 16–17, 95, 141
Ambler, Tim, 35
American Theocracy (Phillips), 231
Andrieu, Joe, 9, 15, 46, 168, 191, 193
Android platform, 134, 138
Apache, 170
APIs. *See* application programming
  interfaces
Apple
    approach to smartphones,
      133–135, 140
    being different and, 235
    customer focus, 242
    evolution of software for telephones
      and, 127–128
    future of, 143
    vertical monopoly, 137
Apple Stores, 136
application programming interfaces
  (APIs)
    businesses modeled as a fort,
      198–199

ACKNOWLEDGMENTS

These are the credits, which I've sorted into categories, even though many people I list defy categorization.

My wife Joyce, without whose faith and gentle pressure (over more than twenty years), this book would not have been written. Also, our son Jeffrey, who compiled the bibliography and who has been patient with my nonparental preoccupations. And our older kids, Colette, Jennine, Allen, and their families (including grandkids), who have endured the same neglect.

The quartet of good people who inseminated, incubated, and guided the book into existence. In order of appearance, they are:

- Rick Segal, who pushed me hard to make this book happen. He also gave it the title.

- Jeff Kehoe, my editor at Harvard Business Press, who showed up at my talk by this same title and suggested that the talk become a book. Jeff rocks.

- David Miller, my agent—and much more. He was with us for *Cluetrain* thirteen years ago, and he's with me now for this book.

- Adele Menichella, the friend and editor I called on in the last month of drafting, to help bang the book into its final shape.

The Berkman Center for Internet & Society and Harvard University, which took me on as a fellow in 2006 and patiently gave me four-plus years of runway to get ProjectVRM off the ground. Among my many friends and colleagues there (or with whom I've connected through the center), I'd especially like to thank:

- John Clippinger, Colin Maclay, and John Palfrey, who brought me in as a fellow (and Paul Trevithick, who helped behind the scenes).

- The faculty board that approved my return as a fellow for three years after the first one.

- My fellow fellows, with whom I met weekly and who have provided abundant help and encouragement.

- The Berkman staff, which has always gone out of its way to make Berkman the welcoming, valuable, and well-run place it is. I'd especially like to thank Urs Gasser, Colin Maclay, Phil Malone, Rebecca Tabasky (ably assisted by her cat Nancy), Amar Ashar, Catherine Bracy, Seth Young, Jon Murley, Rob Faris, Dan Jones, Caroline Nolan, Karyn Glemaud, and Carey Anderson, all of whom have never been less than extra helpful, as well as great fun to hang out with.

- The Geek Cave, especially Sebastian Diaz, Ed Popko, Dan Collis-Puro, Danny Silverman, and Isaac Miester.

- My two law school interns, Doug Kochelek and Alan Gregory (both now full-fledged attorneys, practicing in the world).

- John Deighton, Karim Lakhani, and Jose Alvarez of Harvard Business School, Andy McAfee of MIT Sloan School of Management (and formerly of HBS), Doug Rauch of Harvard's Advanced Leadership Initiative (ALI), and John Taysom, also of the ALI.

Developers with whom I've worked directly on code. These include David Karger, Oshani Seneviratne, and Adam Marcus of MIT/CSAIL, and Ahmad Bakhiet of King's College London, for their work on Emancy/EmanciPay/Tipsy, and Dan Choi for his work on ListenLog. I also thank Google Summer of Code (GSoC), through the Berkman Center, for supporting Ahmad and his work. Among Berkman folk, I'd also like to single out Anita Patel, who coordinated our work both with the center and GSoC.

My friends, benefactors, and collaborators in the public media world, starting with Keith Hopper of NPR. Keith is the brainfather of ListenLog and a heavy contributor of time and energy to ProjectVRM, starting with our very first meeting at Berkman. Next are Jake Shapiro and his team at PRX, including Matt McDonald, Andrew Kuklewicz, and Rekha Murthy, who together put ListenLog in the Public Radio Player, plus Kerri Hoffman, who coordinated with Berkman and ProjectVRM. I'd also like to thank Robin Lubbock of WBUR, who was an early supporter of VRM work. And, neither last nor least, is the Surdna Foundation, which provided a grant supporting work on ListenLog and EmanciPay. Vince Stehle led that effort and has continued to provide helpful encouragement.

The companies and organizations working on VRM from the corporate (including the CRM) side. Among those I'd especially like to thank BT, where JP Rangaswami led a number of remarkable efforts, one of which was to get Jeremy Ruston and the Osmosoft team on the VRM case. Also the Innotribe group at SWIFT (Society for Worldwide Interbank Financial Telecommunication), where Peter Vander Auwera and his colleagues worked with a number of VRM developers on the DAG (Digital Asset Grid).

My fellow members of the Berkman Center authors group, without whose help this book would be far less focused and organized than it is now. In alphabetical order by first name, they are:

- Christian Sandvig
- Colin Maclay
- David Weinberger
- Ethan Zuckerman
- Jason Goldman
- Judith Donath
- Lokman Tsui
- Wendy Seltzer
- Zeynep Tufekci

My unclassifiable collaborators and sources of much help, inspiration, or both:

- Craig Burton
- Dave Winer
- Dean Landsman
- Don Marti
- Eric S. Raymond
- Erik Cecil
- Jay Rosen
- Jeff Jarvis

- Jerry Michalski

- JP Rangaswami

- Kaliya Hamlin

- Mary Hodder

- Renee Lloyd

- Stephen E. Lewis

- Steve Gillmor

VRM developers and related organizations:

- Azigo, led by Paul Trevithick

- Buyosphere, led by Tara Hunt

- Connect.Me, led by Drummond Reed and Joe Johnston

- Getabl, led by Mark Slater

- Hover and Ting, led by Ross Rader and Elliot Noss

- Kantara, led into existence by Brett McDowell, and within Kantara the Information Sharing Workgroup, whose members are also listed elsewhere in the credits here

- Kynetx, led by Phil Windley

- MyDex, The Customer's Voice, and Ctrl-SHIFT, especially Iain Henderson, Alan Mitchell, and William Heath

- MyInfo.cl, led by Sebastian Reisch

- NewGov.us, led by Britt Blaser

- Paoga, led by Graham Saad

- Pegasus, led by William Dyson

- Personal Data Ecosystem Consortium, led by Kaliya Hamlin

- Personal.com, led by Shane Green

- Sceneverse, led by David de Weerdt

- Switchbook, led by Joe Andrieu

- Synergetics, led by Luk Vervenne

- The Banyan Project, led by Tom Stites

- Project Danube, and much more, led by Markus Sabadello

- The Locker Project, Telehash and Singly, led by Jeremie Miller

- The Mine! Project, led by Adriana Lukas and Alec Muffett

- Thumbtack, co-led by Sander Daniels

- TiddlyWiki, led by Jeremy Ruston

- Trustfabric, led by Joe Botha

- UMA, led by Eve Maler

Friends in the CRM community, including Paul Greenberg, Larry Augustin, Dan Miller, Mitch Lieberman, Denis Pombriant, Josh Weinberger and John McKean.

ProjectVRM's and Customer Commons' committee members, whose faith and guidance has sustained both me and the whole project. They include:

- Chris Carfi
- Craig Burton
- Dean Landsman
- Deb Schultz
- Iain Henderson
- Joe Andrieu

- Joyce Searls
- Judi Clarke
- Kaliya Hamlin
- Mary Hodder
- Sean Bohan

The rest of the VRM community list. At the risk of insulting any one of them, I'll list the members alphabetically by first name (including some of those already listed):

- Adam Carson
- Adrian Gropper
- Adriana Lukas
- Alan Mitchell
- Alan Patrick

- Aldo Casteneda
- Alec Muffett
- Alicia Wu
- Allan Gregory
- Allan Hoving

- Andre Durand
- Andrew Vitvitsky
- Ankit Kapasi
- Asa Hardcastle
- Bart Stevens
- Ben Laurie
- Ben Rubin
- Bernard Lunn
- Bill Densmore
- Bill Washburn
- Bill Wendell
- Bob Frankston
- Brett McDowell
- Brian Behlendorf
- Brian Benz
- Britt Blaser
- Bruce Kasanoff
- Bruce MacVarish
- Carter F. Smith
- Charles Andres
- Chris Advansun
- Chris Carfi
- Claire Boonstra
- Crosbie Fitch
- Dan Miller
- Dan Whaley
- Daniel Choi
- Daniel Perry
- Daniel Schmidt
- Darius Dunlap
- Dave Recordon
- David Goldschmidt
- David Karger
- David Scott Williams
- David Siegel
- Davor Meersman
- Dean Landsman
- Deb Schultz
- Denise Howell
- Devon Loffreto
- Don Marti
- Don Thorson
- Drummond Reed
- Elias Bizannes
- Elliot Noss
- Eric Norlin
- Erik Cecil
- Ethan Bauley
- Francisco Casas
- Frank Paynter
- Frankxr
- Gabe Wachob
- Gam Dias
- Gerald Beuchelt

- Gon Zifroni
- Greg Biggers
- Greg Oxton
- Guy Higgins
- Hanan Cohen
- Henk Bos
- Henri Asseily
- Jamie Clark
- Jason Cavnar
- Jay Deragon
- Jay Gairson
- Jay Graves
- Jeff Bunch
- Jim Bursch
- Jim Morris
- Jim Pasquale
- Jim Thompson
- Joe Andrieu
- Joe Botha
- Joerg Resch
- Johannes Ernst
- Jon Garfunkel
- Jon Lebkowski
- Jonathan Peterson
- Jonathan MacDonald
- Jorge Jaime
- JP Rangaswami
- Judi Clarke
- Julian Gay
- Katherine Warman Kern
- Keith Hopper
- Ken Shafer
- Kenji Takahashi
- Kevin Barron
- Larry Chaing
- Lorraine Lezama
- Lucas Cioffi
- Luk Vervenne
- Maarten Lens-Fitzgerald
- Mark Lizar
- Mark Scrimshire
- Mark Slater
- Markus Sabadelo
- Marty Heaner
- Mary Hodder
- Mary Ruddy
- Matt Terenzio
- Matteo Brunati
- Matthew Blass
- Matthew Platte
- Maurice Sharp
- Meg Withgott
- Michael Becker
- Michael O'Connor Clarke

- Michael Zeuthen
- Mike Kirkwood
- Mike Ozburn
- Mike Warot
- Mitch Ratcliffe
- Naos Wilbrink
- Neesha Mirchandani
- Nick Givotovsky
- Oshani Seneviratne
- Paul Bouzide
- Paul Chapman
- Paul Hodgson
- Paul Kamp
- Paul Madsen
- Paul Trevithick
- Persephone Miel
- Pete Touschner
- Peter Davis
- Peter Vander Auwera
- Phil Jacob
- Phil Whitehouse
- Phil Windley
- Phil Wolff
- Phillip Sheldrake
- Phillippe Borremans
- Ray Zhu
- Renee Lloyd

- Richard Dale
- Richard Reukema
- Robert Kost
- Robin Lubbock
- Ryan Janssen
- Sara Wedeman
- Scott Pine
- Sean Bohan
- Sebastian Reisch
- Spencer Jackson
- Stuart Henshall
- Stuart Maxwell
- T. J. McDonald
- Tara Hunt
- Ted Shelton
- Tim Pozar
- Thom Hastings
- Tim Hwang
- Todd Carpenter
- Tom Carroll
- Tom Guarriello
- Tom Stites
- Torre Tribout
- Trent Adams
- W. B. McNamara
- Yosem Companys

Two universities dear to my heart and mind. First is the University of California Santa Barbara and, in particular, the Center for Information Technology and Society there. CITS has been waiting patiently for me to return home and get back to research on the Internet and infrastructure, which I began there in 2006 and which I will complete after getting this book done. At CITS, I would especially like to thank Bruce Bimber, Jennifer Earl, and Andrew Flanagin. I would also like to thank Kevin Barron of the Kavli Institute of Theoretical Physics at UCSB, my good friend and collaborator on efforts to make fiber-to-the-premise happen in Santa Barbara and Santa Barbara County. One of these years, it will. Second is Harvard University, where gathered are some of the world's most helpful people and resources. I had never set foot at Harvard before Dave Winer's first Bloggercon there in 2003, when Dave was a fellow at Berkman. Yet I felt welcome and at home from the start. In addition to the people and organizations at Harvard I've already thanked, I'll add two more: (1) Harvard University Health Services (HUHS), which provided excellent care—especially through a couple of emergencies from which I came out more healthy than I went in; and (2) the library system, which claims to be the largest of its kind in the world, and seems even bigger than that.

ABOUT THE AUTHOR

Doc Searls wrote *The Intention Economy* while evangelizing the development of VRM (vendor relationship management) tools and services. This work began in 2006 when he launched ProjectVRM at the Berkman Center for Internet & Society at Harvard University during his fellowship there. Today there are dozens of VRM development projects under way.

When his work on VRM began, Doc had already been covering free software and open source development as senior editor of *Linux Journal*. For that and related work, he won the Google-O'Reilly Open Source Award for Best Communicator in 2005. For his work on VRM, Searls was named a "2010 Influential Leader" by *CRM* Magazine. In *The World is Flat*, Thomas L. Friedman calls Searls "one of the most respected technology writers in America."

In 1999 Doc and three collaborators launched The Cluetrain Manifesto, an iconoclastic Web site that the *Wall Street Journal* called "the future of business." Doc and his collaborators then wrote a book by the same title, which became a business bestseller in 2000. According to Google Books, *Cluetrain* has been cited by more than five thousand other books.

Doc is also one of the Web's longest-serving and widely sourced bloggers. J. D. Lasica, author of *Darknet: Hollywood's War Against the Digital Generation*, calls Doc "one of the deep thinkers in the blog movement."

Since 2006 Doc has also been a fellow at the Center for Information Technology & Society at the University of California, Santa Barbara, where his work focuses on the intersection of Internet and infrastructure.

Through his consulting practice, The Searls Group, Doc has worked with Hitachi, Sun, Apple, Nortel, Borland, BT, Motorola, Acxiom, and other leading companies, in addition to dozens of start-ups. The Searls Group grew out of Doc's work with Hodskins Simone & Searls, which he cofounded in North Carolina and which later became one of Silicon Valley's top advertising agencies.

Doc is also an avid photographer with more than forty thousand photos published online, most shot through the windows of commercial airplanes. More than two hundred of those photos now illustrate articles in Wikipedia. His photos have also appeared in many books, magazines, and other media. NBC used his ice crystal photos as a primary graphical element in its TV coverage of the 2010 Winter Olympics in Vancouver.

Doc and his family divide their time between their home in Santa Barbara and his work in Cambridge, Massachusetts, and elsewhere.